MORE THAN A MUSE

CREATIVE PARTNERSHIPS THAT SOLD TALENTED WOMEN SHORT

MORE
CREATIVE PARTNERSHIPS THAT
THAN A
SOLD TALENTED WOMEN SHORT
MUSE

Katie McCabe

Hardie Grant

QUADRILLE

Publishing Director Sarah Lavelle
Commissioning Editor Zena Alkayat
Editor Susannah Otter
Assistant Editor Stacey Cleworth
Designer Maeve Bargman
Junior Designer Alicia House
Head of Production Stephen Lang
Production Controller Nikolaus Ginelli

Published in 2020 by Quadrille, an imprint
of Hardie Grant Publishing

Quadrille
52–54 Southwark Street
London SE1 1UN
www.quadrille.com

All reasonable effort has been made to contact the
appropriate copyright holders and the publisher will be
happy to correct any omissions.

Cataloguing in Publication Data: a catalogue record
for this book is available from the British Library.

ISBN 9781787134119

Printed in the U.K.

TO MAEVE,
MAEVE AND AVE

CONTENTS

PREFACE

In 1949, New York's Sidney Janis Gallery staged an exhibition with the title *Artists: Man and Wife*. The concept was fairly simple: to pair the works of couples who were making strides in modern art and to display their paintings side-by-side for a group show. But before the exhibition had even opened the doors, a seed of bias had already been planted. While the male artists taking part (Jackson Pollock, Max Ernst, Jean Arp) got to remain in the default identifier of 'Man', the women involved (Lee Krasner, Dorothea Tanning and Sophie Taeuber-Arp) were reduced to 'Wife'. Any sense of parity was out the window. The message was clear since it was right there in the name – this was not about the artistic partnership of husbands and wives, it was a stage they had set for men, where their partners had been cast in a supporting role. Instead of a creative exchange, it served as a condescending shrug of, 'Oh look, she paints too'.

The paintings produced by the men became the standard for their partners to be measured against and the art critics that came to review skipped right into the trap that was laid out for them. 'Here are works by well known painter-husbands and their wives', said *The New York Times*, 'On the whole husbands are the more adventurous, giving ideas their heads, whereas the wives are apt to hold them back by the short reins of the particular scheme of design or color [*sic*] on which they are based. This is noticeably true of Jackson Pollock as opposed to Lee Krasner's conglomeration of little forms'[1].

Pollock's ideas, according to the writer, commanded the label of serious, while Krasner, along with most women involved in the show, is dismissed as careful and tidy in her approach. There was no consideration of difference, that the use of restraint in these 'little forms' was Krasner's exact intention, worthy of its own analysis. Instead, they were seen through the prism of her husband. It was a catch-22 for women living within a creative partnership with a more famous man – share inspiration and be considered a pale imitation; produce entirely different work and see it compared to theirs regardless.

With a cursory glance, the critic found his affirmation for what he'd already believed to be true. This is what happens when 'genius' is considered male; women are left to compete against a contrived status quo, resulting in feeble, half-baked readings of their art.

The exhibition might have taken place in 1949, but the message it perpetuated around artist couples still lingers today. It calls to mind a term coined by the journalist Lili Loofbourow: 'the male glance'. Although Loofbourow used the term for the treatment of stories by women writers, the male glance can equally be used to describe readings of visual art. 'The male glance is the opposite of the male gaze,'[2] writes Loofbourow, 'Rather than linger lovingly on the parts it wants most to penetrate, it looks, assumes, and moves on.'[3] In the case of *Artists: Man and Wife,* the male glance was in full force; having already consumed the supposedly 'serious' work of the men, the mind of the critic had already been made up when it came to the paintings of Lee Krasner and other participating women artists. It is not to say that their work did not require critique, in fact, the opposite: their art deserved deeper, more thoughtful criticism.

Instead, it received sweeping categorisation that set a dangerous precedent. Krasner was a well-known and respected painter in New York avant-garde circles by 1949, but this was the show that presented her to the public as Pollock's 'wife'. 'The slope from taxonomy to dismissal is deceptively gentle, and ends with a shrug. The danger of the male glance is that it is reasonable. It's not always or necessarily incorrect,'[4] Loofbourow writes, 'It feeds an inchoate, almost erotic hunger to know without attending – to reject without taking the trouble of analytical labour because our intuition is so searingly accurate it doesn't require it'[5]. The male glance is a mental heuristic that causes some to quickly classify work made by women as 'lesser', and move on. It says, here is the serious work, and here is the secondary. There is no need for you to dig any deeper.

Why couples?

The aim of this book is the inverse of *Artists: Man and Wife*; it is an attempt to foreground important, talented women whose work has often been overshadowed by that of their romantic partners. The idea is to traverse stories of women who worked in different creative disciplines: visual art, literature, composition and film, exploring the 'couple' as an editorial theme. Creative 'genius' is so often defined by the image of the solo male artist, set apart from the herd, working in isolation. The context of the 'couple' places a spotlight on gender imbalance, and on the obstacles to independent creative productivity these women faced as a consequence of their relationships with more prominent men.

Not every woman in this book fits neatly into the perceived meaning of muse, a person who supposedly embodies the source of inspiration for an artist's offering. But each of them aided the creative impetus of her partner – whether through emotional support, modelling for his artworks, editing his writing, or working to further his career – usually at the cost of her own. One outlier inclusion is that of New York Dada artist Baroness Elsa von Freytag-Loringhoven, whose career has been overshadowed by that of Marcel Duchamp's for reasons far more complicated than romance.

In each couple, this dichotomy manifests itself in a different way. I am not here to make a case for equal fame for all couples mentioned (they are, after all, individuals, not part of a cohesive unit) but to investigate how we look at their work, the way we speak about them, and the differences in the opportunities they were offered or given.

Chapters are guided by high-profile art movements and creative epochs that are more loosely defined, each exploring the contributions women made within them. There are chapters contextualised in Romantic-era composition, the Pre-Raphaelite Brotherhood, French Impressionism, the early days of the Slade School of Fine Art, Russian Constructivism, Surrealism, the Harlem Renaissance, the Jazz Age of the 1920s and the early days of British silent film. The time period jumps from the mid-nineteenth century right up to the 1980s.

In some cases, I focus on multiple women within a movement (Surrealism, in particular, had more complex artist couples than I could discuss in one chapter).

For others, the focus is on just one woman, such as Clara Schumann, a virtuoso composer of the Romantic era who remains lesser known than her husband, Robert Schumann. Throughout these pages, I discuss the work of Russian artist Varvara Stepanova, filmmaker Alma Reville, jazz pianist and composer Lil Hardin Armstrong, painter Josephine Hopper and playwright Shirley Graham Du Bois.

For the most part, these stories stand alone, but there is one thing the couples have in common: with the exception of Surrealists André Breton and Jacqueline Lamba (he being the writer, she the painter) they all, at some point, worked in the same artistic discipline. This is to demonstrate the difference in the expectations placed upon them, and the loaded readings of their work. Although there are huge contrasts and gaps in time between these stories, there is a theme that continues to rear its head. In almost every art movement, in every shift in a creative industry, there are women who contributed and were never given due recognition. Those who did, continue to have their work read as secondary to that of their partners. The scenario is far from unique to artist couples but allows us to see the sharp contrast in the way they were perceived, despite producing work in the same time period, socialising in the same circles and sometimes even working out of the same studio.

The culture of men centring themselves (or, in some cases, being centred by art historians after the fact) as the main 'masters and thinkers' of art movements – be it French Impressionism, Dadaism or Surrealism – has had a disastrous effect on the perception of women within them, leaving us to sift through the archives for names that should have been given top billing.

Why artists?

Overwhelmingly, you will find painters, photographers and sculptors in these pages, and the reason is simple: the case of a woman being eclipsed by her male partner is depressingly prevalent in the visual arts. Almost every high-profile art movement from the nineteenth century onwards (starting with the Pre-Raphaelite Brotherhood, who, again, had it right there in the name) features women whose contributions have been erased or defined by their erstwhile role as 'muses'.

As art historian Griselda Pollock put it in her feminist art polemic *Differencing the Canon*, 'The Story of Art is an illustrated Story of Man ... To that end, and paradoxically, it needs to invoke femininity as the neglected other that alone allows the unexplained synonymity of man and artist'[6]. One of the most obvious reasons for the gender imbalance in the history of visual art, is the artform's reliance on training academies who actively blocked women out. In her 1971 essay, *Why Have There Been No Great Women Artists?*, Linda Nochlin redrew the lines for feminist art historians everywhere when she carefully stated the obstacles women had faced in visual art throughout history.

The Royal Academy of Arts in London was founded in 1768 but did not admit its first female student until 1860, and even then, women were barred from what was then considered the most important aspect of an artist's training: life-drawing classes. It was unthinkable that a woman be exposed to the male nude; the only way a woman was allowed to enter the realm of a proper life-drawing class was as a nude model. Things weren't much better in Paris, where the only 'serious' academy class that allowed women to draw the nude male form was at the private Académie Julian, which did not open until 1868. And over in the US, American painter Thomas Eakins was fired from his job at the Pennsylvania Academy in 1886 when he removed a male model's loincloth to allow his female students to sketch his form; before this, the women had to settle for cows, which were regularly hauled in to serve as nude 'models', udders and all.

Why was the ability to master 'nude' so important? At the time, it offered a potential path to 'greatness', to the big, grand history paintings. Baroque masterpieces of perfectly rendered saints. Women who were not connected or wealthy enough to receive private tuition or a place at a high-profile art academy might be lucky enough to attend a class that specialised in 'feminine' media. 'Let women occupy themselves with those types of art they have always preferred such as pastels, portraits or miniatures,'[7] French art critic Léon Legrange wrote in the *Gazette des Beaux-Arts*, in 1860.

The classification of 'greatness' was defined early: women in flower-painting school, men sketching male nudes in the academy. There is, as Griselda Pollock and co-author Rozsika Parker observed in their book *Old Mistresses: Women, Art and Ideology*, no recognised female equivalent for the reverential term 'Old Master'.

We built the foundation of bias early, and from one century to the next, so many behaved as though the obstacles never existed, asking again and again, with myopic ignorance, what could be the reason for this absence of great women artists? By laying out the answers for the world to see, Nochlin challenged the banal assumption that perhaps there is some innate, male energy that is better suited to the visual arts. That men are simply 'more adventurous'. Better at 'giving their ideas heads'.

But what about those who did make it through? Nochlin saw that the 'small band of heroic women' who did manage to achieve fame as artists, 'were either the daughters of artist fathers, or later, in the nineteenth and twentieth centuries, had a close personal connection with a strong or dominant male artist'[8]. Italian Baroque painters Elisabetta Sirani and Artemisia Gentileschi were both trained by their fathers. Neoclassical portrait painter Elisabeth Vigée Le Brun was the daughter of an artist, as was founding member of the Royal Academy of Arts Angelica Kauffmann.

Only as we edge into the nineteenth century do artist couples become more common, which is why I chose to begin *More than a Muse* at this point, investigating the life and work of Elizabeth Siddall, a painter and poet aligned with the Victorian artists of the Pre-Raphaelite Brotherhood. The Brotherhood is one of the earliest examples of a British art movement that included women in its ranks, but some were mythologised by muse-hood to the point that they scarcely maintained their humanity, let alone an artistic identity of their own. Elizabeth Siddall's image is known not through the self-portrait she produced, but through the works of her husband, Dante Gabriel Rossetti. When she died, her body was committed to the earth with a book of his poetry. Later, he would have Siddall exhumed so he could retrieve the collection for publishing.

Then there is Camille Claudel, a French sculptor and genius whose reputation as an artist has been in rehabilitation since the 1980s. As an eighteen-year-old student, she found work in the studio of Auguste Rodin and began a relationship that would go on to define her career. As an assistant in Rodin's studio, Claudel moulded the hands and feet of world-famous Rodin sculptures. She developed a deeply sensual style of her own, producing sculptures like *The Waltz*, an impressively rendered model of lovers intertwined. While the overt sexuality of Rodin's work was celebrated, hers were considered too realistic and raw for public display, just by virtue of being sculpted by a woman. As Rodin ascended to greatness, Claudel spent the final thirty years of her life in an asylum and was buried in a common grave.

Impressionist painters Berthe Morisot, Marie Bracquemond and Mary Cassatt were called 'the three women' of Impressionism. And still, modern Impressionist exhibitions keep them on the peripheries, their work corridor inclusions to the 'great men' of the movement: Monet, Renoir, Degas.

The least recognisable name of the three is Marie Bracquemond, whose husband, printmaker Félix Bracquemond is thought to have discouraged her involvement with the group. After her marriage, the production of her art slowly dwindled and was eventually extinguished as she struggled to balance and maintain her independence as an artist with the heavy weight of expectations placed on the role of wife.

Two women in particular who faced the burden of this expectation were Ida Nettleship and Hilda Carline. Both studied at the Slade School of Fine Art a generation apart and yet their experiences are remarkably similar. Both married profoundly egotistical male painters (Nettleship to Augustus John, Carline to Stanley Spencer), and endured the hypocrisy that a faux British bohemianism created for women of the late-nineteenth/early-twentieth century. They entered into unpredictable, artful 'bohemian' marriages, but unlike their husbands, they did not have the luxury of escaping family life, childcare and housework to meditate on their own ideas. They were not afforded the same space, time, and independence to pursue painting. Nettleship's story is one of the paintings we never got to see, because she was never really given the space or freedom to make them. Her ideas stayed inside, half-formed, fermenting, clawing away at her until her death, at the age of thirty. It brings us to another recurring theme: female guilt.

The sense of guilt and self-dismissal is everywhere in this book. The feeling of: if I wanted to, I could have found a way. But when you're tasked with the responsibility of keeping a house together, feeling guilt about painting, guilt about not painting, and trying to make room for yourself in a field where so few women have come before, when you're sharing space with someone who is getting the work done, how hard it must be to ignore the voice of self-doubt that says: I'm not good enough. It's not happening. Why not let him be the one to thrive? Maybe I don't deserve it, or it just isn't meant to be. After all, the supposed paucity of 'great' women in the arts was there to feed that flawed hypothesis.

The limitations

For the parameters of this book, I chose to focus on opposite-sex couples, to investigate the gendered readings of the work, as well as the different opportunities presented to men and women living side-by-side. These parameters, as is always the case, come with frustrating limitations. Though not nearly as common, the 'eclipsing' of one partner has of course occured within queer relationships too. One such example is Marcel Moore and Claude Cahun, an artistic duo and couple who staged their own micro fight against the Nazis during World War Two. Together they typed up notes denouncing the conflict, signing them 'The Soldier With No Name', as though they were written by a disillusioned German soldier. They found ways to slip these messages of rebellion into the pockets and cigarette packets of the occupying forces. They are considered Surrealist artists, but Moore and Cahun operated as their own formidable unit.

Together, they produced photography that served as protests against gender norms. With Cahun as the primary subject, they toyed with identity and self-image, experimenting with androgynous clothing and personae. Both adopted names that could not be recognised as male or female. There is no question that

Moore was instrumental in taking the photographs for which Cahun is better known and was the illustrator of Cahun's poetry books. As acknowledged by the curator of the exhibition, *Acting Out: Claude Cahun and Marcel Moore*, the Cahun photographs were frequently classified as 'self-portraiture', when Moore's very shadow is visible in some of the images, showing clear collaboration. For the show, the curator asked, 'What social prejudices and artistic hierarchies does the erasure of Moore accommodate and to what extent did the two artists foresee, forestall, foreclose (or, on the contrary, foreordain) this erasure?'[9]. Beyond the cast of that shadow, Moore has work which is rarely discussed, outside the context of the relationship to Cahun. Their partnership and approach to the work was seemingly equal but when it comes to analysing the art, it still falls into the narrow societal perception of art: as a solo pursuit. One person is given the authority of ownership, rather than it being judged as a collaboration. The masculine ideal of the solo and solitary artist has, arguably, been projected onto them, framing their work in a way that fits a potentially damaging status quo. It is not the story of a woman being overshadowed by her partner, but an example of how art history can have a flattening effect that erases the complexities of queer artists' lives.

Focusing on visual art presented another glaring limitation. Highlighting art couples, particularly modern art couples, has meant the majority of subjects are Euro-centric. Avant-garde art movements were overwhelmingly white. I felt it was especially important to re-examine the stories of women like Suzanne Césaire, one of the only black women connected to Surrealism in the 1940s. Césaire reimagined Surrealist language as a means of articulating the horrors of colonialism, and saw its ideas about 'unlocking the subconscious' as a way to tackle the irrationality of racism. Her ex-husband, Aimé Césaire, became a respected Martiniquan politician, poet and writer. Suzannes Césaire's writing has remained peripheral, with only seven published essays in existence. But her experience of gender bias is compounded by racial oppression. We cannot ignore the bias or institutional racism that further marginalises the work produced by black women artists. Of all the subjects I discuss in the Surrealism chapter, Césaire is the least recognisable name.

And then, there is 'the contradiction'. In order to discuss these women, their experiences and their work, I have to step into the very thing I am criticising – the categorisation of 'muse', and the annexation to a partner. The grouping together of women in this way, could in itself be considered problematic. After all, these are different women, different relationships and different experiences of different realities.

There were women I considered leaving out, such as Lee Krasner, as her reputation as an artist has, in recent years, finally met with the reverence it was due. But elements of Krasner's experience is mirrored by so many others in this book whose careers have not had the same revival. When her retrospective was announced in 2018, one newspaper ran with the headline 'Jackson Pollock's artist wife Lee Krasner to get major Barbican exhibition'. Clearly, we still have a way to go.

Modern couples

The launch of the exhibition *Modern Couples: Art, Intimacy and the Avant-garde* which opened at the Barbican Centre in London in 2018 took a very different approach to the artist couples seen in the *Artists: Man and Wife*. It attempted to explore the 'playground for creativity' that reveals itself when artists fall in love, but did not shy away from the obvious, recurring theme of the imbalance. Jane Alison, the exhibition's curator told me that the intention was 'to counter the idea that Modern art is just about solo genius working alone'. She continued, 'In telling that story and making that argument, inevitably you begin to foreground the female artists in a partnership who were frequently overshadowed or marginalised in relation to their often legendary, acclaimed partners… One of the ideas that underpinned the exhibition was that if you're in a relationship where there is love and desire and psychological and physical intimacy, the other often becomes the subject.'[10]

Much like this book, *Modern Couples* explored the lives of women writers and designers as well as artists, but throughout the exhibition, familiar stories emerged. Stories of men taking credit for their partner's work. Of women being placed in the role of Pygmalion's Galatea, sculpted and painted into the work of men, siphoned off from their own identity into the creative vision of another. Of women who had careers of their own but immediately took a backseat to focus on the men. Many of the subjects of that exhibition are included here. One example is Lucia Moholy, a photographer and collaborator of László Moholy-Nagy, her husband. Together they developed game-changing new ideas in the developing field of photography, co-writing and publishing celebrated articles on the subject which only carried his name. Moholy had lived at the famous German school of art and design, the Bauhaus, before the breakout of World War Two, taking artful photographs of its original architecture. When the reputation of the Bauhaus began to soar in the USA after the war, Lucia Moholy's images of the buildings were used in multiple exhibitions and journals, with no trace of credit to her name. Her negatives were kept from her by the school's founder Walter Gropius, who stored them in his basement while Moholy struggled to establish her reputation as a photographer and make a living in the UK.

The theme of misattribution is a common one, but reaches a new extreme in the case of Margaret Keane. For almost twenty years, Keane's husband took credit for her 'big eye' paintings, achieving rock-star level fame. He promoted the two as an artist couple in the press, framing Margaret as the muse and hobbyist painter in his shadow. Meanwhile, he was pressuring her in secret to churn out one painting after another. An article in *Life* magazine condescendingly compared her work to 'his', describing how she mimicked his technique, completely unaware they were all Margaret Keane's. He hadn't contributed so much as a brushstroke.

A question of balance

As I was putting together this book, everyone I spoke to about it assumed that I would focus on the dickhead painter trope – the egotistical male artist who resents his lover's attempt at being anything more than a muse. And yes, they are very much here. But even in the most supportive, balanced unions, where men have used their position of privilege to elevate the woman's achievements, the art world still largely failed to acknowledge them.

I felt it was important to include the harmonious relationships, as well as the imbalanced, complicated and destructive, as the factors that led to these women being eclipsed are societal, as well as personal.

Russian artists Varvara Stepanova and Alexander Rodchenko were part of the short-lived radicalism of the avant-garde art movement that developed in Moscow in the aftermath of the 1917 Russian Revolution. Their relationship was an unusually progressive one for the period; they mocked traditional gender roles and expressed horror at the subjugation of women in the west. Stepanova was a key player in the Constructivist art movement, which sought to unite art with the modern industrial world. Unsurprisingly, she and her colleagues were focused on the construction of artworks, rather than autonomous creation, branching into architecture, textiles and design. She was a skilled textile and graphic artist, but also took on the role of documentarian, organising their joint creative work and acting as a secretary to the Constructivist art group. As her grandson Professor Alexander Laventiev told me, Stepanova 'committed herself totally to his work'. Stepanova's art focused mainly on her (in hindsight, ulta-modern) textiles, a historically undervalued artform. Her work has been under-examined, and still she is known primarily as Rodchenko's collaborator and partner rather than as an independent artist.

Echoes of her experience can be seen in the case of Shigeko Kubota, a pioneering video artist of the 1970s and 80s who, along with her husband, Nam June Paik, pushed the boundaries of video as a medium, and was one of the first to produce video sculpture. Paik actively supported her career, but her innovations were largely sidelined by his global fame.

The overshadowing, in these cases, brings us back to the male glance. It is down to a troubling legacy of a lack of investigation and interest from critics and historians, and to poor archiving and lack of inclusion in permanent gallery collections. Cases like these turn the focus away from the relationships themselves, and on to us.

1
PRE-RAPHAELITE WOMEN: BREAKING THROUGH THE MYTHS

The Victorian artistic alliance known as the Pre-Raphaelite movement was by definition a 'Brotherhood', but it is known best for its images of women: usually red haired and pale-skinned. They can be found looking worried while holding fleshy pieces of fruit, floating hopelessly on rivers, or staring vacantly out of stained-glass windows. It's a style that has seen millions of maudlin teenagers decorate their bedrooms with poorly reproduced posters and filled library shelves with biographies on the 'secrets' of the Pre-Raphaelite circle. 'The Victorian Avant-garde' is a generous tagline sometimes used to sum up the Pre-Raphs – a label of rebellion and artistic upheaval that would probably have delighted its founding brothers, Dante Gabriel Rossetti, William Holman Hunt and John Everett Millais. It formed in 1848, when these men, all students of the Royal Academy in London, took issue with the state of painting in their time. They rejected work created after Raphael, deeming it dull and lax, they dismissed the trend for paintings with black backgrounds and brown tones. While other Academy artists and the French Impressionists next door were leaning into an experimental, loose brushwork style, the PR boys were having their heads turned by the fifteenth century, admiring the detailed approach of Italian greats like Sandro Botticelli. Anything else was branded stale or mediocre; they even nicknamed the founder of the Royal Academy of Arts, Sir Joshua Reynolds, 'Sir Sloshua' because of his supposedly sloppy (what others might call painterly) approach to portraiture.

The painters of the Pre-Raphaelite Brotherhood (PRB) mined Arthurian literature for themes and English poet Alfred, Lord Tennyson's ballad *The Lady of Shalott* was like a Pre-Raphaelite starter pack. Tennyson's rhyme tells the story of a cursed woman who is fated to live alone in a tower and cannot look directly at the outside world. She sits at a loom with only a mirror for company, weaving images of the comings and goings that pass her window that are reflected in the mirror's glass. Her world is upended by the sight of Sir Lancelot du Lac across her reflector, and she decides to escape the tower to explore the city of Camelot, curse be damned. It has all the key ingredients of a Pre-Raphaelite masterpiece: the surrounds of nature, the inflated notions of romance, the foreboding and the final seasoning: a woman on the brink of a tragedy.

With almost every one of the famous works from this period, the women who posed for them were real-life figures who helped shape the Pre-Raphaelite movement. They are everywhere – in the watercolours, oil paintings, in the text of the books about the men's lives – but it's like they met eyes with the Gorgons and turned to stone. Suspended in these portraits, they have no real voice of their own. Admittedly, in some cases, we never stop hearing their story – like that of artist and model Elizabeth Siddall, a woman so consumed by Pre-Raphaelite mythologising that people can scarcely separate her from a character in *Hamlet*.

For most, the first encounter with Siddall is in John Millais' *Ophelia*, a febrile portrait of a woman drowning in a river. With a viewing of this work usually comes the well-worn yarn about Siddall's torturous experience posing for Millais. For hours, she lay in a bath set up to mimic Ophelia's watery grave, with nothing but a few broken lamps beneath to keep her warm. As Millais lost himself conjuring Shakespeare's words in pigment, the temperature of the water she was submerged in began to plummet, causing a hypothermia that almost killed her. Now it's just an anecdote to be doled out to tour groups at London's Tate Britain. Other stories lean into the morbid fascination with Siddall's life. When she died of an overdose of laudanum at the age of thirty-two, her husband Dante Gabriel Rossetti had her buried with a bound notebook of his poetry in Highgate Cemetery. With Lizzie (as she was known) gone, he claimed, there would be no more use for them. He must have changed his mind; seven years after her body was committed to the earth, he had her exhumed to retrieve the works and have them published. When his poems were eventually released in 1870, they earned him £800 in the first year. Rossetti did not attend the exhumation. Everything we have come to know about Siddall has been aligned, and defined, by the men in her life – even down to her own name. She was christened Elizabeth Siddall, but dropped the second 'l' at Rossetti's suggestion. The single-L Elizabeth is the one that has been absorbed and dehumanised by the PRB myth-making, and defined by Rossetti's desires, so here, we will refer to her by her original name.

There are conflicting stories about Siddall's 'discovery' by the Pre-Raphaelites. One legend tells us that an artist associated with the Brotherhood, Walter Deverell, spotted the twenty-year-old Siddall working in a milliner's shop in Cranbourn Alley off Leicester Square, and was so struck by her 'stately neck'[1] and unusual features that he asked her to model for him. The other is that Siddall introduced herself to Deverell's father (then the principal of the School of Design in London) by showing him a collection of her sketches. The account that paints Siddall as a woman with confidence, agency and artistic ambition of her own is the lesser told. Siddall was the daughter of an ironmonger and did not have the advantages afforded to some other female artists of the Victorian period such as Henrietta Ward, who came from a family of artists, or military painter Elizabeth Thompson, who studied art in England and Italy, and received private training.

There have been so many breathless interpretations of Siddall's early life, even by those who knew her, that perpetuate the idea of her as some winsome feminine icon and a Pre-Raphaelite supermodel in the making. Painter William Holman Hunt, another Brotherhood crony, wrote in his autobiography that the day she was discovered, Deverell ran into the studio of Dante Gabriel Rossetti claiming, 'What a stupendously beautiful creature I have found. By jove! She is like a queen'[2].

When looking for models, the Pre-Raphaelite m.o. was to search for true-to-life authenticity, to avoid antique forms. Siddall was asked to model precisely because of her normality, but was turned into an idealised symbol of a flame-haired Pre-Raphaelite beauty anyway. She went from working with Millais to sitting regularly for father of the Pre-Raphaelites Dante Gabriel Rossetti, and the two began to develop a creative partnership; by 1852, she was his pupil, receiving advice on draughtsmanship and image making.

Though the earlier artworks Siddall produced have a naive edge, in some ways they surpass the Pre-Raphaelites' ambition to push the boundaries of their academic training. Siddall was not able to access the institutions where they learned their craft, and so she did not have the same formal rules to 'unlearn'.

That freedom from convention doesn't change the fact that, when it came to art education, she was at a disadvantage. In her drawing *Clerk Saunders*, an image plucked from a traditional child ballad, her line is rough, erratic and experimental. The flat figures and stained-glass colours seen in her creations *Lady Affixing Pennant to a Knight's Spear* and the watercolour for *Clerk Saunders* have shades of the drawings seen in medieval illuminated manuscripts. These rough-hewn works are far removed from the hot colours and elaborate realism found in the paintings of Millais and Rossetti.

As she moved in Pre-Raphaelite circles, Siddall's work quickly caught the attention of art critic John Ruskin (an early PRB champion during a time when the Brotherhood were heavily criticised). He agreed to be Siddall's patron, and paid her £150 for a year in exchange for any paintings or drawings she might produce to that value.

Members of Rossetti's friendship circle were preoccupied with Siddall's supposed ill-health, treating her as vulnerable and sickly, eager to have her examined by doctors and fed prescriptions. But Rossetti was supportive of Siddall's motivation to make art, maybe even too much so, as PRB expert Dr Jan Marsh argued, 'If anything he was too encouraging, too lavish in his praise, too ready to persuade her to paint before she had learnt to draw… She never seems to have mastered figures, and most of the people in her pictures have no legs'[3]. A lot of Siddall's work could be dismissed as crude and amateurish composition, but her *Self-portrait* (1853-1854) in oils is evidence of her artistic promise – she paints herself stiffly on a moss green backdrop with loosely tied hair, dark, bulbous eyes staring out from the canvas. For once she is in control of her own image, instead of being source material for the Pre-Raphaelite canon.

Things began to deteriorate between Rossetti and Siddall as their relationship became romantic, he delayed committing to her in any meaningful way. They separated for two years. An ally of Siddall's, the nineteenth-century artist and feminist Barbara Leigh Smith Bodichon wrote: '[Miss Siddall] is a genius and will, if she lives, be an artist. Alas! Her life has been hard and full of trials, her home unhappy and her whole fate hard. DR [Dante Rossetti] has been an honourable friend to her, and I do not doubt if circumstances were favourable, he would marry her'[4]. They did eventually marry in 1860 but Siddall died from a laudanum overdose just two years later.

'Dead Love'

After her death, Siddall was portrayed as either an ailing Pre-Raphaelite muse or an emboldened temptress whose very existence proved torturous for Rossetti; you'd wonder how she could possibly be both. Her husband obsessively painted her image, aligning their relationship with the work of Italian poet Dante Alighieri. In *Beata Beatrix*, a work Rossetti painted after Siddall's death, he reimagines her as Dante's deceased lover. Siddall, merged with Beatrice Portinari (the inspiration for Dante's *La Vita Nuova*), is painted in a saintly pose, frozen in a moment of spiritual transfiguration. It's the kind of mythologising which allowed Siddall's life to become inseparable from the perpetuation of PRB legend. In a 1947 catalogue of a PRB exhibition in Birmingham (which included four of her works), she is credited as one of the elements that helped dissolve the Brotherhood. It was the work of feminist art historians like Griselda Pollock and later Dr Jan Marsh that helped revive her status in the 1980s as an artist, firmly asserting Siddall's importance and influence within the PRB movement. Up until this point, much of her life was documented in the writing of William Rossetti (Dante Gabriel's brother) who positioned himself as the arbiter of the Pre-Raphaelite legend. One positive of this was the reclaiming of Siddall's extant poetry, which remained unpublished until after her death. It was unfortunate that William Rossetti had taken it upon himself to heavily edit Siddall's words, sometimes changing or omitting entire lines. With just sixteen poems, her output is small, but her words are crafted with irony, caustic wit and the kind of fatalistic melancholy that comes with a shorter life expectancy. The Victorian poet, her sister-in-law Christina Rossetti, said one of Siddall's poems, *Dead Love*, had a 'cool, bitter sarcasm'[5].

In 2018, the full unedited collection of Siddall's poetry was published for the first time thanks to the work of Dr Serena Trowbridge, who trawled through the archives of the Ashmolean Museum in Oxford trying to decipher Siddall's handwriting. 'I think we need to try and see Siddall's poetry in terms of Victorian women's poetry. [It's important] we don't see it as this one-off thing, as if she is a special case,' Trowbridge told me. 'She is essentially one of two Pre-Raphaelite women poets, Christina Rossetti being the other.' Siddall's poetry has not been taken seriously by scholars but has been analysed by some biographers trying to squeeze out some 'facts' about her life as though it were historical evidence. 'Poetry can never be evidence,' says Trowbridge, 'Until we can get past these man-made – literally man-made – myths, and all these ideas about her, I don't think we'll ever see her as an historical figure'[6].

Beyond Siddall

The renewed interest and repositioning of Siddall's story is welcome and long overdue, but the fascination with her life has elevated her work, sometimes at the expense of other Pre-Raphaelite women artists. Out of the 250 works included in the Pre-Raphaelites exhibition at Tate Britain in 1984, there were only two pieces by a woman; both were by Elizabeth Siddall, primarily as a signifier for her position as a muse, a satellite orbiting the men in the room.

In reality, more than eighteen women painters, embroiderers and photographers crossed three generations of the Pre-Raphaelite movement. One of the most significant was Joanna Mary Boyce, a painter tangentially associated with the PRB. She was married to another well-known artist of the period, miniature-portraitist Henry Tanworth Wells, and because of the custom of erasing the woman's entire name to adopt the husband's, she is sometimes referred to as 'Mrs HT Wells'. Boyce's rich, painterly approach to portraiture brought her a lot of acclaim during her short lifetime (she died at just twenty-nine);

and she actually sold her work. While the male counterparts of the PRB were busy filling canvases with garish colours, Boyce was more subtle and restrained. She handled portraits with delicate, warm tones and a gentle execution that feels more human than the gleaming porcelain faces of the early PRB works. Her subjects tended to be female sitters, or images of her own children, but when she received praise for her work, it was for painting 'like a man'. 'Without sinning on the side of the masculine, Miss Boyce paints with a manliness which there are few men to emulate'[7], *The Spectator* wrote of her work in 1855.

One of her sitters, Fanny Eaton, was a hugely important Pre-Raphaelite model, a woman of mixed-race heritage born in Jamaica in 1835, just one year after emancipation. Before this, Fanny's mother, Matilda, had been enslaved in the country by white British colonialists. Fanny travelled to the UK in the 1840s, where she married a Londoner, and found work as a cleaner. Not much is known about how she entered the world of the Pre-Raphaelite Brotherhood but she began sitting as a model for a number of PRB artists, appearing in Biblical scenes by Rossetti and Ford Madox Brown, though she is frequently referred to as artist Simeon Solomon's muse. Solomon produced numerous pencil drawings of Eaton, but the most well-known portrait of her is his 1860 painting *The Mother of Moses*. Rebecca Solomon, an artist who had enormous success in the nineteenth century (and also happened to be Simeon's sister) depicted Fanny with two children in her painting *A Young Teacher*, which shows a small, blonde, pale child 'teaching' Fanny from an open book, a stark and shameful representation of a downward colonialist gaze. Conversely, Joanna Mary Boyce painted *The Head of Fanny Eaton*, a regal side-view of Fanny's face, thought to be a study for a full-length portrait of a Libyan queen.

Eaton modelled for the PRB for almost ten years, but very little is known about her life; a census revealed that she was working as a cook in the Isle of Wight at the age of sixty-three, but died in London at eighty-eight. The fact that we know so little about Eaton, but have multiple biographies at our disposal for Siddall, is an example of the more extreme erasure of women of colour from these histories. It's essential that stories like Fanny Eaton's are written into the narrative of the Pre-Raphaelite movement.

The second generation

The second wave of Pre-Raphaelitism (1860s–1890s) – an era awash with Romantic symbolism and medieval legends – is tied to the work of Edward Burne-Jones and designer William Morris. Cherry-picking from PRB ideas, Burne-Jones shifted the focus toward the cult of beauty, a vision wrapped up in the 1860s Aesthetic movement of Oscar Wilde. A key carry-over from that first PRB wave was the belief in the model, the need to find a woman to fixate on. Georgiana Macdonald attended the Government School of Design and was a budding painter and etcher until her marriage to Burne-Jones. The birth of her first son and pressure of domestic life precipitated the end of her artistic career. Few of her works exist today, other than the poignant *Dead Bird*, a watercolour painting held in Tate Britain. Georgiana endured Edward's infatuation with his models (whom he called 'pets'), in particular Maria Zambaco, who is usually labelled as a 'temptress' muse that plagued Burne-Jones. Zambaco was from a wealthy Greek family that lived in London. She was friends with the writer and cartoonist George du Maurier, and had the means and freedom to pursue a career in the applied arts; she focused her talent on medal art, casting metal bust portraits on to small coins, including one of fellow woman PRB artist, Marie Stillman. She exhibited work at the Paris Salon in 1888 and her medals are held in the British Museum collection. As with Siddall and Rossetti, Zambaco's story has been tangled up with her appearances in Burne-Jones' art. Her life is described in the context of fraught sexual allegory in paintings like *The Beguiling of Merlin*, where Zambaco's likeness fuses her with the character of Nimue, a siren who imprisons Merlin in a hawthorn tree while she reads to him from a book of spells. Her biography has been aligned with the role of the muse, a character that submerged the art she created.

Breaking into Camelot

Efforts have been made over the past thirty years to revise Pre-Raphaelite history, and place women within it. An exhibition called *Pre-Raphaelite Women Artists* was held at the Manchester City Art Gallery in 1997, and Dr Jan Marsh curated the extensive *Pre-Raphaelite Sisters* exhibition at the National Portrait

Gallery in 2019. But on each occasion, we are presented with a group of forgotten women. Instead of these artists being absorbed into the artistic canon once rediscovered, feminist historians have again and again been tasked with flying the flag for these long-gone artists, calling for them to be taken seriously, instead of treated like a cohort of muses with an occasional talented anomaly among its ranks. They are woven into *The Lady of Shalott* realm of Pre-Raphaelitism, when they should be running riot in Camelot.

2
CLARA SCHUMANN: THE VIRTUOSO

Clara Schumann was one of the most important virtuoso pianists and composers of the nineteenth century, and in her own way, she was also a formidable music critic. She called Wagner's *Tristan und Isolde*, 'The most repulsive thing I ever saw or heard in my life'[1], dismissed a sextet by German pianist Friedrich Kalkbrenner as 'miserably composed, so poor, so feeble, and so lacking in all imagination'[2]. While Russian keymaster Nikolai Rubinstein had 'an amazing technique, though his fingers are quite short and thick.'[3] Even when her hearing began to fail her Schumann could deliver a put-down sharp enough to puncture the hide of a rhinoceros. In a letter to her close friend the composer Johannes Brahms, Schumann described a recent piano concert she'd attended declaring, 'What I did hear left me so utterly cold that again I had to leave at the end of the first part.'[4]

Funny, withering comments like these can be found peppered throughout her letters and diaries, and are far removed from the nineteenth-century public perception of Clara as the quiet, melancholic concert pianist whose life had been marred by tragedy. Her words don't exactly come from a place of love, but they are not entirely drawn from spite either. Schumann was a deeply serious woman when it came to piano composition. In another letter to Brahms in 1864, she wrote, 'I have come across nobody who is heart and soul an artist. They treat everything superficially, the good with the bad, nothing moves them deeply, and of reverence they know nothing.'[5] She did not suffer fools or tolerate half measures. Once, when she was encouraged by a group of friends to play a small section of her husband Robert Schumann's composition *Carnaval* at a party, she retorted: '*wenn man den Carnaval spielt, spielt man ihn ganz*', meaning 'if you play the Carnaval, you play it completely'[6], and sat at the keys to deliver all twenty-one short pieces that make up the opus.

Her high standards and sacred attitude to piano composition are easier to comprehend when you learn how she was brought up. Clara's father, Friedrich Wieck, was a respected piano and singing teacher in Germany, and had designs on turning his daughter Clara into a pianist. From the moment she was born, he set out to create a *wunderkind*. Until around age four, Clara struggled to form words, claiming later in adulthood that 'my ear became more sensitive to musical sounds than to those of speech'[7]. At just five years of age, she could pick up small tunes and play by ear. Wieck wanted a child prodigy, and that's exactly what he got.

Clara made her formal debut at the Gewandhaus concert hall in Leipzig when she was just nine years old. She travelled to Paris for piano recitals, and performed for the writer Johann Wolfgang von Goethe. The Polish composer and professor, Theodor Leschetizky claimed that she was the first pianist ever to play from memory. In his book *The Great Pianists*, Harold C. Schonberg writes, 'she began playing Bach and [Robert] Schumann in public ... She also introduced a good deal of Chopin's work to Germany. Her father fortunately let her develop musically as her instincts dictated'[8]. More importantly, she had begun to create music of her own. Thanks to the methodical lessons of her father, which involved violin, theory and singing, Clara understood the nature of composition. In 1831, at twelve years of age, she produced *Quatre Polonaises pour le pianoforte*, a cheerful, technically sound piece of her own. At this early stage in her career, she was handling the works of crowd-pleasing composers like Henri Herz and Franz Hünten with a stylistic grace, but she wanted to be part of the dawn of a 'New Poetic Age', the kind of literary, soulful approach to composition that was being written about in *Die Neue Zeitschrift Für Musik*, a magazine edited by Robert Schumann that he co-founded with her father.

Robert was a student of Friedrich Wieck, and his life was intertwined with the Wieck family. When he first met Clara, she was around nine, and he was eighteen. Despite the completely inappropriate age gap, he fell in love with her as she reached adolescence, and the love was reciprocated. As soon as

Clara turned eighteen, he proposed, but while she accepted, her father refused. Wieck disapproved of the relationship (understandably so, given that Robert Schumann was a mentee and colleague, and had known Clara since she was a child). He would not give his blessing, and so they brought a court case against Wieck for the right to get married.

The couple won the case and Clara Wieck became Clara Schumann, but the dispute started their relationship on a bitter note, creating a rift between Clara and her father. As she committed herself to the relationship with Robert, she began to express some doubt about her abilities that seemed at odds with the bravura of her early career. In 1839, she wrote in her diary, 'I once believed I had creative talent but I have given up the idea; a woman must not wish to compose—there was never one able to do it. Am I intended to be the one? It would be arrogant to believe that…'[9] They married in 1840, lumbering Clara with a complex dual identity that would throw up endless challenges in her sixteen years of married life: the revered concert pianist and the 'dutiful' wife.

The Schumanns

Clara and Robert's relationship has been a goldmine for biographers and filmmakers looking to dramatise their love story; they made everyone's job incredibly easy by making the unusual choice to keep a 'marriage diary' for the first four years. Its pages are obsessively detailed (Robert was meticulous with note-taking and archiving), to the point that it contains some cringeworthy entries about their sex life. But when Robert was immersed in composing, the diary entries were left to Clara, falling in line with that predictable tradition of the 'wife as a biographer'. She expressed elation in the first four months of marriage, but the fractured relationship with her father loomed large. And though Clara continued to perform and compose, the pressures of a domestic life began to hamper her output. Robert locked himself away for days to work on his first symphony, always uninterrupted, while Clara was left with the household and administrative duties. In her diaries at least, she was effusive about her happiness, 'my father always mocked at the so-called domestic bliss. How I pity those who do not know it, they are only half alive'[10], but Robert's love couldn't offer the sense of self-fulfilment and adulation Clara received from the public after a successful concert. Up until this point, she had been the more famous of the two. Robert was well-regarded as a composer, not a performer. And when he was shut away, feverishly stringing notes together, he would not allow Clara to preview the music, a decision that must have been hurtful to the woman who had premiered his works to huge crowds at her own concerts.

On 2 June 1841, she complained to her diary about her craft being neglected, 'my piano is falling behind. This always happens when Robert is composing. There is not even one little hour to be found in the whole day for myself! If only I don't fall too far behind. Score reading has also been given up once again, but I hope that won't be for long this time.'[11] By that point, Robert had thrown himself into his 'year of song', sketching out *Symphony No. 1* in just four days. This was the same year that they had their first child, Marie, and the year that Clara held her first solo concert since marrying Robert.

At the time, it was extremely unusual for a married woman with children to pursue a career, but by now Clara was twenty-two and no longer a 'child prodigy'. Paranoia about the rise of young stars like Anton Rubinstein was seeping in and she needed to keep herself visible to the public if she was going to survive as a pianist. With the very privileged support of an additional handmaid and a wet nurse, Clara was able to continue touring and began making efforts to revive her solo career in 1842. As a nineteenth-century woman she had to make considerations that would never even occur to a male pianist. Women of that time were not easily able to travel alone: it was considered inappropriate for a woman of her class. Robert had to accompany her. Once, when she decided to travel without Robert to perform in Copenhagen, she wrote to her friend Emilie List expressing a mix of shame and defiance. She tries to justify her need to share her talent, and her identity, with the need for money, 'I am a woman, am not neglecting anything at home, earn nothing, why shouldn't I use my talent for once to contribute my mite to Robert? Could anyone blame me for this? Or my husband for going home to his child and his business?'[12].

Though Robert was enthusiastic about his wife's genius, and wrote about how proud he was of her playing, he had a galling habit of sending her guilt-provoking letters whilst she travelled, something which must have pained Clara, given that she was already away from her children and defying social norms to pursue her career. 'Still no news from you my Clara. Have you forgotten me already? Yesterday I could hardly bear the melancholy that overwhelmed me. This desolation in the house; this emptiness in me! Letting you go was one of the most foolish things I ever did in my life and it certainly won't happen again'[13]. He did not always play the wounded husband, many of his letters were filled with love and recognition of Clara's achievements: 'you write so little about yourself as an artist, where you have played and whether you were understood.'[14]

Clara was groomed to be a concert pianist by her father, it was her *raison d'etre*, and while her husband might have been happier to see her settle into life as at home, she was unwilling, and unable, to let her vocation go.

Robert accompanied Clara on a working trip to St Petersburg in 1844, a place she had longed to tour. The journey was hellish, something Clara took in her stride, performing for the Tsar and a Tsarina in a Russian palace. It all took its toll on Robert, who suffered a breakdown that was given the very sheepish nineteenth-century diagnosis of 'nerve fever'. It was an early sign of deterioration in Robert's mental health. After the nerve fever incident, they moved from Leipzig to Dresden. There was more heartbreak when, in 1846, Clara had a miscarriage while the couple were spending the summer on the island of Norderney. It was during this time that Clara managed to compose the *Piano Trio Op. 17*, a poetic, polyphonic masterpiece that is now considered her most accomplished composition.

The Düsseldorf years

Clara had not composed for some time when she and Robert met Joseph Joachim, a precocious young violinist from Hungary, in 1853. Hearing him play Beethoven's *Violin Concerto* gave her the motivation to pick up a pen and complete the *Three Romances for Violin and Piano*, a lyrical piece of work that swells with sincere emotion and is fraught with contrasting musical styles. It shifts from languid, poignant moments to a rousing complex urgency, positioning Clara as a firm equal among the great Romantic composers. So what brought her here?

Aside from the help of Joachim, Clara finally had a creative space that was hers alone. A move to Düsseldorf (where Robert Schumann succeeded Ferdinand Hiller as municipal music director) allowed them to buy a new spacious apartment where Clara composed freely at the piano without having to 'disturb' her husband. Through Joachim, they were led to Brahms, then a young and hopeful composer keen to study under Robert. The moment the couple first encountered Brahms is dramatically embellished for the 1947 Clarence Brown film *A Song of Love*. Clara, played by Katharine Hepburn, is seen prancing down the stairs, Pied Pipered by the sound of Brahms' notes in the air. She grips Robert's biceps as she asks, 'Who is he?' (in an inexplicable American accent). According to the writings of their daughter Marie, the visible excitement at Brahms' arrival was very real – from that moment, he became an inseparable part of the Schumann story. Brahms had a deep admiration for them both, but developed feelings for Clara, with whom he had a lasting friendship and a sort of co-dependent artistic bond.

It was in Düsseldorf that Robert's mental health took a turn for the worst. He struggled to fulfill his role conducting the municipal orchestra. A recurring finger injury prevented him from playing the piano, and so Clara stepped in to support him, attending rehearsals to accompany the chorus – work that was far removed from her stature as a world-famous concert pianist.

We have to remember that, at this point, she was a thirty-three-year-old woman trying to balance an unstable husband and a career of her own, as well as being a mother to (by that point) seven children. Ruppert Becker, concertmaster of the Düsseldorf orchestra, expressed concern about Robert's poor mental health and advancing auditory hallucinations, writing in his diary, 'Today Schumann spoke about a peculiar phenomenon that he has noticed for several days now. It is the inner hearing of beautiful music in the form of entire works!'[15]. It eventually led to a full breakdown. For ten days, Clara would not leave his side. Becker wrote, 'Frau Schumann looks as if she is suffering as she never has before… she is in the eighth month of pregnancy'[16] (it would actually have been her sixth month, with their eighth child). Breaking point came in 1854, when Robert was admitted to the Endenich asylum near Bonn after attempting to throw himself into the Rhine. Public perception of Clara's behaviour around this time has been exceptionally unfair. Doctors at Endenich forbade Clara from visiting Robert, feeling it would be too distressing for husband and wife, and still she has been labelled as cruel and selfish for not being by his side. Dissuaded from visiting her husband, and effectively left a single parent, Clara threw herself back into her solo career. As recently as 2006, *The Independent* has run the subheadline 'Clara Schumann resumed her piano career even as her husband Robert lay dying in an asylum. Devoted wife or damaged prodigy?'[17]. Clara had eight children to support at this traumatic period in her life, and while it's true she was offered financial support by friends like Brahms, there was little consideration for the fact that Clara may have needed to tour in order to grieve for her husband. Perhaps returning to her original identity helped her take back some control over a devastating situation.

The final movement

In May 1856, Clara Schumann played to a packed Town Hall in Manchester. The following day, a rave review appeared in *The Manchester Guardian*, 'Comparing Madame Schumann with the leading pianists of the day, we would say at once that she surpasses them all in that great quality which we sum up expressively by the word "*soul*." She is all music; and, as she bends over her instrument, it is very easy to see, from her expressive gestures, that the wooden instrument, with its bits of ivory in front and its steel wires behind, has become a golden gate through which her spirit passes into the purest regions of harmony.'[18] Months later, after a brief reunion with his wife (which took some persuasion of the doctors) Robert died in the asylum at Endenich, two and a half years after he'd been admitted. Clara has been further criticised for the edits she made to Robert's work after his death, in particular her decision to destroy one of his last works, the Five Romances for cello and piano, and rightly so, but it is worth employing some empathy here. These works – tangled in the filigree of her husband's delusions – exemplified his ill-health to Clara and symbolised the disappearance of the man she loved. It explains, to some extent, why she wouldn't want them recorded, performed, and absorbed into his oeuvre for eternity. After his death, she no longer composed, save for one piece called *March*, written for a friend in 1879. Clara continued to tour into old age, keeping Robert's compositions alive through her performances.

Though she is well regarded as a pianist today, and still widely revered in classical music circles (before the euro, her face appeared on the 100 Deutsche Mark), as a composer, Clara Schumann's work remains eclipsed by that of Robert's.

A good measure of this is seen in filmmaking, a medium that has introduced so many cinemagoers to orchestral scores, conciertos and symphonies they might otherwise never have heard. Robert Schumann's work appears on more than 206 film soundtracks, including Hitchcock's *Notorious* and Pakula's *Sophie's Choice*. Clara's work, on the other hand, appears in just six films, one of which is a biopic on her own life, *Beloved Clara*. For a long stretch of time after her death, the world appeared to forget about her compositions altogether; in 1952, *The New York Times* ran a review of her *Piano Trio* with the headline 'Clara Schumann: Wife of Robert was also a composer'[19]. Robert is afforded the title of the troubled virtuoso, the composer that rang in the new world of German Romanticism. His pieces are explosive, melancholic, unpredictable; Clara's technically sound, polished and poetic. If he was a lightning bolt, she was a clear dark sky. Clara was a child prodigy, a teen composer, a touring piano soloist and a mother to eight children. And still she couldn't get past the idea that she wasn't capable of great composition, that a woman couldn't quite grasp the gift afforded to men like Robert. That cloud of self-doubt robbed us of all the Clara Schumann works that never made it to the page, and we owe it to her to make the most of the masterpieces that managed to escape the storm.

3
IMPRESSIONISM: MARIE BRACQUEMOND AND THE FEMININE INFLUENCE

Impressionism started as an insult. Like a lot of moments that changed the way we view painting, the art movement stemmed from some form of rejection: in this scenario, the rejected paintings of Monet and Renoir, which weren't getting past the gatekeeping judges for the Paris Salons. And so they set up their own exhibition, presenting as a group of independent artists. The old studio of photographer Gaspard-Félix Tournachon (also known as Nadar) was filled with the paintings of Cézanne, Pissarro, Degas and Sisley, and just one woman, Berthe Morisot for the event. Some critics came with noses already upturned, sniffing at the scratchy, *non fini* images, chastising the artists as nothing more than 'Impressionists' masquerading half-arsed studies as finished works.

Impressionism's detractors looked down on its nervous physicality, the candid handling of the paint and the need for the artist to be guided by their senses. In 1891, French critic Théodor de Wyzewa wrote an article that suggested that the lightness and elegance of Impressionist imagery made it inherently feminine. He didn't seem to believe women could give their talent to the depths of 'real', explorative art and threw to the table a crumb that women could instead see the universe 'like a gracious, mobile surface, infinitely nuanced … Only a woman has the right to rigorously practice the Impressionist system, she alone can limit her effort to the translation of Impressions'[1]. To label Impressionism as feminine was to undermine it. Femininity, at least as critics like de Wyzewa appeared to perceive it, was characterised as sometimes beautiful, but always superficial. But we all know this 'derogatory' label didn't last. Impressionism revolutionised painting, becoming the single most important art movement of the nineteenth century. Monet, Renoir, Degas, Cézanne and many of the male artists even loosely associated with the Impressionist circle became household names. As its 'genius' was confirmed, the notion of this inherent 'femininity' faded, and so did the names of artists Berthe Morisot, Marie Bracquemond, Mary Cassatt – the women who created Impressionism alongside them.

The three women of Impressionism

The assertion that Impressionism was suitable for women might have been couched in sexist ideation, but it wasn't completely off the mark. At the time of the movement's genesis in Paris, the state-funded and respected École des Beaux-Arts (where Degas, Seurat and Renoir studied) did not accept women. Institutions that did allow female students were generally the reserve of elite women who dabbled in drawing and watercolours of floral still-lifes. Impressionism's emphasis on *plein air* (outdoor) painting, gave women artists a chance to pursue painting beyond studios and academic settings. We have to remember that the 1860s in France was a period where bourgeois women were generally expected to be accompanied by a chaperone – they didn't have the freedom to gather in Parisian cafés to argue about Manet's *Olympia* over absinthe. Impressionism gave an invitation to move away from historical, academy-based painting subjects and lean into outdoor landscape scenes, still-life and portraits. It might have been by coincidence rather than design, but by venturing outside the confines of the studio, Impressionism allowed women a way in.

In writer Henri Focillon's survey of new French art in 1928, he listed the three women of Impressionism. One was Berthe Morisot, an educated, upper-middle-class painter who, along with her sister Edma, had access to private lessons from the grand bourgeoisie of the Parisian artworld, and was taught by Joseph Benoît Guichard. In a letter to Morisot's mother, he warned, 'My teaching will not endow them with minor drawing room accomplishments; they will become painters. Do you realise what this means? In the upper class milieu to which you belong, this will be revolutionary — I might almost say catastrophic'[2]. Her mother held weekly salons where a selection of Parisian artists would gather at the Morisot family home, allowing Berthe to discuss and develop her craft with some of the biggest names in the city's art scene. It was considered proper for ladies of her class to experiment with drawing and watercolour, but breaking out of dilettante mode to be regarded as a professional artist proved an insurmountable challenge for most, regardless of talent and class status. Morisot was the first woman to enter the Impressionism fold, exhibiting ten of her paintings in the very first of the eight renowned Impressionist exhibitions; her work appeared in all except one, in 1879, owing to the birth of her daughter. Later this French coterie of painters found an American addition in the form of Mary Cassatt, a Pennsylvanian artist known for her original, rapturous portraits of women and recalcitrant children, seen in the defiant mini personality slouched between billowing cushions in one of her best paintings *Little Girl in a Blue Armchair*. Like Morisot, she came from an extremely wealthy background and had the rare opportunity of training at the Pennsylvania Academy of the Fine Arts from the age of sixteen. Her languid, intimate figures and experimental painting style flies in the face of the cosy images of rosy-cheeked Victorian cherub children and maternal perfection that were so common at the time. She showed her work at the Paris Salons, when she managed to get it past the judges, until her good friend Degas invited her to exhibit with the Impressionists. That invitation, as she would later admit, had a huge impact on her work. Griselda Pollock has written extensively about her career, crediting her importance as a radical member of the Impressionist set. Her female figures are defiant in their introversion, rarely meeting the viewer's gaze. Paul Durand-Ruel, the art dealer who devoted himself to the Impressionist cause by buying up works by its artists in huge numbers, revered her. He had as many pieces by Cassatt as he did Degas, purchasing around 400 of her paintings. Cassatt is arguably better-known in the context of American Impressionism; despite her success in France in her lifetime, her reputation in Europe diminished over time. Feminist art historians like Pollock have helped to reinstate Cassatt's fame, and if capital worth is a reflection of relevance, Cassatt has ripped off the bonnet: in 1996, she broke the world record for the most expensive painting by a female artist when her work *In the Box* sold at auction for more than $4 million (the record, at the time of writing, is held by Georgia O'Keeffe). Then in 2018, her pastel drawing *A Goodnight Hug* fetched $4.5 million at a Sotheby's auction.

Not included in the 'trio' mentioned by Henri Focillon was artist Eva Gonzalès, the only formal student of Édouard Manet, and one of his many models. In *Eva Gonzalès* Manet depicts her at her easel, painting a still-life of flowers, in a very impractical fancy white empire-line dress whose hem collides with the splattered pools of paint at her feet. Morisot sat for Manet many times, though he always chose to portray her like a lacklustre debutante, usually spread across a chaise lounge, instead of at the easel, where she spent so much of her time. As with her teacher Manet, Gonzalès never exhibited with the Impressionists, choosing instead to submit her work to the Salon judges. But she is, laterally, associated with the group.

So who was that third woman Henri was talking about? Marie Bracquemond, the lesser-known pillar of the painterly troika.

Marie Bracquemond (née Quivoron)

Painting should never be the preserve of the wealthy, but there's no getting away from the fact that an upper-middle-class upbringing could help chip away at certain obstacles facing women artists in the nineteenth century. Can't get into the École des Beaux-Arts? Just pay for private training from the best artists in the country. Can't be seen having indecorous debates in cafés? No problem, your mother just invited him around for an art salon in the family home. Unlike Morisot and Cassatt, Marie Quivoron did not have the ready finances for this kind of support, or the benefit of their stable, fancy upbringing. Her sea captain father died after joining an expedition to the Marquesas Islands when she was just a baby, leaving her mother to quickly remarry and move a young Marie to the Jura Mountains in Switzerland. It wasn't until they settled in Étampes, France, that Quivoron produced her first piece of art: by crushing and scraping field flowers, she produced her own pigments to paint a birthday present for her mother. A family friend took notice of her resourcefulness, and rewarded her with a box of watercolours. The painting obsession stretched into her teens and though Quivoron got some insight into the art-making process working alongside a local art restorer, she was largely self-taught. She might not have had the grand infrastructure of her peers, but her big break did come from that other all important boon: connections. Another helpful family friend had recognised her talent, but instead of a box of watercolours, she got an introduction to Jean-Auguste-Dominique Ingres, the giant of French Neoclassicism. Ingres would have been in his late seventies at the time, probably dressed with a popped white shirt collar framing his face and a morose, hangdog expression – an intimidating figure for any sixteen-year-old girl. He was impressed with her work and invited Quivoron to work in his studio and enter two drawings to the Salon of 1857 as a 'student of Ingres'. Just as wealth shouldn't be the only means of having your art recognised, proximity to a man shouldn't be the only means for a woman artist to have her talent seen, but in that climate, with no experience, having Ingres' name attached gave Quivoron's work real clout. Her drawings made it into the Salon, and landed her a commission as a 'copyist' in the Louvre.

Working with Ingres gave an undoubtable boost that allowed Quivoron to finesse her drawing style, seen in the considered lines of *Head of a Muse* and an early etching *Portrait of my Sister*, but she was stunted by the dark, heavy tones and restricted academic values of the Ingresian approach. He may have supported her but he still viewed her work through a gendered lens. He advised her to study with the wife of his student Jean-Hippolyte Flandrin, who ran a school that, as Quivoron put it, was just a place where 'some rich young ladies try their hand at painting some flowers. But I quickly understood that I could take no part in that school except to waste my time'[3]. Quivoron was faced with an internal tug of war with career versus creative freedom. What use was it to continue receiving the support of Ingres, when his outlook was placing a stranglehold on her output? To grow as a painter, she needed to sever ties with him. 'The severity of Monsieur Ingres frightened me … because he doubted the courage and perseverance of a woman in the field of painting … He would assign to them only the painting of flowers, of fruits, of still-lifes, portraits and genre scenes,'[4] she wrote, 'There is in me a strong determination to overcome all obstacles. I wish to work at painting, not to paint some flowers, but to express those feelings that art inspires in me… All this will not come to pass in a year, but in any event, I do not wish to return to Monsieur Ingres'[5]. Moving away from someone as influential as Ingres is testament to Quivoron's gumption: she wasn't willing to churn out the anodyne watercolours expected of her. Understanding what feels wrong to an artist can be instinctive but the real challenge comes in finding what feels right.

It was a turning event in her personal life that would eventually lead Marie down the verdant path of Impressionism. While busy sketching baroque masterpieces in the echoey galleries of the Louvre, Marie met Félix Bracquemond, a successful artist who led the etching revival in France. Although his work was not Impressionist in the way we understand it today, he was one of the artists on the roster for that first exhibition out of Nadar's studio. Bracquemond moved between classic and decorative arts, producing a series of plates with ducks on for Eugène Rousseau, all loosely inspired by the Ukiyo-e prints of Japanese masters like Katsushika Hokusai (there's a story that Bracquemond 'discovered' Hokusai's work in a print shop, sparking the popularity of Japanese art in France, but the latter claim is likely overblown). When he wasn't decorating plates with bird motifs, he was rolling with the avant-garde boys' club that had Charles Baudelaire, Alfred Sisley, Jean-Baptiste-Camille Corot, Henri Fantin-Latour and Edgar Degas for members. Quivoron's eventual marriage to Félix introduced her to artists who were satisfying the desire she'd been denied – breaking out of the academic fold and finding a new means of expression. She developed a friendship with Claude Monet, and he encouraged her to detach herself from the dark, buttoned-up Ingresian ways and step into the lightness and giddy brushwork of the Impressionists.

'All at once a window opens'

Parasols, lace and swathes of sunlight feature heavily in the paintings of Marie Bracquemond. Space played a big part in the work she produced, as she could only work from subjects found in the areas deemed appropriate for women – dining rooms, drawing rooms, manicured gardens and other realms of the domestic sphere. One thing all three of these women of Impressionism have in common is that they all painted their sisters. This is not because they made such compelling sitters but to give them freedom to stare. For bourgeoise women, keeping sustained eye contact with a man was not 'proper', since a gaze could mean seduction, and a loss of male control. Women could be both subject and object, but unless he were a close friend or family member, a man could not play the same role. Marie's painting *The Lady in White* demonstrates her gradual, and slightly tentative move into Impressionism. It is a *plein air* portrait but the woman looks as though she could have been posing in a studio. It is extremely detailed and well-composed, down to the full, layered ruffles of her bright white dress. But look closely, and you'll see how Marie has begun to toy with subtle touches of movement, surrounding the sitter in a soft halo of sunlight. One of her 'official' Impressionist works *Tea Time* shows Marie's sister, Louise, relaxing with a book in the Bracquemond garden in a whirl of energetic brushmarks and modulated colour. Louise's downward gaze becomes the pictorial locus, her white dress superimposing the layers of daylight worked into the canvas. Bracquemond might have been limited to typical aesthetically pleasing middle-class scenes of ladies living in the Third Republic, but this style allowed her to shake up this static, poised portrayal of women and betray some of that inner female world. Bracquemond's work appeared in three of the eight Impressionist exhibitions, and she first took part in 1879, the same year as Mary Cassatt. In a letter to Félix ahead of the fifth Impressionist show in 1880, Degas expressed his anger at the 'idiotic'[6] decision not to include the names of the three women taking part on the posters, urging Félix and Marie to fight for her name to be equally represented.

They shared artistic friendships, but when it came to artistic styles, Marie and Félix were not in sync. Even though her husband had exhibited with Impressionists himself, he looked down on them. In an essay on Marie Bracquemond, historian Jane R. Becker wrote how Félix claimed 'that the Impressionism so dear to her had never produced a composed painting, only slices of life'[7]. He failed to see that these very slices of life are what give the works their vigour, capturing blurred moments and half-formed memories, summoned

by a flick of horsehair. Marie believed that 'Impressionism has produced …
not only a new, but a very useful way of looking at things. It is as though all at
once a window opens and the sun and air enter your house in torrents.'[8]

Nobody can ever really know the inner workings of a marriage and the
toll it takes on a person's ambition. If an unpublished manuscript by Félix
and Marie's son Pierre Bracquemond, *La Vie de Félix et Marie Bracquemond*, is
to be trusted, Félix's antagonistic behaviour and moments of jealousy over
Marie's talent slowly caused her to drift away from the painting and resolve
herself to the expectations of domestic life: 'She who never leaves Sèvres, no
longer visits exhibitions, lives closed up in her house, confined to her solitary
thoughts, tormented by her regrets.'[9], Pierre wrote. A similar take on Félix's
curmudgeonly personality is seen in the writing of the couple's friend Gustave
Geffroy, who described Félix as quick tempered, especially when discussing art.
And if we don't believe it, here's what we do know: Marie Bracquemond lived
as an effective recluse for the last twenty-five years of her life, and produced
very little. She firmly closed the window on those torrents of light.

An egalitarian movement?

You could put a Bracquemond or Morisot beside a Monet and claim the latter
is simply the better painter, but that cannot be used as an easy explanation for
why their work has been so poorly represented in the gamut of Impressionism.
What we should be asking ourselves is why, in the nineteenth century, were
Impressionist exhibitions more radically inclusive of the women who helped
found and elevate the movement, than the Impressionist exhibitions staged at
London's National Gallery some 130 years later? Art historian Griselda Pollock
called it 'the first affirmatively and consistently egalitarian art movement'[10],
but nowhere is that represented in modern exhibition taglines and titles like
'From Manet to Cézanne' and 'Painting the Modern Garden: From Monet to
Matisse' (you can see the pattern).

Even when these women's paintings are included in these landmark
shows, they are rarely presented as key works, if mentioned at all. They exist
unexpressed in the 'to', that space between the recognisable male names. When

London's National Gallery mounted the exhibition *Inventing Impressionism: The Man Who Sold a Thousand Monets*, themed around the art dealer Paul Durand-Ruel, in 2015, Pollock called them out for including just one female Impressionist, a single painting by Mary Cassatt (as mentioned earlier, Durand-Ruel owned 399 more than that).

Is it really a surprise that so many outside the art world (and many in it) struggle to name a female Impressionist other than Mary Cassatt? The presence of women in Impressionist exhibitions should not be a point-scoring addition – it should be central to them. Throwing a couple of Morisots or Bracquemonds on a side corridor off a room filled with Monet's *Haystacks* might give curators something to point to in an exhibition brochure when called out on erasure, but it does not address the issue. If the goal really is to represent the inner workings of the movement, and the artists who represented it, Berthe Morisot, Mary Cassatt, Eva Gonzalès, and Marie Bracquemond must be on that list. Just as Degas argued in 1880, it is idiotic for their names to be dropped from the posters.

4
CAMILLE CLAUDEL: MASTER SCULPTOR

When Parisian artist Camille Claudel first presented her sculpture *The Waltz* to the Ministry of Fine Arts, it was criticised on account of the 'closeness of the sexual organs'[1] on display. *The Waltz* captures an erotic moment between two lovers intertwined, and Claudel was apparently too adept at crafting their bodies. The nudity was deemed too real to ever appear in a public place.

Nineteenth century French sculptors like Claudel depended on state commissions to have their works cast in bronze, and she was desperately seeking the approval of the Ministry of Fine Arts' inspector, Armand Dayot, to help secure the funds. But the sight of two bare, heterosexual bodies, shaped by the hands of a woman in her twenties, was just too much for Dayot, who found it indecent and rejected it, all the while claiming those dangerously close sex organs had been 'rendered with a surprising sensuality'[2]. The surprise being that such sensuality was rendered by a young woman.

You'd be forgiven for thinking the ability to conjure two naked human forms realistic enough to shock, in a pose accurate enough to evoke an arresting sensuality would be seen as valuable attributes for a sculptor. Not so for Claudel. She suffered from the extreme paradox of her gender. To be accepted as a woman and a sculptor, she had to be exceptional. And she was, but she remained caught between two worlds: she dared to express eroticism from a female perspective, but what made her exceptional broke the boundaries of supposed social respectability. The same rules did not apply to her oblong-bearded lover and sometime teacher, Auguste Rodin. When he chiselled the intimate figures of two bare, adulterous lovers from Dante's *Divine Comedy* for his sculpture *The Kiss*, it was seen as a masterpiece. After it was first exhibited in 1887, *The Kiss* became an instant hit; it was copied in bronze and had more than 300 casts made of it in the space of thirty years.

When Armand Dayot observed *The Waltz*, he measured Claudel against her teacher, saying, 'Rodin himself could not have studied with more artistic finesse and consciousness the quivering life of muscles and skin'[3]. High praise, and still, she did not get the commission. Claudel was determined to pursue the nude as a subject, but conceded to Dayot's proposal that she clothe the figures of *The Waltz* in draperies. With the 'closeness of the organs' concealed by her new composition, Claudel's request for marble was accepted.

Frustratingly, as the request reached the upper echelons of the Ministry of Arts, the money she had been promised, along with the opportunity to produce the work in marble, was blocked. Even with Dayot's renewed support, she did not fit the Ministry's narrow view of what a woman artist could be. In Odile Ayral-Clause's excellent biography of the sculptor, *Camille Claudel: A Life* she quotes French art critic Louis Vauxcelles's accurate take on Claudel's circumstance: 'If Camille Claudel had stooped to sculpting elegant dancers, of a socialite elegance... her success would have been sudden and fabulous.'[4]

Claudel refused to limit herself to these prescribed 'feminine' subjects. Instead, she pursued what Vauxcelles recognised as a 'rhythm, melody and intoxication'[5] in her sculptures that gave the men at the Ministry cause for alarm. Rodin had a similar style, but enjoyed reverence and acceptance for it that she was denied. It was an imbalance that set the tone for their relationship, and eventually, her downfall.

Claudel had begun sculpting at the age of twelve, working with local clay in her hometown of Nogent-sur-Seine. Curious to see if she had real talent, her father put the question to a neighbour, sculptor and friend of Rodin, Alfred Boucher. He declared the child had something, and so the family got behind Claudel's work, moving to Paris so she could knuckle down and study her craft. At this time – around 1881 – anyone in Europe pursuing sculpture with any kind of conviction put their roots in the academies of Paris. Claudel knew the kind of career she wanted but the opportunities for women were minimal. The most highly regarded school, the École des Beaux-Arts, only admitted men, and so she settled on the Académie Colarossi. There was no real culture of sculpting among women in Paris at the time, few notable foremothers of the craft to inspire. So Claudel decided to create something of her own, setting up a studio with a group of similarly ambitious young female sculptors.

A master

Not long after her arrival in Paris, Boucher set up an introduction between Claudel and Rodin. For the meeting, she brought two pieces to show him, a realist-style bust called *La vieille Hélène*, and a bust of her brother, the poet Paul Claudel. She was eighteen, Rodin forty-two. He immediately recognised her abilities, employing Claudel to work as an assistant in his studio. Soon, she fell into the nebulous world of colleague-meets-muse. She modelled for Rodin, spending long, laborious hours on a podium, sacrificing time for her own sculpture. He was in a relationship with Rose Beuret, but began a tempestuous affair with Claudel that became an open secret in Paris. His letters to her read like the urgent scribblings of a teenager possessed, filled with the panicked air that he has fallen for someone he cannot control, 'My fierce friend ... My poor head is sick, and I can't get up any more this morning. This evening I wandered (for hours) in our favourite places without finding you, how sweet death would be and how long is my agony ... My Camille be assured that I feel love for no other woman, and that my soul belongs to you ... You don't believe my suffering. I weep and you question it.'[6]

In the first months of his affair with Claudel, Rodin was enjoying some of the most lucrative commissions of his career. She continued to work in his studio (along with fellow artists, like British sculptor Jessie Lipscomb), modelling parts of some of his most recognisable pieces. The hands and feet of *The Burghers of Calais* are thought to be her work. One of Claudel's bronze sculptures, a detailed head called *Giganti*, is now held in the collection of the Kunsthalle Bremen but it was originally misattributed to Rodin. His signature had been scrawled on its neck, to drive up its price.

She had annexed herself to him, perhaps for love, but also for mentorship and a means to ingratiate herself into his world, to find her place within it.

Claudel was determined not to live on the vapour of Rodin's perceived genius.

The couple were learning from one another's style. Women in Rodin's sculptures were often passive, merely receiving the lust of men, or created for their eyes (see The Bather); in Claudel's aesthetic, female figures had vibrant sexual agency. In her hands, clay could be used to encapsulate private female world, absent of men, such as in The Gossips, where a group of women huddle together completely naked, spilling the tea of the day.

Her approach to sculpture transcended the expectations of femininity that permeated the period in which she lived. She was not afraid to carve strong, muscular female bodies that wilfully gave themselves to erotic moments. The stars of her moulds were not just fallen women of Greek mythology or submissive objects of desire – they were complex, thoughtful and free from reductive categorisation. They were also more realistic. When Rodin sculpted Crouching Woman, which shows a model in an uncomfortable squatting pose, he captured an idealised female form. Her body is contorted and yet is smooth and slender, with no visible imperfections. Claudel crafted a more true-to-life image of the female body for her Crouching Woman: the rippled layer of stomach and breasts that droop naturally towards the floor.

Rodin may have been obsessed with Claudel's youth and beauty, but he was no fool; he knew how exceptional she was and made significant attempts to elevate her career. But it was Mathias Morhardt, an art critic, who went on to become one of Claudel's biggest champions. Upon seeing her work The Little Chatelaine, he wrote, 'There is… in the very disproportion of this too powerful, too lifelike head, already much too open to the eternal mysteries and the delicately childish shoulders which it reveals, something undefinable which communicates a deep anguish … The bust proves … that Miss Camille Claudel is henceforth a master'[7]. While critic Louis Vauxcelles claimed 'I don't know what to admire most … Camille Claudel is without contradiction the single female sculptor upon whose brow sparkles the sign of genius'[8]. Morhardt claimed, 'She is of the race of heroes'[9], meaning she was an exception of her gender, an anomalous infiltration of the 'masculine' world of real creativity, rather than proof of what women artists had to offer, given half the chance.

Such adulation means little when it can't carry through to the public, or to the Ministry of Fine Arts who refused her a commission. Claudel had her fans, but being tethered to the lionised Rodin often marred perception of her. When her style flourished, some critics assumed she was merely imitating him, feeding on the scraps of his tutelage.

As knowledge of their relationship spread, life became increasingly complicated for Claudel. The affair was a scandal in her social circle, and the risk was all hers. When her relatives discovered the truth about the affair with Rodin, she was turfed out of the family apartment and faced bitter derision from them, especially from her brother Paul, who had become a strict Catholic.

Claudel went from promising student to the objectified, ethereal muse-on-the-side. Her name became inseparable from Rodin's, but not for her work alone – when they looked at Claudel, they saw her through his sexualised gaze.

In Rodin's portrait *Thought*, Claudel's face emerges from a hacked block of marble with a chilling likeness, frozen in time. Her eyes look to the floor, crestfallen, but not devoid of hope. The hope was that talent was enough, that eventually these men would look beyond her gender, and her sex life, and recognise the quality of her sculpture, but her work was almost always seen in the context of his.

To make things worse, her relationship with the 'master' began to deteriorate. A battered sense of self-worth, coupled with his feckless promises to leave Rose, had begun to cloud Claudel's view of the relationship. In 1886, she drafted a contract ordering that he renounce other women, bring her on his travels, leave his partner and marry her a year later. These were the conditions Rodin had to meet if he wanted to sleep with her in her studio four times a month. He agreed of course, but the two never married, and he never left Rose.

Claudel eventually grew sick of his ill treatment and infuriating influence on her reputation, and ended their relationship. His response was to fashion her head in plaster, placing her hands over her lips and making her eyes wide with worry for his sculpture *Farewell*.

Meanwhile Claudel grew reclusive. Morhardt and Rodin continued to try and fund her studio time, offering stipends and commissions, but her mental health started to deteriorate. She became an iconoclast of her own work, smashing up much of her corpus, believing that 'Rodin and his gang' were hellbent on stealing her ideas. Claudel's father, her first patron, died in 1913. As it turned out, he was also her last protector. Within days of his passing, her brother, Paul, the subject of many of her bust portraits, had her institutionalised. In the asylum, she refused art materials for fear Rodin would get his hands on them, but Claudel's mental health issues were not the only cause of her marginalisation. The affair with Rodin made her a *persona non grata* among members of her family, and left her with no financial support once her father died. Institutionalisation was the end of Claudel; she remained incarcerated for thirty years, until her death in 1943, and was buried in a communal grave.

'Finished only when it is done in marble'

Can Rodin be blamed for Claudel's spiral into obscurity? The imbalance in their partnership chipped away at her confidence and her mental wellbeing, but there were much broader issues of institutional sexism that kept her away from the fame she deserved. Though we cannot gloss over the reality that when they met she was eighteen and that he was twenty-four years her senior. If their explosive partnership had just remained a platonic union of mentor and student, Claudel might have found a different path, but the devastating, erotically charged work they both produced at the height of their love might have taken a very different form. Maybe she would have been lauded for her daring, countercultural representation of female nudes, instead of shamed for them. Or maybe she'd just have been another student in the Rodin studio, chiseling the feet of seminal works to bear his signature.

How devastating it must have been for her, to have had such an important, formative exchange of ideas with Rodin, and watch him take them into the stratosphere while she was sequestered in an asylum. Once, when writing to the Ministry of Fine Arts to secure a commission for a marble version of her sculpture *Sakuntala*, she said, 'I still hope you will help me to complete this group, which will truly be finished only when it is done in marble'[10]. Her sculpture was revolutionary, but it too was sequestered, and left incomplete.

Claudel might have died in obscurity, but her story has succeeded her, albeit still tethered to Rodin's. Her old admirer Morhardt suggested a room at the Rodin Museum be dedicated to her work, and eventually one opened in 1952, a literal Claudel annex to a Rodin castle.

Books about 'Rodin's lover' that told of their fateful encounter, and the ruination of the great sculptor's 'muse and mistress' filled shelves in art gallery gift shops. Gérard Depardieu played a colossus Rodin in the Academy Award-nominated film *Camille Claudel*, with Isabelle Adjani giving a fey depiction of the protagonist.

Recent years have brought greater clarity to this misty, rom-tragi-drama. In 2017, a museum dedicated to Claudel's sculpture opened in her old hometown, Nogent-sur-Seine. They tracked down the pieces she did not manage to destroy, and created a paean to her work, allowing her to emerge from the role of the muse.

Claudel was punished for her modernism, and her excess of feeling. The 'surprising sensuality' of her sculpture was so real it terrified the men who could have made her a master of her own time. And that is the tragedy here, not Camille Claudel.

5
BOHEMIAN DREAMS: IDA NETTLESHIP AND HILDA CARLINE

Ida Nettleship

There's a passage in Alison Thomas' book *Portraits of Women* that describes the moment English painter Augustus John was almost killed by a haystack. At the time, he was in relentless pursuit of Ida Nettleship, a fellow art student at the Slade School of Fine Art and the source of his supposed 'torture'[1]. Nettleship had gone to St Albans in Hertfordshire for a party at the home of her friend Edna Waugh.

Edna and Ida had the kind of intense friendship where a short time apart left them both anxious and unfulfilled, and that night, looking for time alone away from the party, they escaped the socialising by climbing a ladder to swap stories on top of a tall crop of hay. But Augustus John appeared at the ladder in search of Ms Nettleship. He clambered up the rungs to interrupt their bonding, and refused to leave. She told him to get lost, and like an overtired toddler, John launched his body onto the thatch of the haystack, and started sliding headfirst down the dehydrated mound. Worried by the steep drop threatening his skull, Ida and Edna rushed to grab his shoes, but they slipped right off with his socks, 'he wriggled like an eel and then his trousers began to come off'[2], Edna wrote. He was saved by the women's screams for help; someone came and propped up the ladder John had kicked to the ground. After that moment, Edna explained, 'the peace of our solitude was completely shattered'[3].

John would go on to be just as unpredictable and slippery in his six years of marriage to Ida Nettleship. Such is the paradox of the early 'bohemian' British marriage – a world where the man is permitted to fulfil every sexual desire and impulse, and the woman is left grabbing at his socks (the ones she is responsible for washing) as he slips over the edge. While John embodied the caricature of the uninhibited artist, free to pursue affairs untroubled by thoughts of housework or childcare, Nettleship bore the weight of domestic responsibility. In taking his hand she also dropped the paintbrush – there was no time for her art in the 'free' Bohemia. She sought escape from normal married life, and found herself trapped in tradition regardless. In those six years, Ida Nettleship experienced five pregnancies. After the birth of her fifth, she died from puerperal fever at the horrifyingly young age of thirty, in 1907. Augustus John's fragmented memoir, *Chiaroscuro*, hardly mentions her. Writing about the 'talented and highly ornamental girl students of the Slade'[4], he says 'among the more outstanding were Ursula Tyrwhitt , Edna Waugh, Gwen Salmond and Ida Nettleship. I formed an attachment to the last named, which was to fructify in time'. Not exactly a stirring tribute.

Very few examples of Nettleship's work from her days at the Slade have survived, save a pencil self-portrait, and a full-length study of a male model in a loincloth. It would be dishonest to try to recapture her as a 'lost artist', with so little to draw from. She died too young, with a career extinguished before it had a chance to develop – but what we do have shows her promising draughtsmanship. Not much had been written about Nettleship's life until recently, she was usually found in the early pages of an Augustus John biography, an existence described in relation to his. The publication of her own letters for a book called *The Good Bohemian*, helped restore her personality line by line and brought a strong, lyrical and caustically funny woman into view.

'Stir up, look the thing in the face and be a man for a time'

Ida Nettleship was raised in a Pre-Raphaelite mood, part of a wealthy, creative family. They valued the autonomy of the artist, as long as it stayed vaguely within the moral panic room of late-Victorianism and didn't cause too much scandal. Her father, John Nettleship, painted garish images of wild animals – giant bears and jungle cats, or what W.B. Yeats called 'melodramatic lions'[5], and her mother was a respected costume designer. Ida followed suit early on, she was just fifteen when she enrolled at the Slade, one of the first art schools in Britain to accept female students, on a three-year scholarship. Presided over by a Henry Tonks – a critical art tutor who frequently reduced students to tears – the Slade operated on a level of art that valued extreme earnestness. Tonks' insistence that Sladers follow his approach meant that much of the school's output at the time was fairly repetitive. But it allowed women like Nettleship to draw full length nude studies, a practice other academies had reserved for men. Life-drawing sessions were completed in a deathly silence and students were motivated with a sense of fierce competition cultivated by travel scholarships and prizes for composition. Many women thrived in the rigorous surroundings of the Slade, among them Nettleship and her friend from the haystack, Edna Waugh, a star pupil who won the coveted composition prize for her now lost painting *The Rape of the Sabine Women*. In *Portraits of Women*, Alison Thomas writes about their closeness and joint artistic energy. They modelled for each others' projects, and even tied each other to the bed to evoke violent and dramatic scenes for their paintings.

When Waugh wrote to Nettleship asking for advice about whether she should marry solicitor William Clark Hall (she was sixteen at this time, he was around twenty-nine). She responded with a letter full of teasing aphorisms, 'the more your love hops about the better. Good heavens, what do you expect, you *idiot* … you must not think you are not an ordinary mortal… everyone is a fool and a creature of everyday feelings'[6]. Later, with a painful foresight, she warns Edna not to let William distract her from her work, 'I believe you want to paint. Then walk down that road and don't get looking at the sky, and don't get down side paths. You've got to go for your end with your might. Stir up, and look the thing in the face and be a man for a time.'[7]

William promised Edna he would put her art first and not have her 'hampered in any way by stupid domestic details'[8]. He rolled back on their agreement soon after they were married, discouraging her work, sneering at the 'rubbish'[9] paintings taking up space and chastising her for not being the ideal wife he had claimed not to want. Waugh channelled her frustration into deeply moving watercolours illustrating the pages of *Wuthering Heights*, which are now her most well-known works. After children, traumas, a nervous breakdown and other troubles in between, her husband eventually became more supportive of her talent, and set her up with a studio (later destroyed by the Blitz, taking much of her back catalogue with it). Waugh's career was celebrated with small solo exhibitions and retrospectives, culminating with a show at the now closed New Grafton Gallery in London in 1979, the year of her 100th birthday, and her death. By John's own admission, the turn of the twentieth century (what he called the 'Grand Epoch of the Slade'[10]) was a key time for women artists. But other than his sister Gwen John – an important but supposedly 'forgotten' artist who seems to be rediscovered by British galleries and media every other year – none achieved anything close to the fame and infamy of Augustus John.

'Ida full, happy and smoking'

As her friend Waugh accepted a proposal, Nettleship broke off an engagement (to family friend, Clement Salaman), took up a travelling scholarship she'd won at the Slade, and moved to Florence in 1897, taking in new experiences and Old Masters she copied for drawing practice in the galleries of Palazzo Pitti. 'I am so bold and unafraid in the way I work that all the keepers and all the visitors and all the copyists come and gape'[11]. Afternoons were spent people-watching the 'queerest' characters around her, 'Americans and poets and grey haired spinsters who drink hot water'[12]. At the same time her writing betrays a creeping self-doubt about her work, 'an inborn perverseness... something in me which ties down my hand'[13]. Self-deprecation aside, she still has that urgent but inconsistent energy of her twenties, flipping like a Newton's Cradle between carefree and contented to melancholic and insecure. Letters are filled with lines like, 'Dinner over. Ida full, happy and smoking'[14].

The European adventures continued the following year, when Nettleship and 'the two Gwens' – Gwen Salmond and Gwen John – went to Paris to broaden their studies of Post-Impressionism and symbolism. They lived in a powder-puff cloud of Belle Epoque Paris, visiting cafés, painting each others' portraits ('We all go suddenly daft with lovely pictures we see or imagine, and want to do'[15]) and going to dances at Whistler's studio. It's Nettleship at her most adventurous and hopeful – her real Bohemian years, still sketchbook scratching out her voice as an artist. 'I almost think I am beginning to paint – but I have not begun to really draw yet. I am always on the verge,'[16] she wrote to friend Michael Salaman. Gwen John ended up spending the majority of her life in France, where she would go on to produce her most important work, have a destructive creative partnership with Auguste Rodin, and resign herself to life as a recluse. Nuns and local school children became her subjects in Meudon, a Paris suburb, and she devoted herself to a pious, painterly solitude. For Ida, it was back to England, where she would fall into a relationship with Augustus John.

'Duty is so wearing'

Nettleship and John eloped in 1901. Her family weren't pleased about their relationship and would not have given their blessing, given John's reputation as an oversexed emotional powder keg.

John and his sister Gwen were brought up within a straight-backed, draconian household in Wales, with a strict father who extolled the value of reserved behaviour. John wanted none of this Victorian priggishness, and tried everything he could to become the inverse of his own upbringing. That meant earrings in, hair grown out. Wine, women and song … along with occasional collapses and disappearances. Everyone at the Slade seems to have a story about him: about how he would scale buildings to pop into open windows if he lost his key, or the time he went careering over flower beds in Hyde Park to escape the police. Writer Wyndham Lewis thought of him as 'a great man of action into whose hands the fairies had placed a paintbrush instead of a sword'[17]. I picture him like a hot-headed Beano character thundering through the Slade with a pointed beard and oval palette under his arm. In any case, Ida and Augustus were married – her father conceded, attending a party for the couple. John, however, was nowhere to be seen; he'd dipped off to have a bath, appearing later that night with a check suit to match his earrings.

Things started out happily. Nettleship now went by the name Ida John and letters to friends in that first year make life at their new home in Liverpool (where Augustus had taken up a teaching job at the University College) sound like a joyful experiment fueled by pots of handmade soup and sloe gin; she was expecting her first baby, and still producing 'drawings – mostly portraits'[18].

Pregnancies for Ida were then practically annual (condoms could hardly be bought in Boots). They couldn't afford to hire help and between the immense task of crowd control childcare and the mammoth labour of household chores in the 1900s, Ida could not sustain painting as well. Her husband had little interest in the ever-turning carousel of crying babies and nappy changes: 'When not painting [he] lies reading or playing with a toy boat'[19], Ida wrote. Augustus made up much of his oeuvre creating portraits of his own children, the great advantage of the artist who gets to father from behind the easel. His wife kept a cautious ambivalence and rarely uttered a criticism against him, always sympathetic to the will of the artist: 'I think, well, how could he paint if he had to be on duty in between, duty is so wearing'[20]. Ida didn't seem to think she was deserving of the same space away from 'duty' to produce work – she had faith in the abilities of the 'child genius'[21], as she called him, but did not appear to have the same faith in her own.

'Shall we laugh at all this when we're fifty?'

It'll come as a shock to no one that a woman of the early twentieth century was expected to give up her talent to focus on family life with an absence of support from her husband. But the complexity of their relationship would transcend the usual domestic oppression. Enter Dorelia McNeill: then a secretary and student at the Westminster College of Art. Gwen John was the first to encounter Dorelia, and she became something of an obsession in the lives of the John siblings. They each painted her portrait. Gwen invited her to walk the distance from Toulouse to Rome, an offer she accepted. Both Gwen and Augustus wanted to possess her, and be possessed by her. Like Maria Zambaco to Edward Burne-Jones, she was reimagined as a Nimue figure. Augustus was so preoccupied with her that he didn't bother to conceal his feelings from Ida. Instead Dorelia became a part of their marriage, and Ida effectively became the manager of a love triangle.

Coaxing this woman into their world became a family effort, Gwen told her: 'You are necessary for his development and for Ida's, and he is necessary for yours'[22]. The mirage of bohemia provided a convenient armour against cries of infidelity – this was not a 'conventional' family – they were radical, they did things differently, with rebellion that neatly served the desires of Augustus. Peering at her marriage through this John-adjusted viewfinder, Ida took on the persona of the Edwardian cool girl, and joined the pursuit to keep Dorelia in their lives.

Writing to Dorelia, Ida does not steer into feelings of victimhood, instead moving between a sensual aggression ('to the prettiest little bitch in the world'[23]) and black humour about their situation ('shall we laugh at all this when we're fifty? Maybe – but at fifty the passions are burnt low'[24]). The honesty is raw and stark; she confides in her, admits feelings of tenderness as well as hate, and expresses a need to leave Augustus. When Dorelia had lived with the family for a period, then deserted, Ida writes like a jilted lover begging her to return (which later, she did). She chastises herself for her moments of jealousy toward Dorelia. Showing immense insensitivity about the pressure he was placing on his wife, Augustus began a double portrait of the two women, and later painted Ida out.

'To live with a girlfriend & have lovers would be almost perfect'

Augustus romanticised the Roma way of life. So much so that he decided to cart this newly assembled family off to live in a wagon in Dartmoor. To slip in and out of the artistic nomadic existence, while real Roma travellers faced social exclusion, was the privilege of middle-class Bohemia. Maybe if they travelled as far away from the bore of convention as possible the wilderness would fix problems of his own creation.

The birth of Dorelia's and Augustus's baby created a tectonic shift in the relationship between her and Ida. In an idealistic escape of their own, Ida and Dorelia decided to take the children and put over 450 miles between them and Augustus by moving to Paris, where he would visit from London. Ida expressed more than once how much she enjoyed living with women. 'To live with a girlfriend & have lovers would be almost perfect,'[25] she wrote to Mary Dowdall in 1903.

This departure from the world Augustus had contrived for them may have been an attempt to rewind to the more hopeful Paris with the two Gwens. Life was undeniably more complicated now – she was living with her husband's mistress, caring for six children between them (by now, Dorelia had two children with Augustus) but they both showed unimaginable strength taking this risk – Ida in particular. She frequently wrote to her mother and sisters, and with extreme empathy, would try to placate their distress about her situation. The days of trying to save Augustus by his socks were innocent compared to this. While untangling the jumbled marionette strings of her life, she managed to carve out independence for herself in Paris, gently explaining to her husband that they were better apart. She was now the one securing the borders of Bohemia.

But they didn't hold. In 1907, while pregnant with her fifth child, Ida felt the jolt of labour pains, and walked herself to the hospital. She died there five days later.

Hilda Carline

The burden of Bohemia had got no lighter by 1925, when artist Hilda Carline married Berkshire painter, Stanley Spencer. Ida Nettleship and Hilda enrolled at the Slade School twenty-six years apart, but little had changed in the circumstance of the married woman artist in the post-World War One landscape. The altar became the finishing line for so many careers as women lost painting time to mothering, cleaning and management of male egos. It's a cycle so vicious it could be represented by a serpent eating its own tail. For Hilda and Stanley, the artist-marriage could be more accurately depicted by a comic book cloud of smoke with clenched fists poking out of it, only the characters here have made amends by the final frame.

Stanley Spencer always wanted 'more' from the ordinary. He was the kind of man who could pontificate for hours about the sight of nightingales circling the roof of a barn, and saw his birthplace of Cookham not as a pretty southern village, but a microcosm of world feeling. In *The Resurrection, Cookham*, an overwhelming 9 x 18ft painting and his best known work, he turns the calm, folksy community into a rapturous Biblical scene.

Hilda would poke fun at Stanley's habit of talking big about himself and his big pictures. In a letter to Hilda in 1922, he reasoned that this was not the consequence of a swelled head of self importance but a 'natural exuberance and desire to tell everybody everything'[26]. That desire for 'everything' found its way into their relationship too.

Hilda came from a family that had been producing artists since the eighteenth century; the family home at Downshire Hill in Hampstead was like a very British version of the Café Guerbois in Paris (probably with less absinthe), where characters like painter Henry Lamb, Paul Nash and the Spencer brothers (Gilbert and Stanley) might drop in for soup and arguments. Lamb called the meetings '*cercle pan-artistique* of Downshire Hill' but the intellectual gatherings never really took off as a 'movement' like the Camden Town Group or the Bloomsbury set. Like their father George Carline, Hilda and her brothers (Richard and Sydney) all painted, but Hilda came to training late; her father initially discouraged her from attending art school, keen that she support her mother around the house.

When she was around twenty-four, he gave in, allowing Hilda to develop her already impressive skill for landscape painting with two years at Percyval Tudor-Hart's art school in Hampstead. And after her service in the Land Army in 1916, where she spent her wartime days planting vegetables on a farm in Suffolk, Hilda found her way to the Slade School of Fine Art.

For a burgeoning artist, the set-up was undeniably cushty, but expectations were higher for the men of the family. Her parents rented two large studio spaces for her father and brothers in an old church school. Hilda took over a side corridor in the building, giving her the name of the 'passage artist'. The early 1920s was a productive time for Hilda, when she painted some of her most ambitious landscapes, like the morose but original scene *Return from the Farm* or the unusual oil work *Cliffs, Seaford*, a vertical seaside view that looks as though it were snapped from the window of a nosediving Spitfire.

'To produce an epic one's thoughts and convictions have to be positive'

Hilda first met Stanley properly over dinner with her family at Downshire Hill and he fell hard for her, almost in an instant: 'I saw life with her'[27]. Hilda's connection wasn't so immediate. Another *cercle* regular James (Jas) Wood was apparently in love with her too, as was Stanley's brother, Gilbert. When things ended with Jas, in a move of *telenovela* drama that would flash into their lives more than once, Gilbert whisked Hilda off to Cookham to present her with an ultimatum: she had to choose between the two brothers. Stanley would later tell Hilda that, if she had chosen Gilbert, he'd hoped she'd be a kind of sister to him, and that he could 'come in for little bits of crumbs of affection'[28]. There was no need for thumbing up crumbs, in the end, Stanley was her choice. It was on a painting holiday with Hilda and her family in Sarajevo, where the two made landscapes side-by-side, that Stanley proposed. Once Hilda said yes things did not move smoothly. Stanley kept getting spooked, breaking off the engagement several times. His habit of sharing every given feeling meant he had little in the way of a filter. He could be painfully blunt; letters to Hilda moved violently from sincere expressions of love, 'You have had a wonderful effect on me too Hilda; you have put a new song into my mouth'[29], to criticism that could cause even the most self-assured painter to grind their molars to dust, 'I feel that you also fail to express yourself in landscape as compared with your ideas'[30].

Funny that the criticism rarely extended to his own work. 'It is rather comical that I hate myself and love my ideas, whereas with you I hate your ideas and love you'[31]. Given Hilda had struggled with depression and self-doubt about her work in the past, this must have been a bracing punch to the gut.

The two were artistic sparring partners, and would spend hours arguing over religion on Hampstead Heath. Hilda was a firm Christian Scientist for her whole adult life. But perhaps his critiques were galvanising for her work too. During the early helter-skelter years of her relationship with Stanley, Hilda created her most arresting painting – an impressively detailed and claustrophobic *Self-Portrait*. Her stare is made more pensive by the dark and sunken shadows painted beneath her eyes. The painting is now held in the Tate collection. Hilda produced a portrait of Stanley the same year, where he sits with his head tilted and an indirect gaze, painted in the kind of earthy ochre tones that were popular with the Camden Town Group. The jolt of productivity didn't last. Very soon after the wedding, Hilda became pregnant with their first child, Shirin, and Stanley was off trying to turn himself into the Bruegel of Berkshire with the three-year creation of Biblical behemoth *The Resurrection, Cookham*. Hilda appears in this painting again and again, all in different guises, like a prophetic *Where's Wally?* (we find Hilda in a white wedding dress, Hilda sleeping on a bed of ivy, Hilda frozen in the church doorway, with the hand of a god-like figure resting upon her head). It has an erotic and spiritual charge, a churchyard anthem to the loss of virginity. Though the relationship was essentially happy, and Hilda was championing her husband's success, she did not have the same divine inspiration. 'My whole idea of art and production is of an epic order and to produce an epic one's thoughts and convictions have to be positive and vital'[32], she wrote. The arrival of a new baby and the marriage to Stanley (whose *Resurrection, Cookham* consumed most of the available work space) meant Hilda stopped painting for almost four years.

'I just wonder whether you ought to try to be like me?'

The impossible compromise of this artist-on-artist marriage was exhausting for Hilda. Stanley wanted her to be better at cooking and management of the house. When they hired a maid, Elsie, he measured Hilda's shortcomings against her. And when she worked in the garden, he chastised her for procrastinating from painting. You might as well clip the wings of a heron and get angry when it refuses to fly.

How could she expect harmony between them, he asked 'when to my symphonic efforts you keep up a dreary beating of old tin cans which is all your sewing and gardening means to me'[33]. Here he was, a marvel in action, why couldn't she just be the same, and also manage to keep the sheets folded? He wanted her to transcend the normal and menial to match his 'big' feelings, while keeping the day-to-day dullness of life in check so he didn't have to.

Even before they were married, Stanley would alternate between loving words and hurtful comments. When advising her about her about work, he once asked, without a hint of satire, 'I just wonder whether you ought to try to be like me?'[34].

As Simon Schama pointed out in his essay on Spencer 'The Church of Me', one of the figures in *The Resurrection, Cookham* appears to be a hybrid of Hilda's body grafted with Stanley's head, a taxidermy union of husband and wife. He seemed to want their partnership welded together in love and in art – painting what she painted – and criticising for what she didn't.

When Hilda executed her most technically accomplished and detailed full-length portrait, *Elsie*, Stanley set up his easel behind his wife to capture their maid from a different angle. The image was one Stanley had a deep admiration for, telling Hilda 'the way you have painted Elsie's skirt is a revelation to me'[35]. He kept the portrait with him after Hilda's death, and until his own. According to Nancy Carline, a British artist who was married to Hilda's brother, one reviewer would later praise and mistakenly attribute *Elsie* to Stanley Spencer[36].

Seeking breathing space away from her husband to rediscover her work in 1930, Hilda returned to her parents' house in Hampstead. Away from the intensity of her home with Stanley in Burghclere, she created *Portrait of the Artist's Mother*, months after the death of her brother, Sydney, from pneumonia. Her mother's face is cavernous and drawn, loosely painted with defiance not flattery. Hilda evokes the deep physical depression of grief, as though an unknown force is pushing down on her mother's shoulders.

Cookham feelings

The gravitational pull of Stanley's beloved village was guiding him home with the strength of a neutron star. He couldn't ignore his irrepressible 'Cookham feelings', or endure Hilda's supposed ambiguity about them any longer. The family move to Cookham was the catalyst that would eventually derail their relationship for good; the village became the backdrop to the soap opera that would cloud Hilda's career as an artist, and have her better known as the 'first wife' of Stanley Spencer.

The 'second' was Patricia Preece, a Cookham painter popular with Roger Fry and the Bloomsbury Group. She lived in the village with her long-term partner, Dorothy Hepworth. Only Patricia was not the main artist: in a case of seemingly willing overshadowing, the limelight-shy Dorothy would produce most of the work, and let Patricia sign her name. It's difficult to know what power-dynamics were at play here, but the fact that Dorothy continued to sign her works 'Patricia Preece' even after Preece had died suggests she was content with their set-up. Stanley was completely enraptured by Patricia Preece, and was either too naive to notice, or too attracted to care that she was in a committed relationship with Dorothy Hepworth.

There's a photo of Stanley Spencer and Patricia Preece on their wedding day, a *mise-en-scène* so full of unusual characters it could have been a screenshot from a screwball comedy, only the plot that went with it would not have made it past the enforcers of the Hays Code. Four figures stand in the frame: Stanley at the centre, trousers fastened above his belly button, a funnelled fisherman's cap obscuring half his head. The flash of the camera has turned his round-framed specs into two headlights, as though he were wearing mirrored sunglasses. Best man and witness Jas Wood is to his left, Patricia to his right, wearing a floppy sun hat with a rim so wide it extends beyond her frame. Standing beside her, a few inches removed, body tilted away from them all at an obtuse angle, is Dorothy Hepworth, clutching her bag as though she's been trying to leave the pub for the last half hour, if only her partner would stop chatting. Dorothy and Patricia spent the Spencer-Preece honeymoon together in St Ives, with Stanley in the next room, alone. He would go on to sign over his Cookham home to Patricia, leaving himself and his family with Hilda impecunious as he struggled to make maintenance payments.

The wedding took place mere days after the divorce with Hilda had been finalised. In the years before this, a characteristically filter-free Stanley had agonised over his infatuation with Patricia by sharing his feelings with Hilda. Similarly to Ida Nettleship and Dorelia, the women, at least initially, forged a kind of friendship. In an interview with *The Telegraph*, Hilda's sister-in-law Nancy Carline noted that 'ironically enough, Patricia admired Hilda's work more than Stanley's'[37]. Trying to spin the plates of caring for a young family and her husband's explosive obsession with a different woman must have been intensely draining for Hilda.

When writing about her parent's atypical relationship in her book *Lucky to be an Artist*, Unity Spencer observed that her mother 'put too much pressure on herself to love, against all odds – not only Stanley, but Patricia as well' and was 'expecting things for herself that even a saint would find difficult'[38]. As with Ida and Augustus John's situation, Stanley (and also Patricia) suggested they turn the marriage into a *ménage à trois*, relegating her from wife to mistress, but for Hilda, an extremely religious woman, that was pushing even her sainthood too far.

Stanley's double nude portraits of himself and Patricia are among his most famous. Grotesquely erotic like a Lucian Freud, vaguely comic like a Beryl Cook, the heavy, abundant fleshiness of them is almost kinetic – drooping muscle and skin ripple across the canvas. The nicknamed 'Leg of Mutton' painting (real name *Double Nude Portrait: The Artist and His Second Wife*) was considered too carnal and explicit to exhibit at the time it was made. In *Self-portrait with Patricia Preece*, we see Stanley's little head pop up, inquisitive and avian; he's staring just beyond the site of Patricia's reclining, naked body, looking for answers in the beige floral wallpaper behind. It didn't get a full thumbs up from Sister Wendy, the habit-wearing TV art critic, who dismissed Patricia's pubic hair as 'unconvincing'.

Aggressive use of a painter's biography can put a stranglehold on their art's ability to breathe. As Surrealist Dorothea Tanning put it, 'I think we're prisoners of our events'. But when you look at these intensely sexual (or rather, explicit but strangely asexual) paintings, it's of no small significance when you learn that Stanley and Patricia's marriage was never consummated.

Hilda, on the other hand, is a posthumous 'prisoner of her own events' without the artistic importance that comes with it. As her marriage was imploding, she channelled her emotions into her work just as Stanley had, creating a portrait of Patricia Preece called *Lady in Green*. By that point Hilda had left the village for Hampstead, but made Cookham returns for sittings with Patricia to complete the portrait. Dour, dark and sharp – it is a ferocious, if slightly unfinished image of Patricia. The dappled light on her face and brown shades show some similarities to Stanley's style, a fluidity between the two painters, but here is a chance to see the situation through her eyes. Hilda's artistic output is, admittedly, patchy at times, but the talent in her portraiture is vivid, we can only imagine the work she might have produced if she'd had the space for the independent ego afforded to her husband. A collection of Hilda's work was not assembled for exhibition until 1999, at the Usher Gallery in Lincoln, almost fifty years after her death.

Hilda experienced a deterioration in her mental health in the early 1940s, and was admitted to Banstead Hospital. It was during this period that she and Stanley made amends; he visited her regularly and wrote letters to her incessantly. For a decade after she died, the letters continued, *memento mori*, correspondence with his own grief and to happier times with Hilda.

The fallout caused by Stanley Spencer created unstoppable gossip about Spencer and the Carline family, and almost clouded her career completely. While Stanley's paintings from this period in his life hang in the Fitzwilliam Museum and Tate collections, Hilda's have scarcely been seen since that revisionist solo show in 1999. In their joint, overwhelming 'biography', she is buried among the paragraphs. The passage artist in the church of Stanley Spencer.

6
GABRIELE MÜNTER: THE BLUE RIDER

In the final sighs of the nineteenth century, artist Gabriele Münter could be found cutting through the dirt roads and scorched plains of the Texas Panhandle. After the loss of both parents, Münter and her sister had decided to leave Berlin for an American adventure to visit their remaining family, funded by a large inheritance. During the American Civil War, their father had brought his immediate family back to Germany, leaving relatives behind. On her American journey, Münter travelled through St Louis and Texas, riding on a wagon to a cowboy reunion (to the uninitiated, that's a yee-haw gathering of cowhands designed to keep cowboy traditions alive). Along with her sketchbook, she was armed with a new Kodak camera to photograph her surroundings, capturing images of her young cousins or people 'planting taters' in the sun. These were candid snaps of American life: children with muddy faces straddling broken fences, women in cartwheel hats running to catch the last steamboat, little girls scratching their backsides through the skirts of their Sunday best. Münter would later make disparaging remarks about the camera as a medium, 'Photographs make clear how superficial, often even false, outward appearance can be,'[1] she wrote in 1952. Münter may not have thought much of the Kodak as a medium but the visual diary formed by her photographs of the old west is anything but superficial. It gives us insight into her early development as an artist, her spontaneity, her keen eye for composition and her fascination with the inner lives of children. It's an independent side to her work that's hardly seen. Münter was one of the leading painters in German Expressionism and founding member of Munich art group The Blue Rider (Der Blaue Reiter), but when her artwork is shown there is, consistently, one prominent theme: the landscapes she painted alongside Wassily Kandinsky.

'Genuine lyrical magic'

Münter always had ambitions to study art but the official academy in Düsseldorf did not accept women in 1898. If a woman was lucky enough to have the wealth (which she did) she could try private lessons, or attend the Ladies' Art School (which she did) but the hobbyist atmosphere left Münter frustrated. 'I found the teaching of its academy, however, very uninspiring, still dominated by the ideas and tastes of the later Romantics; besides, nobody there seemed to take seriously the artistic ambitions of a mere girl'[2]. She was living in the era of the *Malweiber*, a dismissive term for a woman artist exemplified in a cartoon by Bruno Paul. Underneath the sketch of a man and a woman at a painting easel was the caption: 'You see, miss, there are two types of women painters: those who want to marry, and those who also have no talent'[3].

The Ladies' Art School felt like an exercise in keeping middle-class women busy before marriage. While Münter was studying there, growing increasingly bored by the day, fires of modernism were being lit all over Europe, and she had no interest in being trapped in traditionalism.

It was a German cabaret called 'Eleven Executioners' that gave her the push she needed to try a new path. Sitting in the audience, watching the performers leap around in masks, she explained, 'my fingers began to tingle, a sculptor I would be'[4]. She found a place at the Phalanx Schule, a small, private and progressive new art school in Munich, taking part in a sculpture class where she had the opportunity to draw nude models and, finally, be taken seriously. Her supervisor was the Russian painter Wassily Kandinsky, who took an enlightened approach to teaching that had been lacking in the Ladies' Art School. He treated Münter 'as though I were a consciously striving person who can set herself problems and goals'[5], and gave her the respect of an actual artist instead of a young woman just passing the time. 'German painters refused to believe that a woman could have real talent, and I was even denied access, as a student, to the Munich Academy. In those days women could study art, in Munich, only privately or in the studios of the *Künstlerinnenverein*, the association of professional women artists. It is significant that the first Munich artist who took the trouble to encourage me was Kandinsky, himself no German but a recent arrival from Russia'[6], she said.

Wassily Kandinsky was eleven years older than Münter, and was married (to his cousin Anna Chemyakina), but somewhere between student and teacher bike rides through the Bavarian countryside and afternoons out *plein air* sketching, they fell in love. On art trips with other students, Kandinsky and Münter would catch moments together through an adjoining room. At one stage, she quit the class at Phalanx to ease Kandinsky's awkwardness about his wife showing up, but soon rejoined. He promised to divorce Chemyakina for Münter, and they were effectively engaged. The relationship lasted twelve years, living on borrowed time.

The teacher-dating-student set-up isn't remotely original. In their letters, he could slip from supportive to condescending; at one point, he told her trying out woodcuts would be 'much too much for the small, poor (lazy) Ella'[7] and got sniffy and jealous when she expressed how Picasso had influenced her work.

Still the relationship was formative for both artists. In 1906, they went to Paris and spent fourteen months absorbing the ideas of the Fauvists, the visual language of Picasso, Van Gogh and Gauguin. They were filling up their modernist shopping baskets, and working out the formula that would later form the Munich art group The Blue Rider.

Kandinsky was dead wrong about those woodcuts, though. Münter excelled with the technique; woodcut prints make up an important part of her body of work, and show just how multifaceted she can be. One reviewer of the Munich New Artist's Association exhibition called them, 'first class, completely lovely, naive fairy-tale poetic works full of genuine lyrical magic'[8], but managed to get in a few digs about her painting, 'It is difficult to understand how someone, succeeding in such cabinet pieces, then again in the manner of this same Gabriele Münter is able to mess about on the canvas with foolish colours and wild lines'. It's those 'foolish colours' and 'wild lines' that would make Münter's name, and leave her endlessly compared to Kandinsky.

'Still life is the piano – landscape the orchestra'

It was in a little market town nestled in the shadow of the Bavarian alps that Gabriele Münter created her best-known paintings, the Murnau landscapes. The surrounding lakeland, the blue of the mountains and the colourful log houses helped her make the leap to Expressionism, producing hundreds of landscape paintings through simple licks of paint. Kandinsky and Münter spent their summers in Murnau with another art couple, Russian artists Marianne von Werefkin and Alexej von Jawlensky. Like Münter, Werefkin's work has been subsumed by that of her partner. She was once called the 'Russian Rembrandt', and trained with realist master Ilya Repin before a hunting accident injured her hand and put an end to her tight academic brushwork. Werefkin settled into life as a hostess of art salons and focused on Jawlensky's career, before rediscovering her talent through a looser, Expressionist mode of painting.

The time between 1908–1909 was a productive one for the foursome in Murnau; Münter even bought a house there that became known locally as 'the Russians' house' (even though Münter, the owner, was German). Their friendship wasn't always easy. In her letters to Kandinsky, Münter doesn't pull her punches when discussing her fallouts with them, 'Has Marianne suddenly gone off her head? The Baroness had at any rate been acting differently toward me … I'm not going to make the first move. They can go hang, for all I care'[9].

Fallouts and feuds aside, the Murnau period was pivotal in Münter's journey as a painter. When she captured the area's landscape, Münter used thick contour lines of paint for the shape, filling them in with flat planes of unglazed and unshaded colour.

The landscapes are intentionally naive, illustrated with the simplest possible forms, like a half-remembered dream. The bendy roads and houses of her landscapes are similar to the ones Alfred Wallis would paint in St Ives twenty years later. They are created in a jump, a flash of colour and spontaneity, that burns slow. 'Still life is the piano, landscape the orchestra'[10] she wrote in her diary in 1954.

Münter's skills as a colourist were heavily informed by her discovery of *Hinterglasmalerei*, Bavarian glass painting. 'In Murnau I was the first, as far as

I know, in the entire circle [of Munich artists], who took panes of glass and made some [glass paintings] myself. At first copies, then various ones of my own …'[11]. All four of them tried the technique, but it was Münter who would carry it into the rest of her career. In so many of her pieces, she mimics the piercing colours, pyramidal forms and segmented planes of those Bavarian glass works. The Murnau landscapes of Kandinsky and Münter are a visual dialogue: there is so much crossover in technique, with slight variations in approach to colour. His landscapes are squished late-summer fruits, hers the darker autumn harvest of orange and umber.

Münter has often been given credit simply for being present while the great Kandinsky was producing his semi-abstract landscapes, some of the most vibrant of his career. It created a millstone that's been hung around the neck of her career since. Since they painted in sync, her work was treated like an extension of his, facing comparisons Kandinsky's did not. The landscapes are treated like 'evidence' that he was the better painter, when in reality, the couple were headed in different artistic directions.

'Short holidays in the realm of abstraction'

Münter had a deep interest in children's art; between herself and Kandinsky, they collected more than 300 children's drawings. It's a simplicity she integrated into her painting, merging it with a Fauvist approach to colour, and the pattern-making of Russian and German folk art. She collected German folk toys, such as *Schepperdocken*, hollowed-out wooden dolls with a stone placed inside to give a slightly nightmarish rattle. Like so many of her portraits, the *Schepperdocke* has two blue dots to denote its eyes. Unlike Kandinsky, her motifs brush up against the front door of abstraction without ever stepping over the threshold completely.

Münter's real talent always lay in figuration, something she acknowledged herself: 'I also tried my hand, of course, at a few improvisations of the same general nature as his. But I believe I had developed a figurative style of my own, or at least one that suited my temperament, and I have remained faithful to it ever since, with occasional short holidays in the realm of abstraction'[12].

The majority of her portraits are of women, usually captured in thoughtful poses, cheek in hand, reflecting. Portraits of children are painted on flat backgrounds of pinks and yellows, and look as modern today as when they were first painted.

Though Gabriele Münter was a founding member of The Blue Rider group in 1911, the 'almanac' they created was edited by Kandinsky and Franz Marc, and so they have together gone down in history as its most prominent members. The group even took its name from a Kandinsky painting, *Der Blaue Reiter* but it was a wholly collective effort. It grew out of a desire to connect the dots between the past and the then-present of revolutionary art movements across Europe. As a movement The Blue Rider was a melting pot of Expressionism, Russian Mysticism and German Romanticism. They wanted to form a new way of seeing, for people to hear the inner sound of colour, and feel in painting the same heartfelt sincerity as felt through folk song. As Münter put it 'we were all more interested in being honest than being modern'[13].

There was no didactic style among the Blue Riders; they were proud of their individualism, but because of her links to Kandinsky, Münter was continually denied hers. 'In the eyes of many, I was only an unnecessary side-dish to Kandinsky. It is all too easily forgotten that a woman can be a creative artist with a real, original talent of her own. A woman standing alone … can never gain recognition through her own efforts. Other "authorities" have to stand up for her'[14], she wrote in her diary.

In their final correspondence before the outbreak of World War One, Kandinsky and Münter are sharing ideas about what they should have for dinner when they next see each other, 'Mother finds the idea of chops very acceptable', Kandinsky wrote on 18 April 1914. The war had other plans, putting a blockade on their relationship. Kandinsky was forced to emigrate to Russia, and promised to return, but Münter was devastated when she heard through a mutual friend that he'd married someone else (despite their informal engagement). They never saw each other again, though they did have a protracted legal battle over Kandinsky's works (Münter withheld them on moral grounds, though did end up returning the majority to Kandinsky).

Those she held onto she kept safe from the Nazis in the basement of the Murnau house she had bought for their old age, risking arrest or worse.

Münter eventually donated 1,000 Blue Rider works with 300 drawings and ninety oil paintings by Kandinsky to the Städtische Galerie in the Lenbachhaus, which, while slightly reviving her own artistic reputation, only served to further connect her to Kandinsky in the public consciousness.

One of the last interviews with Gabriele Münter was with critic Edouard Roditi, in 1958, when she was over eighty, later transcribed from his scribbled notes for the book he published in 1960, *Dialogues on Art*. In a later edition, he even opens with a kind of disclaimer that says Münter was chosen for inclusion by a happy accident of circumstance. 'I have been asked why I chose to include … Gabriele Münter, whose name and work, as a companion of Kandinsky, at the time of his decisive shift from figurative art to his earliest and more expressionist style of abstraction, were still scarcely known, except to a few specialists, beyond the frontiers of West Germany'[15]. Although Münter comes across as shrewd, carefully crafting her answers to redirect the focus to her work, the entire interview is preoccupied with Kandinsky's career, his influences and practice. Roditi treats Münter like a living archive to clarify points in Kandinsky's biography.

Münter has had more than twenty-one solo exhibitions across the world, but Kandinsky's presence endures. It is treated as a necessity, to explain her journey, and while to an extent this is true, male artists are rarely expected to pay ode to their mentors and influences in the same way. Russian author and occultist Helena Petrovna Blavatsky was likely an influence on Kandinsky. Does Blavatsky get a mention in every Kandinsky retrospective? Does Münter? She was gracious about the man who abandoned her, claiming, 'When I begin to paint, it's like leaping suddenly into deep waters, and I never know beforehand whether I will be able to swim. Well, it was Kandinsky who taught me the technique of swimming'[16], but from 1914 she swam alone.

No artist is free from influence, at some point in their journey, they all stand on another's shoulders to see the next destination. When he met Münter, Roditi spoke about how youthful she seemed like 'one of those spry pioneering grandmothers' you might meet in the Old West. And that's how I like to imagine her, back on the dirt roads of the Texas Panhandle, her converted wagon packed with her canvases, hitched to no one.

7
VARVARA STEPANOVA: CONSTRUCTING RUSSIAN ART

In the years before and after the Russian Revolution in 1917, Varvara Stepanova was one of the most radical figures in the Russian avant-garde art scene.

You couldn't move for 'isms' in Russia back then; by the 1910s, the avant-garde crowd were hoovering up ideas from Italian Futurism, Cubism and the Malevich-patented Suprematism faster than an art-history student cramming for finals. Stepanova was the youngest in an experimental constellation of creators but was instrumental in the formation of Constructivism, one of the most important artistic movements of the early twentieth century. Among the Constructivist ranks were artists Olga Rozanova, Kazimir Malevich, Natalia Goncharova, Lyubov Popova, poet Vladimir Mayakovsky and Alexander Rodchenko – Stepanova's artistic collaborator and later, her husband.

For a short time after the Revolution, these artists were suspended in a bubble of conceptual discovery, searching for an artistic philosophy that would reflect this socialist life-in-progress, the hope of a new and better society under the Bolsheviks. Constructivism was the answer to that half-formed question, a rejection of the 'elitist' art barricaded in academies and museums. Instead, they would embrace productivist, egalitarian art, work that could find a place in the factories, streets and squares of Moscow.

Constructivist art branched into painting, sculpture, architecture and printmaking, but Stepanova's contribution found a home in textile production. Her creations were absorbed by industry, and could be manufactured into objects that were used by the people.

In a way, she and Lyubov Popova were among the few artists in the group to truly execute the promises of Constructivism in their work, but their textile designs remain under-recognised in the written history of the movement. Echoes of 'applied' Constructivist art in the mainstream favours the flapping wings of Vladimir Tatlin's Soviet flying sculpture *Letatlin* or Alexander Rodchenko's collaged, call-to-action portrait of Lilya Brik, an image that's continually referenced in popular culture, for example, in the album art of the band Franz Ferdinand's *You Could Have it So Much Better*.

And then there is the difficult issue of partnership. Regardless of her independent achievements, Stepanova's entire artistic output is all too readily tethered to Rodchenko's. You can understand why. They shared the same studio, the same materials, friendships, ideology and artistic influences. Photographs of the two together make for wholesome social media posts: there are endless shots of them mucking around in their studio, posing with upside-down guitars and giant paint brushes, wearing matching heavy-knit jumpers. Fodder for 'couple goals' captions.

They had an undeniable visual interdependence, and an equal, productive relationship that fought against the gendered expectations of the West. She was his partner in every sense, not his student. Though she is not well known in the West, Stepanova is a point on a jagged historical line of political Russian artists that travels from the photomontage of the 1920s right up to the guerrilla feminism of Pussy Riot.

The union of Stepanova and Rodchenko and the extensive body of art it produced has been recognised in multiple joint exhibitions but it is Rodchenko who is set apart as a notable figure with international retrospectives and solo shows. Stepanova's name might not be heard as often, but the creative afterglow of her work is everywhere – in the geometric patterns sailing down contemporary catwalks, and the colourful unisex sports clothing lines being rolled out by Adidas and Nike. But her designs were not limited to the textile factories: there was also her painting, book design, photomontage, polygraphic poster art and Stepanova's lesser-discussed innovation, her experimental, visual poetry.

'Creator of the future not the heir to the past'

While in her late teens and studying at the Kazan Art School, Stepanova crafted exceptional poetry with a romantic feel, musing on things like the pale rays of 'silvery moonlight'. Writing to Rodchenko (who at this stage lived in Moscow) she says, 'You are mysterious to the core, elusive like the reflection from a dead opal in a deep mirror of water'[1]. Some of these poems were responses to his graphic designs; Stepanova would write them in a notebook decorated in the curlicues of Art Nouveau.

This early relationship between graphics and poetry would form an important revelation in Stepanova's practice: her non-objective (or, what some might called abstract) visual poetry. In an homage to the Zaum poets of the Russian Futurist art movement who reinvented and toyed with language in their work, Stepanova explored a type of communication that would up-end conventional poetry. By combining phonemes in a radical linguistic pattern, she created her own free verse with works like *Rtny Kholme*, which went on display as a series of graphic illustrations at a State Exhibition in 1918.

These were heavily influenced by the Zaum poetry artworks of Suprematist painter Olga Rozanova, another underappreciated female member of the Russian avant-garde.

Stepanova's poetic 'sounds' were visualised by graphic illustrations, where Cyrillic text would be splashed across the page at different angles. She found verse in the space between the letters, and criss-crossed lines. They had their own texture, their own colour, the syllables moved from hot to cold. It was a way of grabbing the expressive sound of the vowels in a closed fist and throwing the consonants onto paper. Instead of an Art Nouveau notebook, the poems were committed to the surface of torn-out newspaper pages, graph paper and small collages. Stepanova was one of the first to show visual poetry of this kind as part of an organised art exhibition.

Writing in the State Exhibition's catalogue she explained, 'By turning the monotony of printed letters upside down and fusing them with painterly graphics, I am approaching a new type of creativity'[2]. The painterly look – a premonition of the angular aesthetic of Soviet prints and Constructivist ideas that would develop in the 1920s – found its way into her poster art too. One splashy, blue and pink collage from 1919 shouts the slogan, 'The proletariat is the creator of the future not the heir to the past'[3], in dancing white hand-painted letters. As her grandson (and professor of the Moscow State Stroganov Academy of Design and Applied Arts), Alexander Lavrentiev put it, she was intentionally paring down an enormous amount of visual information ready to 'explode as the "supernova" star of a new style'[4].

Move your foot forward

The supernova explosion came quickly and with a stellar death. At the *5x5 = 25* exhibition in Moscow in 1921 (which showed works by Aleksandra Ekster, Lyubov Popova, Alexander Rodchenko and Alexander Vesnin) Stepanova and her peers declared the 'end' of easel painting in favour of design. Her contribution to this wake for artistic tradition was her *Figure* series, geometric images exploring human biomechanics, each made up of a 'linear skeleton'. Professor Lavrentiev (who has compiled a book on the complete works of Stepanova and Rodchenko) explains they were never intended to be representational or realistic; the figures are instead 'a reconstruction of the human figure from the elements of abstract art developed by Rodchenko: plane, line, circle, texture.'[5]

Building on the declaration of painting's death, Stepanova wrote, 'the "sanctity" of a work as a single entity is destroyed. The museum which was a treasury of this entity is now transformed into an archive'[6]. It was a theoretical footbridge into the working artistic world of Constructivism, key parts of which were built on Stepanova's ideas.

With an article on the subject of non-objectivity creativity that she composed in 1918, we can see her thoughts on the theory taking shape. She takes aim at elitism in art, and rejects the obsession with subject matter in painting. If the viewer was not 'corrupted by subject matter' she writes, and 'not being so cultured that he demands representation everywhere in art' they would be able to connect with their creativity while standing before that painting, and understand 'his unspoiled intuition as a new beauty, a beauty born of painting's liberation from centuries of accursed subject matter and the depiction of what is visible'[7].

The goal was to push beyond museum structures and art-world cliques. Not only was she against interpretation, she was fighting against the need to find clear meaning in art. 'You won't be able to find anything "familiar" or "comprehensible" but don't let this exasperate you, come to love art, grow to understand the tenet "to live for art". Don't just study and learn to discriminate, to look for subject matter that you understand, the representation of themes you may wish for'[8].

The founding of Constructivism as an art movement is attributed to Vladimir Tatlin (who took his cue from Picasso's Cubism) but it was Stepanova and her colleagues who formed them into art theory at the Institute of Artistic Culture (INKhUK) in 1920–21. In *Who We Are: Manifesto of the Constructivist Group*, released in 1922, they called for an end to art for art's sake and declared, 'We came – the first working group of Constructivists – Aleksei Gan, Rodchenko, Stepanova, and we simply said. This is – today … We are not dreamers from art who build in the imagination …'[9].

With no esteemed academic title at the institution, Stepanova took on the job of secretary at INKhUK, recording notes from their meetings and lectures. Though at the time this was an important organisational role with invaluable contribution to how the group was recorded and later perceived, it makes her appear more peripheral, and less influential than she actually was.

In 1921, she was the only woman to take part in a lecture series that provided, according to Professor Lavrentiev, 'one of the early general theoretical statements about Constructivism'[10] at INKhUK. Stepanova urged her listeners not to indulge in the historic notion of the genius who is struck by the apparition of a muse in his studio and instead see art as an agent of social change. Useful not superfluous, collective not individualistic. Turn 'subconscious inspiration' and the 'spirituality' of artistic activity into 'organised activity'. This would reconfigure the meaning of beauty, so that which was considered beautiful, would be the most useful and constructive.

It's easy to dismiss this productivist approach to art as a play into the homogeneity of industry and mass-production, but for Stepanova, it was about breaking down boundaries between classes by integrating art into all levels of society. The 'new society' would puncture the closed cycle of artworks moving from studio to gallery or museum, operating outside the public sphere, instead of within it. As she told the audience at her lecture 'On Constructivism', 'If you move your foot forward, you declare yourself to be outside the process of continuity'[11].

Sportodezhda

Stepanova put her ideas into action almost immediately with her costume and set design for the stage production of *The Death of Tarelkin* by Aleksandr Sukhovo-Kobylin. She had the skills of an advanced tailor and treated her Singer sewing machine and scissors as artistic tools equal to the paintbrush. Distilling the biometric studies from the 'linear skeletons' of her *Figure* series, she mocked up simple outfits with striking black and white lines that would emphasise the actors' movements.

The story of Tarelkin follows the protagonist as he fakes his own death and assumes the identity of a recently deceased neighbour. Theatre director Vsevolod Meyerhold's 1922 adaptation took aim at life in pre-revolutionary Russia. Stepanova's hyper-modern sets of painted white frames created the surreal slapstick nature of a Charlie Chaplin film. She designed tables that were booby-trapped to surprise the actors, producing sharp acrobatic movements in their monochromatic outfits. It remains one of the most famous stagings of Sukhovo-Kobylin's work.

Soon Stepanova began to apply the idea of costume design to everyday life; she wanted to create 'production' outfits that could offer functional fashion to specific areas of work, leisure and sport – a response to the political atmosphere of the 1920s. Lenin viewed physical fitness and competitive sport as an essential part of the new Soviet life, and ushered in the dawn of *fizkultura*, (physical culture) a communist upbringing to form the new generation. It was all part of the image of the healthy *Novyi Sovetsky chelovek* (new Soviet man).

Cherry-picking ideas from Constructivism, Futurism, Russian decorative art and the clothes of the proletariat, Stepanova created her vision of the ideal *Sportodezhda*. These sports costumes – comfortable, easy-wear unisex jumpsuits – were decorated with bold black and yellow or white and red stripes placed at hypnotic optic angles. It's not a million miles away from the striking pattern configuration on Nigeria's sell-out World Cup men's football strip for 2018, only Stepanova's vision for the cut and style was gender-neutral.

She continued to apply Constructivist theory to fashion, focusing her energy on textile design. Along with Lyubov Popova, she kept to her own Constructivist concept of 'art into production'; she felt that the 'artist' should be involved in every level of textile creation – not in some glass-fronted office overseeing sketches for fabric designs. Stepanova believed the artist should be in the 'organs' of production on the factory floor, dyeing the material and cutting the fabric. Working at the First Textile Printing Factory for just over a year, she conceived more than 150 original textile designs, covering material with the kind of bright sequential patterns and lysergic rhythms you might see through the lens of a child's kaleidoscope.

Most of them were too complicated to ever be fully realised in the machinery of a Soviet factory. But her inventions were so prescient, predicting the optical art of Victor Vasarely in the 1940s and Bridget Riley in the 1960s. Stepanova was made Professor of Composition in the textile department of the Vkhutemas (a Russian state art and technical school) in 1923, where Rodchenko was also on the faculty.

On a tour of the Vkhutemas, Lenin wasn't thrilled by the intensely abstract innovations of the Constructivists, saying, 'Tastes differ… I am an old man'[12]. Under Stalinist rule, the avant-garde received serious threats, satire was high risk, and Constructivism was seen as too alien and far removed from the party line. The bright lights of the Vkhutemas went out in 1930, and by 1932, Stalin had issued a decree that all art must express Soviet ideology. An era of stark Social Realism in art collapsed on the avant-garde like Stepanova's booby-trapped tables.

The only means of conveying reality

There's a photograph of Stepanova at her desk (taken, as so many were, by Rodchenko): she is hunched in a c-shape over its surface, where stray magazine pages lie sliced and diced and scrunched. Gripping the end of her cigarette to her lips, it looks as though an unwelcome stranger has just asked for a drag. Another cigarette, half smoked, sits partly on the ashtray, partly on a pencil sketch for what looks like a book cover. Beside it, there is an open box where dozens more *sigaréty* wait patiently for their turn. The artist is every bit the deadline-weary newspaper editor, waiting for a writer to deliver a front-page splash. Around the time it was taken, she had moved from the world of textiles to the practice that would occupy her artistic life for more than thirty years – book and magazine design.

In some ways, the journey into the polygraphic arts was a natural one for her, taking on creative jobs that involved active production and fed the work straight to the public. With Rodchenko, she formed a micro design studio, where they collaborated on covers for magazines and journals like *Book and Revolution*, *Lef*, *Soviet Cinema* and *Kino-Fot*. Much of the distinctive voice of visual Soviet culture was developed by Stepanova's designs; her oversized flat black lettering, the diagonal compositions and the liberal use of photomontage all predicted the covers of 1990s magazines like *The Face*.

Everything Stepanova created had her signature, like her studies of Charlie Chaplin (for the cover of *Kino-Fot*, and later in woodcut illustrations). With his cog-like movements and black-and-white aesthetic, Chaplin's mechanical figure was like a culmination of her entire practice: the biometric figure paintings, the stripy textiles and farcical stage furniture.

Having initially expressed scepticism about the value of the camera, she eventually gave in to the technique of photomontage, too. In an essay on the technique, she referred to Rodchenko as 'the first photomontagist'[13] and wrote that intense mechanisation had, 'forced them to resort to the camera as the only means of conveying reality'[14]. Stepanova also absorbed all the 'admin' duties – she set the typeface, kept track of deadlines, acted as technical editor, a messenger and a secretary. Adopting this background role meant her enormous contribution was not as visible as the front-facing and now instantly recognisable poster works of Rodchenko.

The future is our only goal

Alexander Lavrentiev has become something of an expert on his grandparents. When asked why he feels Stepanova's involvement in Constructivism is less known than her partner's, he told me, 'She fully dissolved her personality in Rodchenko's activities, helping him to execute his projects. The reason was her love and her full trust in what he did as an artist and creative figure. She kept their small artists' and design studio running… she had much less time for her own creative work'[15]. We can't forget that she was younger than the rest of the avant-garde set, and unlike Rodchenko, who spent time as a director of INKhUK, she did not have a high-ranking title there.

Stepanova formed crucial theories on Constructivism, but writing on the movement centred on Rodchenko and his male peers in positions of prestige. And then there's the familiar dismissal of textiles and other supposedly 'feminine' applied arts, which has been happening for centuries, the unseen workers who wove carpets, sewed lace and embroidered skirts. If only more had thought like artist Kazimir Malevich, who, when looking at the materials created by female Ukrainian peasant workers stated, 'Art belonged to them more than the men'[16].

As an offshoot of Constructivism, unlike the prints of Rodchenko or the sculptures of Tatlin, the textiles of Stepanova and Popova are the less seen. But she is finding parity with Rodchenko in her painting. In 2014, thanks to the spike in demand for Russian artworks of the 1920s–1940s, her *Figure with Guitar* sold at Sotheby's for over £1.6 million.

There is frenetic pluralism in Stepanova's work that makes her so difficult to pin down, how she moved from visual poetry to costume-making to book and magazine design and towards the end of her life, back to the emotional easel painting she had denounced. It's too comprehensive, too strange. By her own manifesto, she wasn't out to make superfluous work that could be easily understood. She was always ready to erupt, go back to black, and start over.

Dada was an art movement that made no sense. To try and describe it is to try and catch air in cupped hands. When it was formed in Zürich in 1916, during World War One, the Battle of Verdun was days away, and then came the Somme, a massacre with a body count of more than one million. Reason, rationality and accountability had been hijacked by war, and the Dadaists swooped in, like an airborne virus ready to fill the lacunae with its absurdity. Society, as they saw it, was broken, and Dada was a way of stripping it down to nothing and starting over, right back to the first syllables to leave a baby's mouth.

Today 'Dadaist' is used as shorthand to describe anything weird. Its stamp of influence can be found on the Sex Pistols, the sculptures of Cornelia Parker, the end credits of a Monty Python sketch or the words of a child's joke.

It all began with Cabaret Voltaire, an anarchistic open mic night founded by poet and vaudeville performer Emmy Hennings with writer Hugo Ball. They had a little help from the intellectual exiles that had found themselves in neutral Zürich: the poet Tristan Tzara, artist Marcel Janco and writer Richard Huelsenbeck.

This was 'anti-art' art, a commitment to what artist Francis Picabia called the unaesthetic in the extreme. Nights at Cabaret Voltaire were an upside-down carnival held in a back room at a Zürich tavern where you could hear poetry performed in three languages at once and watch masked dancers throw shapes of literary verse to an apoplectic drum beat. One of the most recognisable moments of Dada is seen in a photograph of Hugo Ball dressed in a magic bishop's outfit of blue cardboard, looking like 'an obelisk'[1] while reciting the gibberish poem 'Karawane', which included such lines as:

Kusa gauma / ba – umf!

Enemy to totalitarian regimes and the bourgeoisie, with one toe dipped in nihilism, Dada was a mess of contradictions. In practice, the whole notion of the movement was a lot like Tzara's how-to guide for writing a Dada poem: cut up an article from a newspaper, he said, throw the words in a bag, shake, take them out and arrange them to make an original Dada verse that will go 'unappreciated by the vulgar herd'[2].

Club Dada

No one person could be held responsible for Dada's creation. The group had given itself permission to be nothing at all, but that didn't stop its members fighting to be the king of nothing. It found its way to Berlin, Paris and New York, with each new group of artists throwing their idea of Dada into a bag and shaking to see what would pop out. The French contingent couldn't stop measuring avant-garde appendages. Its members splintered over who was the true leader of their Parisian Dada supergroup.

The Berlin era was overtly political. At the First International Dada Fair in 1920, artist Rudolf Schlichter strung a pig-headed dummy of a German soldier from the ceiling with a sign that read, 'I come from Heaven, from Heaven on high'. The Berliner group was embarrassingly performative in its machismo; artists George Grosz and John Heartfield only agreed to let artist Hannah Höch into their ranks after the fair's co-organiser, her lover Raoul Hausmann, threatened to drop out. Though the bellicose boys of Berlin's Club Dada did their best to edge her out, Höch's proto-punk photomontage *Cut with the Kitchen Knife Dada through the Last Weimar Beer Belly Cultural Epoch of Germany* turned out to be a smash hit at the fair. Using spliced and diced images, she created a montage of fragmented political moments and feminist thought; in its bottom right-hand corner was a map denoting the countries in Europe where women had, or would soon have, the right to vote.

Whether out of explicit sexism or plain malice, many of Höch's male peers sidelined her in their effusive writings about the the salad days of Dada (self-mythologising was a particular skill of the Dada men). The book *Dada Painters and Poets*, edited by Robert Motherwell, mentions her name and little else. Those that did include her weren't much of an improvement. Hans Richter referred to Höch's 'tiny voice' and 'nun-like'[3] grace compared to the 'heavyweight challenge' of her mentor (Hausmann). He also recast the collagist as a sort of Dada tea lady 'she made herself indispensable… sandwiches, beer and coffee she somehow managed to conjure up despite the shortage of money'[4].

The Dadaists wanted to strip away the worst of society and its conventions, but the all-assuming power of the male ego clung to this clean slate like a stubborn mollusc. Efforts to repress Hannah Höch's relevance did not succeed. Her first major UK show at the Whitechapel Gallery in London in 2014 brought on a slew of admiring articles, bolstering her reputation among a younger audience. With their attacks on the absurdity of gender roles, pressures of maternity and marriage and unrealistic beauty standards, Höch's collages seem as fresh today as they did in the 1920s. She has been reassessed and canonised over the years to the point where her name is equal to – if not more recognisable – than Raoul Hausmann's.

But there is frustration in this need for rediscovery. The culture of men centring themselves as the 'masters and thinkers' had a detrimental effect on the perception of women in Dada. Though they were there from the beginning, the delayed appraisal of their work led to their being treated like an outside force, rather than an intrinsic part of the movement. The exception, not the rule.

For a long time, the stubborn mollusc clung to the work of Sophie Taeuber-Arp, another of the Zürich Dadaists and the only Swiss member of the group. Between her day job as a professor of textile design and techniques at the School of Applied Arts in Zürich, she would take the stage at the Cabaret Voltaire to perform bewitching 'cubist' dances. Dada co-founder Emmy Hennings called her 'a flower that bends to worship the sun'[5].

Dance was only a small aspect of her fluid artistic output. After the early Dada days she was prolific, producing art that traversed textile tapestries, abstract painting, sculpture and puppetry. Taeuber-Arp is one of the most important modernist artists of the twentieth century. Her colourful and abstract innovations like *Rising, Falling, Flying* should be as recognisable as those of Kandinsky or Mondrian but her reputation still lags just behind that of her husband, Jean Arp.

After Taeuber-Arp died from accidental carbon monoxide poisoning at the age of fifty-three, the posthumous handling of her work complicated her oeuvre. Devastated by the loss, Jean Arp strove to keep her legacy alive by asking artist Lili Erzinger to complete Taeuber-Arp's unfinished paintings, dissolving the originality beneath. He also repurposed the couple's *Duo Drawings* by cutting them up to include in his own projects, forming a new 'collaboration' in death. What was intended as a romantic act just tightened the link between her legacy and his own.

Taeuber-Arp's impressive body of work is more diverse than Arp's and thankfully, it managed to stand on its own: New York's Museum of Modern Art, MoMA, held a retrospective for her in 1981, then again in 2014. Her face appeared on a Swiss bank note. Then came a Google Doodle for her 127th 'birthday', prompting multiple headlines asking 'Who was Sophie Taeuber-Arp?'. Even with these mainstream nods, she is still presented as an enigma. If the foundations of Sophie Taeuber-Arp and Hannah Höch's achievements had been properly laid, we wouldn't have to rebuild their reputations for each new generation.

Closing the recognition gap for the women artists of Dada is more complicated for those whose works, like the poetry and dance routines of Dada co-founder Emmy Hennings cannot fill a gallery. Likewise, New York Dadaist Baroness Elsa von Freytag-Loringhoven was a poet who made paintings, collage and sculpture, but very little of it survives. Or does it? The most pressing question raised in relation to the Baroness's legacy is usually one of authorship. For years now, a story has been spinning in the media that she might be the real creator of Marcel Duchamp's famous urinal, the *Fountain*. As I was writing this book, new evidence emerged that challenged this long held theory, but shone a light on other women involved in the creation of *Fountain*. Duchamp and von Freytag-Loringhoven were never in a romantic relationship, but for this chapter, it felt necessary to explore her work in relation to the complex approach to authorship in Dada circles, and how it affected the work created by women. If the Baroness theory were proven, it would have meant the foundation of Duchamp's Readymades and, depending on your outlook, of conceptual art as a whole, were based on a falsehood. We'd have had to rip it all up and start again. It would all have been *so very Dada*.

Emmy Hennings

The men of Dada jostled to establish themselves among its 'founders' once the *ba-umf* years had passed. Huelsenbeck called it 'the battle of the Dada greybeards'[6]. But there would be no Dada without Emmy Hennings. Together with Hugo Ball, she convinced the owner of Zürich bar Holländische Meierei that he'd sell plenty of beer and sausages if he'd just let them put on a show in the back room.

On 5 February 1916, that 'show' exploded into the Cabaret Voltaire. This literary nightclub was the genesis of Dada. Hennings sang French and Danish songs while Ball played the piano, Tzara read poetry in Romanian, a balalaika orchestra played to the (no doubt confused) crowd. Tzara's *Zurich Chronicle* called Hennings 'the star of the Cabaret Voltaire'. She was the only member of the group with any real experience of performing on the variety show scene. When the couple had first arrived in Zürich and were low on cash, Hennings found them a regular gig with a vaudeville troupe. Hidden in a box with nothing on show but her disembodied head surrounded by six black legs, she played Arachne, a truth-speaking spider from Greek Mythology.

Her background taught her exactly how to translate the out-there message of Dada literature to an audience. She'd been moving through literary subcultures for years.

After she lost her first child and faced the end of her first marriage in around 1904, Hennings had travelled constantly. When she gave birth to a daughter during this period in her life, she left the baby to be raised by her mother. Rootless and roving, she made a living appearing in roadshows and operettas. And when she wasn't on stage, she was writing poetry and prose, verse that dealt with her issues with addiction, her life as a dancer and her experience of sex work. When her volume of poetry *The Last Joy* was published in 1913, one reviewer said her words 'really express the last joy of an impoverished Bohemia and Variety based life, without shame, but also without finally divulging the "I"'[7]. Her progressive outlook stands out. In her semi-autobiographical novel, *Prison*, she addresses the hypocrisy surrounding sex work: 'If it is forbidden to accept payment for love by the hour, then it should be forbidden to pay for love by the hour'[8].

She was an established poet long before Ball ever decided to dress up like a magic pencil, but most of the Dada memoirs dissolve her agency as a writer. She is described as the 'madonna' or an ethereal muse: 'Emmy was an extremely perceptive woman, but her intelligence had nothing intellectual about it, she was more of a visionary type'[9], Huelsenbeck wrote of Hennings, 'Hugo wasn't looking for a housewife in Emmy, he was seeking childlike innocence, childhood, the unconscious, the fairy-tale world and the metaphysical'[10].

German painter Hans Richter made it sound as though her life as a writer had not begun until Ball had entered her orbit, 'Emmy Hennings, who had met and inspired some of the best German poets during her lifetime – who had always, as long as I can remember (1912) lived among artists and writers – had become a writer herself'[11]. When she 'lived among' artists, as he says, Hennings herself was a published poet, but her status as a writer did not exist for Richter until Ball had validated it.

The reality is they both founded Cabaret Voltaire, and while her contribution is mentioned in some cases (usually in passing), it always defaults to Hugo Ball as the face of Dada's beginnings. He is seen as the philosopher, the educated theorist of the movement. If Hennings is acknowledged at all, it's usually about her singing, or unconventional dance. Hennings is painted like a medium, channelling the spectre of men's writing through her flailing limbs. She was allowed to be the body of Dada, while Ball was the designated brain.

Hennings' own poetry did not have the nonsensical nature of Dada, but she would still read it on stage at the Cabaret Voltaire. Her words might have been more conventional than 'Karawane', but her performances were the epitome of the Dada mad; dances would integrate the use of her handmade puppets, named Czar and Czarina.

In the beginning, Hennings was deeply invested in the political undercurrent of the movement. The Expressionist art circles she ran in before World War One had initially been supportive of war, viewing it as the ultimate iconoclasm, but Hennings believed in pacifism. In 1914, she was accused of forging passports to help friends dodge the war draft and was thrown in a Munich prison, though she had always maintained her innocence. The Cabaret Voltaire was a reaction to a feeling of helplessness: 'When Emmy Hennings sang "*They kill one another with steam and with knives*" in Switzerland, which was encircled by fighting armies, she was voicing our collective hatred of the inhumanity of war'[12], Huelsenbeck wrote.

Hennings and Ball began to drift away from Dada by 1920. Ball had become disillusioned with his own movement, losing faith in its diverging ideas as members brought it to new extremes. They moved to a quiet spot called Sant'Abbondio in Switzerland, and swapped *ba-umf* chanting for prayer by committing to Catholicism.

There's a widespread assumption that, after Ball died, Hennings began to erase her own identity by immersing herself into his work. It's true that she produced biographies about their life together, and she did try and distance herself from the days of Cabaret Voltaire – those vagabond days didn't tally with her new faith – but the writing never stopped, it's just that the work that didn't directly concern Hugo Ball seemed to carry less weight. Her novel *The Fugitive Game: One Woman's Roads and Detours*, published in 1940, opens with a confession to the reader: 'Many years ago I already planned to make a written confession of my life. I took a lot of notes which I each time rejected. Why? What I produced seemed quite entertaining to me in part, but was not sufficiently sincere enough, not honest enough. I tended, for example, to try to gloss over the most important defects in my nature, to soften them, or to suppress them altogether'[13]. As author Ruth Hemus points out in her book *Dada's Women*, Hennings' 1920 memoir *Das Brandmal* has the subtitle 'A Diary' of Emmy Hennings, but the main character is named Jessy. Divulging the 'I' was not Hennings' style, 'I have never spoken the truth,' she wrote, 'not even as a truth-speaking spider'[14].

Baroness Elsa von Freytag-Loringhoven

The origin of 'found object' in art is somewhere between Pablo Picasso and Marcel Duchamp, but Baroness Elsa was a living example of it. No scrap of New York City detritus was safe in her presence. On a good day in 1913, you might have seen her careering down 14th Street with five dogs on a lead, her hat decorated with spoons, a wooden birdcage around her neck that was home to a live canary, buttons on her fingers, celluloid rings around her wrists. And though she had a name plucked straight out of *Chitty Chitty Bang Bang*, she was not a wealthy eccentric: she had married a German aristocrat, but he was broke.

To support herself, she took up work as an artist's model, toiled in a cigarette factory and did the odd bit of shoplifting. Poet William Carlos Williams described her collector-mania like so, '[A] bride lost the heel of her left shoe at a tube station; lost, it becomes a jewel ... in La Baronne's miscellany'[15]. In a letter to Tristan Tzara, the photographer Man Ray referred to the Baroness's body as her 'performed self'[16], a signifier of 'Americanness/ Dada/the stripping bare of the bride of capitalism'. She embraced androgyny, shaving her head to have it shellacked in vermillion. The artist got wise to the prison of gender restrictions early on: when she landed in Berlin as a runaway at the age of nineteen, she was immediately arrested for smoking a cigarette and wearing men's clothing.

Baroness Elsa made the antics of Cabaret Voltaire look like basement karaoke. She carried Dada on her back wherever she went. Her poetry was littered with her own invented words and James Joyce-inspired scatology, 'And God spoke kindly to mine heart/So kindly spoke He to mine heart/He said: "Thou art allowed to fart!"/So kindly spoke He to mine heart'[17]. The two writers shared page space in *The Little Review* during the serialisation of *Ulysses* that led to an obscenity trial.

The most talked-about piece by the Baroness today, her 'readymade', is a found object sculpture called *God*, created in 1917: a twist of plumbing stuck to a block of wood. It was originally misattributed to Morton Schamberg, until scholar and art dealer Francis M. Naumann figured out that Schamberg merely mounted and recorded the sculpture. *God* took on a new significance with the publication of Irene Gammel's biography of the Baroness, which framed it as a piece of circumstantial evidence that pointed to Baroness Elsa as the originator of Marcel Duchamp's *Fountain*.

Duchamp became part of Dada and wider art world lore when he supposedly sent in a urinal signed 'R. Mutt' to the Society of Independent Artists (of which he was a board member) for an exhibition. When it was suppressed, he quit the Society in protest. Duchamp's friends at Dada journal *The Blind Man* turned the whole saga into a debate about what constitutes 'real art'.

Duchamp had invented the idea of conceptual art and the 'readymade'. Then in 1981, a letter from the artist to his sister, the sculptor Suzanne Duchamp, emerged: 'One of my female friends who had adopted the pseudonym Richard Mutt sent me a porcelain urinal as a sculpture; since there was nothing indecent about it, there was no reason to reject it'[18]. Scholars have since argued that the translation says that the female friend 'sent in' the urinal to the Society, rather than 'sent me', meaning Duchamp.

In her biography of the Baroness, Irene Gammel makes the case that von Freytag-Loringhoven could have been that 'female friend'. Duchamp and von Freytag-Loringhoven had collaborated in the past (once on the semi-erotic film *Baroness Elsa von Freytag-Loringhoven Shaving Her Pubic Hair*, lost forever when the processing of the film was botched). She was completely infatuated with him, and he rejected her sexually, though they had a loving platonic relationship.

Fountain is undeniably similar to *God*: two found object artworks unified by bodily wastes. Scatalogical humour was part of von Freytag-Loringhoven's art make-up. Adding to the suspicion that Duchamp may not have conceived *Fountain* is his claim that he sourced the urinal from J.L. Mott Iron Works on Fifth Avenue in NYC, when the company didn't manufacture that model.

But this 'evidence' is all circumstantial. What we do know for certain is that there were women involved in the making of *Fountain*. To get the debate going, R. Mutt enlisted the Dada-allies to gather round and start filling that urinal to the brim with meaning.

Much of the discourse about the legitimacy of *Fountain* as an artwork came from this frequently quoted but rarely credited defence which appeared in

The Blind Man: 'Whether Mr Mutt with his own hands made the fountain or not has no importance. He CHOSE it. He took an ordinary article of life, placed it so that its useful significance disappeared under the new title and point of view – created a new thought for that object. As for plumbing, that is absurd. The only works of art America has given are her plumbing and her bridges'[19]. The passage was probably written by gifted ceramic artist Beatrice Wood, another little-known member of Dada. Accompanying it was a supporting article by Louise Norton (later Louise Varèse), an important literary translator of Marcel Proust, Julien Gracq and Charles Baudelaire. In her piece 'Buddha of the Bathroom', referring to R. Mutt, she asks, 'Is he serious or is he joking? Perhaps he is both! Is it not possible?' She closes with, 'the most profound word in language and one which cannot be argued — a pacific Perhaps!'[20]

Duchamp was, and is still credited for revolutionising modern culture with his great art prank. But *Fountain* was never just about the porcelain urinal, it's about the debate it started, the publicity it generated; publicity *The Blind Man* was fully complicit in. Without the ideas presented by Wood and Norton, *Fountain* is just an abandoned piss pot in a boardroom. 'A text moves around like an art object. It is unbelievably important. [Wood and Norton] should be really talked about,' art critic Ben Street tells me, 'What happens is the story gets to be "an artist put an object in an art gallery" which isn't what happened. That isn't what the story is. It has become that because it's convenient.'[21]

In William Camfield's 1989 book, *Marcel Duchamp/Fountain*, a deep-dive investigation revealed that the contact details on the submission label for *Fountain* belonged to Louise Norton. A recent discovery of a handwritten draft of an essay by Norton called 'Marcel Duchamp at Play', features her own words about the *Fountain* saga, explaining how Duchamp sent the urinal into the Society of Independent Artists. Before this, it had been suggested that Norton may have submitted *Fountain* on behalf of the Baroness. We may never have one clear author, but what *is* clear is that *Fountain* was a group effort. 'I feel like we have to totally rethink [the way we talk] about art, not as a series of individual outliers but as people who always worked collaboratively. And, I think we could rewrite the whole history of art in that way. None of them worked on their own,'[22] says Street.

When feeling abandoned by her friends in 1923, the Baroness von Freytag-Loringhoven made *Forgotten Like this Parapluie am I by You – Faithless Bernice!*, a painting that features a man walking out of the frame as a pipe-smoking urinal overflows onto the floor. This painting too has been presented as 'evidence' in the Baroness Fountain theory. Could she have been trying to tell us something? All we ever had was a pacific *Perhaps*.

9
LUCIA MOHOLY:
BEHIND THE SCENES AT THE BAUHAUS

Photographs of ghost towns are irresistible to look at. Vacant, dusty and desolate, they are, like negatives, a kind of image in reverse, darkness where there once was light. They are out of tune with the busy family homes and traffic-backed roads to which our eyes are so accustomed. Where did they go? Maybe the trains stopped running, maybe the highway got diverted, or the river ran dry. Maybe miners broke their backs shifting coal until the source had nothing more to offer. Their beauty can be unnerving, and so we populate them with our minds, filling the void with replacement people plucked from long-term memories or scenes from movies. The community is long gone, but even if we know nothing about it, we animate what's in front of us, to imagine what was.

Such is the effect of photographer Lucia Moholy's famous architectural images of the Bauhaus, the radical German school of art and design that spent fourteen years shaping the idea of what it means to be 'modern'. Until the violent oppression of the Nazi party closed its doors in 1933, the teaching faculty of Bauhaus masters was a role call of some of the biggest names in Modern art.

Using a large-format camera, Moholy took hundreds of black-and-white shots of these revolutionary buildings at its campus in Weimar, and later in Dessau, each contained in a clunky 5 x 7-inch plate glass negative. She was a believer in the *Neue Sachlichkeit* (or New Objectivity) philosophy on photography, one that was committed to showing the subject in its real form – no frills. Her outlook was in harmony with her subject; the Bauhaus buildings are assembled like a game of 3D Tetris, a rectilinear formation of clean lines, heavy blocks of concrete and brick with sharp corners and bright glass curtain walls.

The approach was simple, but it captured the buildings with absolute artistry. She lay flat with her stomach resting on the grass opposite, angling her camera upward to fill her lens with the full scope of these harsh shapes like a mathematician guiding a compass. Sometimes, she broke her own carefully held rules of the New Objectivity, using a retouching paint on lines and surfaces of the negative to emphasise areas of darkness.

Instead of photographing the aftermath of an exodus, Moholy preserved the Bauhaus at its most exciting time. Looking at her photographs of the sleek, empty interiors at the homes of the Bauhaus masters designed by the school's founder, Walter Gropius, we picture Paul Klee on the couch putting a new entry in his diary, or Wassily Kandinsky at the full-length bathroom mirror, adjusting his tie.

When Gropius opened the Bauhaus (meaning literally 'building house') school in Weimar in 1919, the same year German women were granted the right to vote, he proposed a new approach to the arts, a chance to erode barriers between the artist and craftsman, known as *Gesamtkunstwerk*. They would integrate art, architecture, craft and design. It arose like a great grey hope from the wreckage of World War One, rejecting the closed-mindedness of the German Empire for a more enlightened, avant-garde way of looking at the world, specifically, by forming a new way of teaching.

Gropius' vision was modelled on the medieval notion of the Bauhütte stonemasons' guild, the idea of collective creativity over individualism – a community of artists and craftsmen would work together to build the 'Cathedral' – no one person would be responsible for the end goal; this was part of the Bauhaus school of thought. Gropius opened the Bauhaus with a speech about 'equality' between the sexes. That first year, more women enrolled into the school than men, though the number of female students would drop steadily over time. It wasn't quite the egalitarian panacea he'd preached. Women were actively discouraged from entering painting, sculpture and architecture classes, and instead were edged towards the weaving workshops, which was deemed a 'woman's class'. It's this kind of segregation of the textile arts that kept it lower on the fine art totem pole.

Anni Albers was dissuaded from joining the painting class at the Bauhaus by artist Oskar Kokoschka ('why do you paint?'[1] was his only response to the sight of one of her portraits). Albers responded by 'painting' at the loom, weaving one geometric innovation after another in wool, essentially creating what we perceive as 'textile arts' today. For much of her career, her abstract art was treated as less valid than that of her husband Josef Albers (a former Bauhaus Young Master). When Albers was alive, she baulked at any suggestion that her career had been hampered by her marriage. When asked about her gender and its impact on her work, she reportedly dismissed it as 'feminist nonsense'[2].

A 2018 Tate retrospective brought Anni Albers' work to a wider audience, and the five-star reviews showed a real change in the perception of textile arts. As *The Guardian*'s art critic Adrian Searle put it, 'Even at its most pictorial, her art is abstract. Even at its most geometric it feels human and alive, less the product of the mechanics of the loom – the construction of a matrix of threads, and fibres, warp and weft – than of the hand and the mind.'[3]

Russian Constructivists Varvara Stepanova and Lyubov Popova actively rejected the notion of individualist artistic genius to focus on textile production, while the men of the movement occupied more prominent positions at educational institutions where they could set the agenda. The same can be said for many of the women of the Bauhaus, like Lucia Moholy, who supported Gropius' own romantic Bauhütte, a vision of group creation. Equally deserving of further attention is Marianne Brandt, the only woman of the Bauhaus metal workshop, or the photographer Florence Henri. The men of the Masters' Council took the Bauhütte school of thinking with a pinch of salt, pursuing their own projects and careers. Unsurprisingly, they remain its recognisable names.

The Bauhaus photographer

When Moholy was lying on that grass, snapping those big angular structures, she was not a member of the Bauhaus faculty, nor one of its students. She had come to Weimar in 1923 with her husband, the Hungarian artist László Moholy-

Nagy, after he was invited by Gropius to join the team of teaching masters (all male, bar master-weaver Gunta Stölzl) to work with the Bauhaus metal workshop. Before this, László and Lucia had been living in Berlin, where she was working as an editor at Ernst Rowohlt's publishing house and was the main earner of the couple.

Though Moholy-Nagy is considered an authority on early-twentieth-century photography, it was Lucia who commanded the dark room at this stage in their lives, and was something of a mentor to him. As she was studying at a Principal Course in Reproduction Technology at an art academy in Leipzig, she had the skills as a photographer and technician.

There is no recorded evidence that Lucia Moholy was given anything in the way of payment or official employment at the school, but as Moholy-Nagy became immersed in teaching, she became the school's core photographer, albeit in an unofficial capacity. When the couple arrived, there wasn't a strong culture of photography at the Bauhaus; formal classes in the discipline didn't even begin until 1929, and Moholy was one of the few on the ground with the necessary talent. Gertrud Arndt, another Bauhaus artist, said in a 1927 interview, 'Nobody could take a photograph when I arrived in Weimar, the only one who could use a camera was Lucia Moholy, she had learned it. She came to the Bauhaus as a photographer'[4].

The work this involved was no casual hobby. Gropius and his wife Ise were committed PRs of the Bauhaus; they knew how important it was to propagate its message in the press. Moholy's photographs were made available to students and to Bauhaus publications for this purpose; she bought into Gropius' grand idea of collective creativity and authorship and was absorbed into the long-term goals of the school as a background collaborator. At the time, she was willing to forgo a position of status for the sake of the 'big picture'. But in the 'big picture' of the Bauhaus, it was the masters who sat front row, with Moholy's blurred silhouette at the edge of the frame.

'Symbiotic alliance'

The role of 'background' collaborator would be a recurring theme in the biography of Lucia Moholy and the Bauhaus. When it came to breaking ground in photographic theory, she and Moholy-Nagy were a partnership. Together, they worked on the book *Malerei, Photographie, Film* in 1925, a text which helped shape early thinking on German photography. Moholy-Nagy was not a native German speaker, and she would help him translate and transmute new ideas onto the page, while feeding in her own.

When it was published, *Malerei, Photographie, Film* was credited to László Moholy-Nagy alone. 'The working arrangements between Moholy-Nagy and myself were unusually close, the wealth and value of the artist's ideas gaining momentum, as it were, from the symbiotic alliance of two diverging temperaments'[5], Lucia Moholy says in her book *Marginal Notes*, a corrective account of László Moholy-Nagy's career, in which she points out the many 'documentary absurdities', taking aim at journalists and biographers getting their facts wrong. Among these is the claim that either Man Ray or László Moholy-Nagy 'invented' the photogram.

A photogram is a means of creating an image without a camera, a technique that was adopted as a form of abstract art. With her extensive academic knowledge of the history of photography, Moholy debunks the idea that either of them could ever have 'invented' anything, seeing that the method has its origins in the early eighteenth century. She recalls how she and Moholy-Nagy adapted, rather than invented, the photogram technique together, in the summer of 1922, using daylight paper, an achievement for which only he gets the glory.

Moholy did, eventually, express regret about the lack of credit she received for her work. On seeing extensive quotation of *Malerei, Photographie, Film* in a catalogue for the Nuremberg Biennale in 1969, where Moholy-Nagy was offered lofty praise for his 'lucid' diction and ideas, she describes feeling 'overcome by guilt'. 'I was made to realise that through all those years we had kept quiet about the extent and manner of our collaboration … How then should friends and colleagues have realised the exact circumstances?'[6] There is a deep sadness to this quote, to see Moholy place the blame entirely on her own head. And a sadness in the reality, that, at the time Moholy-Nagy's star was on the rise, she didn't see fit to join the ascent. She only sought to rectify her omission fifty years later.

Her work as an uncredited editor and producer continued with the Bauhaus book series, of which there were fourteen, as well as her production of the Bauhaus magazine. By Moholy's account, neither Gropius nor László Moholy-Nagy had the interest or freedom to get involved in book production. With her background as an editor at Berlin publishing houses, she had more than enough skills in her arsenal to get the job done. Only one of these books acknowledges Moholy's input, though many feature her Bauhaus photographs of architecture and design objects, which, at this point anyway, had her name attached.

As research curator Adrian Sudhalter acknowledged in her MoMA talk on 'Women and the Bauhaus', Lucia Moholy was not the only unofficial member on this team of Bauhaus myth-makers. Ise Gropius was also a talented spokesperson and editor of the Bauhaus message, helping to navigate and build its public image.

Before marrying Walter Gropius, she went by 'Ilse Frank', until Walter, like Rossetti with Siddall, convinced her to drop the 'L' to make the name sound more modern. Ise's typewriter became an important tool at the Bauhaus, where she would churn out effusive statements about this new phase in its history.

Public perception of the Bauhaus wavered over time; the right-wing German government made multiple attempts to shut it down. In 1925, the Bauhaus lost the first battle: the school in Weimar was dissolved, prompting a move to Dessau. To keep up the Bauhaus reputation, Ise performed linguistic gymnastics editing and reworking releases to spread the word to the press. As Sudhalter put it, she was 'a press agent or public relations secretary, without the title'[7].

To bolster the word of the Bauhaus she needed images, which meant Moholy spending hours in the darkroom developing her shots of the campus buildings and masters' houses in Dessau to have modernist visuals to match the modernist message. In 1926, Ise Gropius wrote in her diary 'Frau Moholy is overworked and works day and night to meet the demand of photos on order'[8].

They were working for a collective purpose, with Ise Gropius and Lucia Moholy's absent credits for production taken as a given. It's a familiar story of the woman as 'secretary' for her husband, reminiscent of all those novel acknowledgements that tell the author's wife 'Thanks for typing'. Presumably, they saw their work as a transmission, rather than a creation of ideas. That changed for Moholy after the war, when the case of her 'missing' glass negatives developed into a Bauhaus film noir.

The missing negatives

The Bauhaus was shut down several times during its existence, but there was no going back after 1933. Nazism sent many of its students and lecturers into exile as far as Switzerland, England, Australia and the US. With its international and transgressive outlook, Bauhaus was a threat to the destructive German nostalgia and regression of the Nazis, and many of its students and teachers were Jewish.

As was the fate of émigrés, those who faced exile had no choice but to leave artworks and personal objects behind. László Moholy-Nagy had to abandon abstract paintings and metal structures, leaving them with a housekeeper who later set them alight and threatened to have him arrested for 'cultural Bolshevism'.

After separating from Moholy-Nagy, Lucia entered into a relationship with Communist Party parliament member Theodor Neubauer, who was captured and killed by the Nazis. Moholy was of Jewish heritage so had to flee the country for London in 1933, leaving her little choice but to entrust some of her possessions to Moholy-Nagy and his new wife, Sybil. Among these possessions were 560 glass negatives.

As art historian Robin Schuldenfrei explains in her extensive research on Lucia Moholy, these negatives would help preserve the Bauhaus legacy abroad. During the Cold War, access to the Bauhaus in Dessau was restricted because of the Iron Curtain, and many of its design objects had been destroyed or simply left behind. Lucia's images were evidence – a pictorial stand-in for what could no longer be accessed, and what the artists had lost.

The Bauhaus had become a ghost town, and these photographs were keeping it alive.

Moholy managed to keep her career afloat in London, taking artful portraits of well-to-do figures like Margot Asquith, Countess of Oxford and Asquith (the image is part of the collection at the National Portrait Gallery in London), and kept up work as a photography educator holding talks and lectures.

In 1939, she published an ambitious book, *A Hundred Years of Photography*, a brief but expertly crafted text exploring the social history of the artform, hopping from the practice of silhouette painting in the eighteenth century, to photography's importance in the Crimean War right up to Man Ray and László Moholy-Nagy's supposed 'invention' of photograms. The book was not republished after the war (though did receive a reissue in 2016, ahead of the Bauhaus centenary three years later).

Overseas, in the USA, where Gropius and Moholy-Nagys had fled, the history of the Bauhaus had begun to penetrate the USA with an overblown Jesse-James-style mythology – but in England, Lucia Moholy was adrift from all this prestige. Moholy-Nagy made attempts to get her work at the art and design school he had established in Chicago, but she was refused passage by immigration as she had not been a professor of photography; she was only considered a 'practising photographer and writer' – another consequence of her commitment to the 'bigger picture'.

Without her negatives, she had no tangible examples of her connection to the school, and the important role she had played in it. She wrote to Moholy-Nagy in an effort to retrieve them, but was told by his wife, Sibyl, they had been left with Walter Gropius, whose home had been hit by a firebomb. Sibyl explained to Lucia that she was sorry, but it was likely they had been destroyed. But in 1938, when MoMA held the large-scale exhibition, 'Bauhaus: 1919–1928', Robin Schuldenfrei[9] notes that Moholy's images were blown up for exhibition displays, stand-ins for the objects no longer accessible under the Nazis. Likewise, the exhibition catalogue included forty-nine of Moholy's images, but nowhere was her name mentioned.

In the 1950s, Moholy noticed high-quality versions of her photographs appearing in different publications and began to get suspicious. Like Harry Lime emerging from the darkness of a Vienna doorway in *The Third Man*, maybe her negatives had survived after all.

Seeking her well-earned bite of the Bauhaus legacy, she wrote to Walter Gropius in 1954 to fish for information, 'If there is the slightest hope that my negatives may still be intact, I must do what I can to trace them … These negatives are irreplaceable documents which could be extremely useful, now more than ever. I am prepared to look into the matter myself … But I can do nothing unless I have a line to work on'[10]. Gropius' reply is enough to make anyone with even a hint of the background story incensed.

'Long years ago in Berlin, you gave all these negatives to me. I have carefully kept them, had copies made of all of them and have given a full set of copies to the Busch-Reisinger Museum at Harvard which has built up a special Bauhaus department which is steadily growing. I have promised them the original negatives with your name attached as soon as I do not need them any more myself. Both Ise and myself remember this clearly. You will imagine that these photographs are extremely useful to me and that I have continuously made use of them; so I hope you will not deprive me of them. Wouldn't it be sufficient if I sent you contact prints of the negatives? There are a great many, but I certainly understand that you want to make use of them yourself. Anyhow it will be a relief to you to know that they are in existence and in good shape'[11].

While Moholy had been turning down orders, commissions and lecture opportunities on the Bauhaus because of her 'missing negatives', they'd been resting in Gropius' basement in Lincoln, Massachusetts, the entire time. And now he'd promised to give her property to the Busch-Reisinger Museum archive 'with her name attached' – a gift she'd never consented to giving. In Gropius' 'bigger picture' of collective creativity, he was the author and auteur, and Moholy did not exist. Her response sounds understandably hurt, questioning how he could have thought he laid claim to the negatives he'd acquired as a result of her exile from a dictatorship: 'Surely you did not expect me to delay my departure in order to draw up a formal contract stipulating date and conditions of return? No formal agreement could have carried more weight than our friendship'[12]. A legal dispute raged between them for three years until a crate of glass negatives arrived on Moholy's doorstep. By which point, it was essentially too late. The Bauhaus legend had been cemented without her.

The fallout from the whole saga was documented by Moholy in a 1983 article in the *British Journal of Photography* called 'The Missing Negatives'. Melissa Venator, a curatorial fellow at the Busch-Reisinger Museum (who has spent years attributing credit to Lucia Moholy and other photographers for the images in the Bauhaus archive that were gifted by Ise Gropius) explains that from the 1930–50s, there was a school of thought that architectural and object photography merely documented other art, and did not count as art itself. Walter Gropius, rather than being insidious, might have thought of the negatives as belonging to him, as documents of the Bauhaus Dessau buildings he designed. Either way, his actions toward Moholy completely undermined her contribution, relegating her to a background administrator for his archive. Gropius never gave photography official status as a course at the Bauhaus, but he clearly recognised its power. Photography acted as a visual talisman for the Bauhaus myth. When we think of the school, many of us picture those black-and-white architectural photographs: a building with the word 'Bauhaus' stamped on its front in Herbert Bayer's Universal font. What doesn't come to mind is the name 'Lucia Moholy'.

'The various apostles'

Lucia Moholy retrospectively criticised the top-down masters' structure of the Bauhaus and its omnipresent image later in her career, referring to the 'various apostles'[13] that made up its history. 'It would not be absurd, if someone were resolved to do so, to write about the role of the masters' wives, those who had no official status and yet played a decisive role in the aftermath of the Bauhaus,'[14] she wrote.

The centenary of the school in 2019 sparked dozens of exhibitions revising its history, putting the focus not only on the Klees and Kandinskys of the Master houses, but on the women too, including a show celebrating the photographs of Lucia Moholy. The Volksbühne in Berlin even organised a 'funeral concert for the Bauhaus' to finally lay the high-minded, romanticised idea of the school to rest. With fresh eyes, and fresh memories about the women who helped construct the Bauhaus legacy, we can repopulate the ghost town.

10
LIL HARDIN ARMSTRONG AND THE JAZZ AGE: BORN TO SWING

Jazz pianist Lil Hardin was once of the most highly regarded players on Chicago's big band scene in the 1920s. She started younger than most. Her introduction to the dark side of the music biz came at just eleven years of age, when she organised her first concert at the Lebanon Baptist Church in Memphis. Once a week, she would play the piano for her Sunday School class, where the pastor would peer disapprovingly over his glasses as she treated its church's ivory keys to a 'definite beat' during her rendition of 'Onward Christian Soldiers'. She didn't know it yet, but that instinctive beat was the one that would lead her into a life in jazz. To try and raise money for the church to buy twelve new hymn books, Hardin convinced a whole gang of kids from the neighbourhood to get dressed up in their starched Sunday best to perform for the congregation. This was not going to be any two-bit school recital; Hardin wanted a crowd, and made everybody involved sell tickets to fill out those pews, including the pastor. When the time came to hand over the dough, the pastor refused. Telling the story later, in 1967, not long before her seventieth birthday, Hardin laughed long and hard as she retold the story, 'I said: "well, I'm not buying any hymn books for the church!"'[1] It didn't matter that she was just a child, and he was a grown man of the cloth – she knew what was right, and wouldn't be intimidated. Hardin played him at his own game, and went home with the twelve dollars she'd raised in her pocket. When church representatives came hammering on her door looking for it, her mother told them, 'I don't know how you're going to get the money, she's dressed up in the twelve dollars'[2]. The pastor tried to shame her in his sermon by preaching hellfire and brimstone about children robbing the church, but Lil wouldn't let up. If the pastor couldn't uphold his celestial principles, then neither would she. Hardin spent that money on a white and blue velvet hat with streamers and two gallons of ice cream for her 'employees' – those neighbourhood kids who performed in the show.

With that gimlet eye for mendacity and her ice cream buckets of charm, Hardin always knew how to handle herself as a musician; she recognised her worth as a player and when the time called for it, she protected her people. It's that kind of mettle that helped her carve out her career as a pianist, composer and big band leader at the height of the Jazz Age, navigating a lot worse than a dollar-pocketing pastor. In the 1920s and '30s, when there were only two known female piano players working out of Chicago (she and Lovie Austin), Hardin led her own band of male players, and won them all over. Looking back on his time in Hardin's line-up, trumpeter Dick Vance said, 'I still think about it as one of the best groups I ever played with'[3].

Her career began in one of the most challenging circumstances possible: she was a young black woman living in Chicago in the wake of the 1919 race riots. Like thousands of other African Americans, her family had left the south hoping to escape its segregation for a better life up north, but many left cities like Memphis and New Orleans to face similar divisons in Chicago: residential segregation, racist employment practices, discriminatory white-owned businesses and police brutality. When working on the big-band jazz scene, Hardin had to contend with the dual oppression of racism and sexism, and still managed to come out on top, building a solid reputation at a time when women musicians were often treated like novelty acts by promoters. Not only did she lead her own band, Hardin composed some of the biggest jazz records around, not least her tune 'Just for a Thrill', which was recorded by Ray Charles in 1959.

You'd think, given the paucity of notable women musicians from the period, her success would make her one of the most recognisable names in 1920s jazz, but accounts of Hardin in the media usually focus on her acquired surname: Armstrong.

Instead of just being celebrated for her own achievements as a leading jazzwoman and blues pianist, she's credited for the role she played in the success of her second husband, Louis. And it's all true. Hardin was the 'guiding force' that helped Louis 'Satchmo' Armstrong get the courage to strike out on his own – but this tendency to define Hardin as a catalyst for his career has distracted from the vibrancy of her own.

Much of what we know about Hardin's background as a musician is gleaned from transcriptions of 'Satchmo and Me', an LP of interviews with Hardin focusing on her life with Louis Armstrong, which is extremely rare. For the only biography of her life, *Just for a Thrill*, the writer had little to work from, admitting that sparse archive material exists about Hardin's life thanks to 'vultures'[4] that made off with some of her personal documents after her death, including pages from her unfinished autobiography. When she was interviewed, it was usually about Louis. There doesn't seem to be an LP recording on Lil Hardin's life dedicated to her perspective alone. But I was able to track down two short clips of Hardin speaking on a tape called 'Hear Me Talkin' to Ya', recorded while she was on holiday in London in 1967. For almost thirty minutes, Hardin is in a constant flow of storytelling, zipping from one incredible Jazz Age moment to another, pausing only to emit howls of laughter or gently tease the interviewer about his questions – 'Is this about Louis, or is this about me – it's about both of us, huh?'[5].

And she was right to jibe. The Armstrong marriage is a tiny slice of the Lil Hardin biography and it lasted just a few years. The more interesting part of the story really starts in 1918, at the Jones' Music Store in Chicago, where punters would gather to see her banging out tunes.

'I played just as hard as I could'

The Jones' Music Store in Chicago got to be Lil Hardin's own personal Carnegie Hall. As a teen, she'd taught herself to read music, and landed a job after she'd impressed the store owner doing her thing on one of the display pianos. She never played by numbers; Hardin was at once fastidious and carefree, she had the confidence to let loose and it came through on the keys – even before she knew what jazz was, she could swing, 'I got to be quite the spectacle in the store'[6], she said.

The defining moment for her piano-playing style came in her late teens, when American jazz pianist Jelly Roll Morton walked through the door. Morton sat at the piano and started hitting the keys hard and heavy with his long skinny fingers. As he played, he stomped his feet, making the walls quiver like his sweet namesake as he covered every inch of the room with the chords. It's a moment Hardin recalled again and again in interviews, 'Goose pimples were sticking out all over me'[7], she said, '[he was] beating out a double rhythm with his feet on the loud pedal. I was thrilled, amazed and scared...'[8]. When he was done, he got up, and looked over at Hardin as if to say 'let that be a lesson to you'[9]. It turned out to be the most important one she would receive.

Jelly Roll Morton was the biggest influence on Hardin's thundering touch on the keys. 'After that I played just as hard as I could ... and to this day I am still a heavy piano player'[10].

Hardin didn't stay the store's novelty act for long. When the New Orleans Creole Jazz Band arrived in Chicago to play a gig in a Chinese restaurant and needed a piano player, she got her first audition. She asked for a key to play in and was told, 'Key, we don't know what key, just when you hear two knocks, start playing!'[11]. The clarinet player looked her way to start the song and said 'boom boom'.

And that was it. Hardin plied her trade by watching those players, feeling the cues, following the electricity of the tune as it fired from node to node, 'After a second I could feel what they were playing, because at that time I don't think they used over four or five chords.'[12] She must have impressed, they asked her to join the outfit as the foundational sound of the New Orleans Creole Jazz Band. They were playing jazz clubs, cafés, famous Chicago venues like Dreamland, for a whole three months before Hardin's mother even knew she'd joined the band. Mrs Hardin did not approve of that 'nasty, filthy, dirty cabaret'[13]. The money she was bringing in every week swayed the deal, but her mother still insisted on embarrassing her in front of the band by turning up at every gig to take her home on the nights she played.

Since the line-up of the bands shifted constantly, Hardin got the chance to cut her teeth with some of the heavyweights from the New Orleans scene as they rotated in and out. Being a woman instrumentalist in jazz meant playing multiple roles – women who were given creative space on stage were usually expected to be soft, sweet, and feminine, decked out in fancy floor-length gowns. But if that sweet, light touch made it into their playing, the tone was dismissed as feminine – not fast and robust enough to keep up with the electricity of the New Orleans sound. Hardin managed to gain respect on every level by pairing her 'sweetness' with her weighted, percussive syncopation; she even got the stage name 'Hot Miss Lil'. She managed to harness that duality, and worked it to her benefit. The same can be said for Lovie Austin, one of the only women piano players working the same scene as Lil in the 1920s. Alberta Hunter, a popular Memphis jazz singer who performed with them both said, 'Lil Armstrong she played a mighty blues, And don't ever forget Lovie Austin. She wrote and played a mess of blues'[14].

Maybe it was her Memphis background mixed with her ability to read music, but Hardin had this natural swinging rhythm, one that gained her major respect among the expatriates of the New Orleans jazz scene now living in Chicago and New York. Writing in his memoirs long after his separation from Hardin, Louis Armstrong wrote, 'She was the best. She would give out with that good ol' New Orleans 4 Beat, which a lot of the Northern piano players couldn't do, to save their lives ... And – for a "woman" there are very few *men* piano players who can swing as good as Lil. And I'm not just saying this – because I was married to her'[15].

'Never mind about him. They know me'

In 1921, Hardin took her career up a notch by landing a spot in the popular King Oliver's Creole Jazz Band. But her position as a pianist might well be one of the reasons she was never a breakout star: it wasn't the style in those times for the piano player to get the spotlight, she was there to be a strong, supporting hand. Not that it stopped Hardin trying, 'Sometimes I'd get the urge to run up and down the piano and I'd make a few runs and things, and Joe [King Oliver] would turn around and look at me and say, "We have a clarinet in the band"'[16].

It was in that same band that she met Louis Armstrong, when he joined as their cornetist in 1922. Hardin didn't think much of him at first, but took notice when someone mentioned on the sly that Armstrong had a better technique than Joe, the band's leader. In recording sessions, the men in the band would place Armstrong right at the back, afraid that he'd steal the show with his blowing. Taking pity on the bullied newcomer, she became a kind of mentor to him. By then Hardin was twenty-four and still youthful in her outlook but she was a seasoned musician, used to dealing with big-band politics. She made an effort to teach him how to read music, brought him out shopping for new clothes, and they 'got to be sweethearts'[17], even though they were both still married at the time. Hardin recognised the difference in Armstrong's technique before he could see it for himself, 'He had the most beautiful shrill whistle and all those riffs that he had later made his music. Such beautiful riffs and runs and trills and things you know. And I said "Maybe someday that guy'll play like that"… You never know when you're crazy the right way, huh?'[18].

Things started to get rocky in the King Oliver family when the band discovered their leader (Joe Oliver) had been pocketing part of the band's fee for himself. Tensions were so high that Oliver started carrying a pistol to work in his trumpet case. Armstrong thought the world of Joe and refused to leave the band, but Hardin gave him the push he needed to strike out on his own, 'He didn't believe in himself. So I was sort of standing at the bottom of the ladder holding it and watching him climb'[19]. Eventually, he left for New York to join Fletcher Henderson's Orchestra, and in the meantime, using her clout at Dreamland Café, she got him a job playing solo for $75 dollars a week. She even convinced the owner Bill Bottoms to put a sign saying 'world's greatest trumpet player' out front. When Bottoms pointed out that nobody had a clue who this guy was, she told him, 'Never mind about him. They know me and they'll come in'[20].

'I only play jobs that I like, and the music I like'

Hardin was a huge part of the Hot Five and Hot Seven recording sessions (1925–1928) that helped make Armstrong's name. He was billed as the 'bandleader', and she was the crew's pianist – transcribing melodies, writing lyrics and organising the band's arrangements. During these years that she put out one jazz composition after another: 'My Heart', 'You're Next', 'I'm gonna Gitcha', 'Droppin' Shucks', 'The King of the Zulus', 'Skid-Dat-de-Dat', 'Jazz Lips' and 'Struttin' with Some Barbecue'. One of the Hot Five recordings even went under the title 'Lil's Hot Shots'. Working as a married couple wasn't easy; now that Hardin was collaborating with her husband, she was seen by the players as his wife instead of the skilled musical director. 'They started calling him [Armstrong] henpecked, henny for short. "Oh henny! Your wife wants ya …" All the musicians would say, "your wife will fire ya!" … I finally had to give the band up. It was just terrible'[21].

She threw her energies into studying instead, getting a teaching diploma from the Chicago College of Music and a postgrad from New York College of Music in 1929, but couldn't give up on the musician's life, so she went it alone, putting together bands of her own. For a time she even had a band of all-women players called the Harlem Harlicans, with Leora Mieux on trombone (Mieux was married to Fletcher Henderson but barely known as a player) and Hazel Scott's mother Alma Long Scott on clarinet. But Hardin appeared to have absorbed those same ideas about 'masculine' vs 'feminine' playing, 'They were a little mild, a little emaciated. They couldn't keep up with me, so I had to get another man's band'[22]. Hardin took over a new group of male players as its band leader and secured a residency in Buffalo, New York, with 'King Louis II' Jonah Jones on trumpet and George Clarke on sax. By then, Hardin and her husband were separated, but she was under the same management, being billed everywhere as Mrs Louis Armstrong with 'a very tiny little Mrs and a huge Louis Armstrong on the placards for the advertisements'[23], remembered her bandmate Dick Vance.

Maybe it was the lack of decent radio play, or a high-profile residency, or maybe the public just couldn't find space in their tastes to accommodate another high-profile Armstrong, but the band never really made it. Hardin got a regular job as a house pianist for Decca Records, then by the 1940s had drifted away from performing, and started trying out new ventures but everything ultimately came back to jazz. Weirdly prescient of a lot of mainstream musicians today, she branched out in clothing design, making pieces like the 'Mad Money cocktail gown' and 'check and double check'[24] coat – she even designed the midnight blue tux Armstrong wore as King Zulu at the 1949 New Orleans' Mardi Gras parade. At one point, she opened a jazz-themed restaurant in Chicago called Swing Shack that serviced up plates of Bebop Black Eyed Peas and High Note Corn Bread (it didn't last long…).

The 1950s ushered in a new era of bebop jazz, and the more esoteric compositions of Dizzy Gillespie and Charlie Parker. Hardin was still invited to perform at the odd musical revue or variety show, but usually, it was to trot out what were by then the golden oldies. Though her name was attached to dozens of Hot Five recordings as a composer, she didn't have the profile for the public to recognise her as the mind behind the songs. It didn't help that Armstrong and Hardin entered a legal battle over the copyright to 'Struttin' with Some Barbecue', one of his most famous recordings. Hardin won the case, and is credited as composer, but some Armstrong experts still try to undermine her efforts by speculating that it was his – up until 1967, the hot trumpet player was insisting that he came up with the idea for the song while eating BBQ ribs with Zutty Singleton.

Legal rifts aside, Hardin never resented her ex-husband. She gave her final performance at a memorial concert for Armstrong, held in 1971, where Hardin collapsed at the piano in the middle of her song. She died later that day.

On the 'Hear Me Talkin' to Ya' tapes, recorded four years before that concert, you can hear the jazzwoman looking back with a kind of ecstatic fondness on her story. She doesn't get the credit she deserves as a songwriter and composer today, but Hardin was well aware of her importance in jazz history. 'Struttin' with Some Barbecue' … That's why I don't have to work too much now,' she said. 'And I'm still strutting'[25].

11
ALMA REVILLE:
THE SILENT PARTNER

It's a sentence we've all heard before, that dreary asseveration: 'Behind every great man is a great woman'. A dispiriting heaviness clings to its cadence, like nine unwanted and slightly too rough pats on the head from the hand of a visiting uncle. It's a way of making male auteurism seem just a little more palatable, but conjures the image of a long-distance runner turning to give a thumbs-up to his competitors from a headstart on the track.

No creative partnership has been more defined by this sententious edict than that of scriptwriter and editor Alma Reville and her husband Alfred Hitchcock. It appears in countless articles about her. The couple were even born one day apart, Hitchcock 24 hours ahead. In the photographs of the couple together, we see it in action. Hitchcock captured from his famous side profile as he pores over the script of *Marnie*, while Alma gestures toward him from behind her desk, slightly out of focus.

Any article that mentioned her during her lifetime seemed to comply with some journalistic convention to mention her height; rarely did writers miss a chance to colour their pieces with descriptions of Reville as a 'tiny', 'bird-like' woman 'who might jump screeching on to a table at the sight of a mouse'[1].

In 2012, there were two Hitchcock biopics back-to-back, each offering up two very different Almas. The Imelda Staunton 'Alma': a milquetoast spouse who hovers in doorways, looking on in exasperation as her husband leches over Tippi Hedren. Then there was the Helen Mirren 'Alma': a commanding figure who was clearly Hitchcock's collaborator as well as his partner. Which was the real Alma? The answer seems to be a frustrating, equivocal bit of both. Their partnership lasted more than fifty years, with one half of the couple going from obscurity to worldwide fame. Alma Reville's life was constantly in flux. How could a private woman like Reville not at times feel overwhelmed in the Hollywood limelight? And equally, how could she not have a strong, intimidating side to her personality, when she had started out in the male-dominated film industry at the age of sixteen, and climbed the ladder to become one of the first female assistant directors in Britain?

One thing the Mirren 'Alma' offered was a revival of Reville-related anecdotes about her involvement in the production of *Psycho*. Without her, the *Psycho* shower scene might have been very different. Those forty-five seconds of footage are so embedded in cinema history that there is a full feature-length documentary dedicated to its seventy-eight set-ups. It's been parodied to death. Today, the pulsating screech of the violin strings Bernard Herrmann composed for it has come to signal the rise and fall of a knife, an instant identifier for horror and violence. But when Hitchcock first heard the score, he wasn't convinced. He wanted to run the whole thing in silence, putting the director and composer in a stalemate. It was Reville who fought on Herrmann's behalf to bring him around. Without her, the only sound you would hear would be, at most, the rush of running water.

This is a fun movie-quiz-level kernel of information, but it doesn't even scratch the surface of how important Reville was to the Hitchcock films. It paints her as the dutiful wife in the background, lovingly guiding her husband toward the 'correct' decision – the great woman behind the man. To see why her opinion was so invaluable to him, we need to roll back and look at the Alma Reville biography in full, right back to her start in the film industry, when she was an up-and-coming film editor, and he was a relative unknown.

'The art of cutting is an Art indeed, with a capital A'

When Reville was sixteen years old, she would cycle through Twickenham to spend her afternoon at the London Film Company. Her family had recently moved from Nottingham through her dad's job as a representative for a lace firm, and he'd landed a position in the studio's costume department. She'd sit quietly in the draughty warehouse space to watch him and the actors working.

To make use of her set loitering, her dad eventually called in a favour to get her a job as a tea girl. From there she climbed the ranks to 'rewind girl' in the cutting room (for a woman in industry in 1915, the -girl title was inescapable) and in less than a year, they'd given Reville a pair of editing scissors of her own. When she was still in her teens, she was entrusted with the snipping of film negatives worth thousands of pounds. 'There were no editors in those days; nobody would take over like they do today. The directors all cut their own movies with assistance from the people in the cutting room'[2], Reville once said.

It was an entry-level job, but one that had Reville working on some major British film productions from the silent film era, like *The Prisoner of Zenda* from 1915. The industry wasn't so heavily unionised then, so it was common for two jobs to be rolled into one, with Reville acquiring another title – 'continuity girl'. 'It sounded a little nicer, but I hadn't the faintest idea what it was. I hadn't a clue. So I said "yes"'[3].

As well as cutting the film, Reville was in charge of keeping the visual consistency of the story in check – was the actress wearing those mittens in the last scene? Is that glass in the right place?

These jobs might not have carried much prestige, but working in cutting and continuity is what developed Reville's intensely visual cinematic mind. During every film she worked on, she developed an intimate relationship with each shot, knowing exactly what it took to connect the dots. It turned Alma Reville into an anomaly of a filmmaker, one who was always thinking about the picture as a whole, and simultaneously moving the cogs of the machine behind the scenes. In an article she wrote for *The Motion Picture News*, she tells the reader that, 'The art of cutting is an Art indeed, with a capital A'. She goes on to explore the neglected nature of the artform, and stressed that this neglect was degrading the value of British films, 'the public, especially the British public, are not hard to please and they know there is something wrong … If Mr Producer would give just a little more forethought to the continuity and cutting of his production before commencing it … how much worry and time he could save in the cutting room'[4].

By the early 1920s, Reville was in demand as an editor in British silent film; she moved from Twickenham to Islington, working at Famous Players-Lasky (which would become Paramount). It was on the set of the (now lost) Donald Crisp film *Appearances* that she first met Alfred Hitchcock; Reville was the film's main editor, whereas he was getting his first break designing the dialogue cards, or 'intertitles' for the silent picture. There was even a profile on Reville in *The Picturegoer* magazine presenting her as a rising star of the British film industry.

The article, published in 1925, is written in that high-octane plummy tone you might find in a government-issue video encouraging women to pitch in to help the war effort, leading with the weirdly self-aware subtitle, 'An interesting article, proving that a woman's place is not always in the home'. 'Little Alma Reville is nothing like as unsophisticated as she looks'[5], it reads. But once you tear away the patronising insulation, it's clear just how highly regarded Alma Reville was. The writer was complaining about how picky female filmgoers had become, 'Mere man, even if he be a high and mighty film director, cannot hope to escape the lash of feminine criticism, unless he has as his assistant a superwoman, whose eye is sharper than an eagle's, whose patience is greater than Job's, whose staying-power is such that it makes the labours of Hercules look like golf as played by an obese retired chartered accountant'[6] – he is talking about Alma Reville. There is a familiar undercurrent here, implying just how well a woman is suited to tidying up after an impulsive director, rather than taking the creative role. But in another sense, the writer is pointing out the need for a female perspective in filmmaking that – until her arrival – was not being served.

'Alma loved it'

It was on the set of the silent drama *Woman to Woman* that Reville and Hitchcock started out as professional collaborators. He'd looked up to her at Lasky, but didn't feel confident approaching her until they were professional equals. When he was appointed assistant director of the production under Graham Cutts, he asked her to be the editor, but Reville dismissed his low-ball offer for the wages. It might have been Hitchcock's first taste of authority on a film project, but she was one of the big dogs in British editing by then, so they had to up the cash to get her on board.

Together they made *Woman to Woman*, an eighty-two minute picture about a soldier who falls in love with a Moulin Rouge dancer, only to lose his memory in the trenches. It had screenings in New York and was well received, proving to sceptical critics that British studios could produce films to rival those coming out of Hollywood. Unfortunately Reville didn't think much of Cutts' directing chops; so she and Hitchcock had to pick up the slack, 'He wasn't really a pleasant man, he knew very little, so we literally carried him'[7]. They were in the same murky situation, both ambitious young people doing the legwork only to watch others snatch the glory on release. Hitchcock's credit for *Woman to Woman* never made the title sequence, and nothing of the film remains today. Still, they stuck with it, making more films with Graham Cutts, with Reville and Hitchcock scrambling to hit six-week production deadlines. She was usually the editor, often helping Hitchcock with the screenplay, he the assistant director, refining the scripts, chipping in with the art department. At some point, they went from 'just co-workers' to a couple. 'He had a Charlie Chaplin moustache ... I made him shave it off'[8], admitted Reville.

Included somewhere in this blizzard of silent pictures from the early twenties was *White Shadow*, made in 1924, about twin sisters who switch roles. The film hit headlines for the first time in eighty-seven years when more than thirty minutes of it was rediscovered in the New Zealand Film Archive in 2011. It had been sitting on a shelf with unlabelled reels of nitrate film, and was revived and restored only once archivists made the connection. So much of what we know about these early films is down to chance findings like these. But the rush of excitement in discovering 'an early Hitchcock' erased other contributions. The all-consuming fame that followed for him meant that everything he touched early in his career acquired a new significance. So, while his days as a lowly title designer in charge of creating and filming the cards of dialogue that popped up on screen for the silent film *Appearances* are there for anyone to see on IMDb, at the time of writing, Reville's name is absent from the crew list. Only when he stepped into the role of director does Reville's hand in the film industry really become visible, as though nothing had preceded it.

It's true that, at least in the early days, Reville's contribution to the Hitchcock films was more high profile than her other projects, as they brought her out of the cutting room. For his first film, *The Pleasure Garden*, she was his second in command. It was the start of a deep co-dependency that would define their working relationship, and their marriage. After every shot, he would stop, look up at Reville and ask, 'Was that alright?'[9].

There were two things that the *Picturegoer* article wanted us to know about Alma Reville. 'The first is that she possesses (but never wears) a pair of horn-rimmed glasses; the second that she has never had time to get married!' Something changed. While travelling on a boat from Germany to England after a location scouting trip for another film, Hitchcock proposed to Reville in the middle of the North Sea. They were married in 1926, the start of a partnership that would see Alma Reville collaborate with Hitchcock on more than fifty productions, jumping about from assistant directing to screenwriting to continuity. There was even the occasional cameo: Reville's twenty-seven-year-old face can be seen emerging from the darkness for a few brief moments in *The Lodger*, filmed in 1926, as a woman listening to the wireless.

And she didn't exclusively work with Hitchcock either; when Reville was pregnant with their only child, Patricia, she was working on the screenplay for Miles Mander's *The First Born*, a boundary-pushing melodrama about a woman who adopts her manicurist's illegitimate child, allowing her absentee husband to believe the baby is his. *The First Born* caused a real stir on release, with audiences shocked by a scene that featured an actress taking a bath (but seemingly not so shocked by the lecherous man creeping into the bathroom to leer at her while she bathes). Around the same time, she adapted *The Constant Nymph*, a bohemian trip of a novel by Margaret Kennedy that explores the labyrinthian landscape of teenage sexuality. In the rich screen version, viewers follow the journey of Tessa, a young girl in love with an older family member, composer Lewis Dodd (played by Ivor Novello).

A rare self-portrait
by Pre-Raphaelite
artist Elizabeth Siddall.

omposer Clara
chumann,
eated at her piano,
, 1850.

The Woman in White, by French Impressionist
Marie Bracquemond, c. 1880.

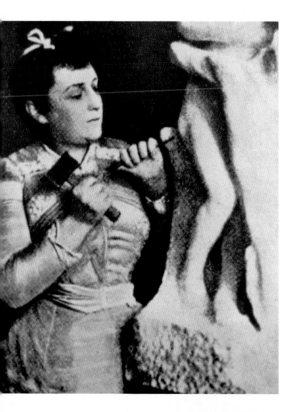

Sculptor Camille
Claudel, c. 1900.

Gabriele Münter,
pictured with her
paintings at her home.

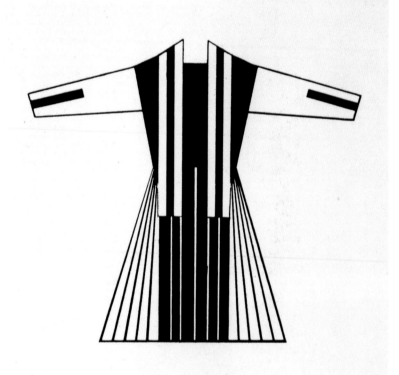

МАВРУША

An ultra-modern costume design by Russian Constructivist Varvara Stepanova, made for a theatre production of *The Death of Tarelkin* by A. Sukhovo-Kobylin, c. 1922.

Bauhaus building, Dessau, photographed by Lucia Moholy, c. 1925–26.

Jazz pianist and composer Lil Hardin at the centre of King Oliver's
Creole Jazz Band, c. 1922.

Film editor and assistant director Alma Reville at work on the set of *The Mountain Eagle* with actor Bernhard Goetzke, c. 1926.

Shirley Graham Du Bois, playwright, biographer and activist, c. 1946.

Lee Krasner, abstract expressionist painter at work in her studio, c. 1981.

Margaret Keane in her studio, with Walter Keane in the shadows, c. 1965.

Pioneering video artist Shigeko Kubota with her Portapak camera, c. 1972.

Reville had this striking ability to distill difficult source material into a filmable structure. Like a chef working in reverse, she could reduce a meal back to its original ingredients and serve up a whole new dish. Producing complex, well-rounded female characters, whose on-screen behaviour got up the noses of the British film censors, became a recurring theme in her work.

'You only need to watch one of the silent films that Reville scripted, such as *The First Born*, to see that what we think of as "Hitchcockian" may really be "Hitchcock-Revillean"'[10], film critic Pamela Hutchinson tells me, adding 'while we think of his work as meticulous, we know that she was the one with the true eye for detail; while we praise his ability to tell stories visually, to adapt text into cinema, that was her gift too'.

It always seemed strange to me that someone with Reville's background, who knew exactly what it took to bring a film together, never attempted to direct one of her own. When asked about this later in an interview with celebrity biographer Charlotte Chandler, she said, 'I'm too small ... not just short, but small. I could never project the image of authority a director has to project. A director has to be able to play the role of a director'[11].

If height had anything to do with it, we'd have a hard time explaining how Danny DeVito managed to direct *Matilda*. It's possible Reville was alluding to how others would perceive her because of her gender. Having worked exclusively with men behind the camera on all her film projects, maybe she couldn't get past the idea of it being a 'male' occupation that wasn't open to her. Perhaps the intense pressure of being one of the few women to direct would have been too much of a burden to carry. It was easier to carve a creative path working alongside directors and swerve the scrutiny.

The turn of the twentieth century had been an explosive epoch for women in cinema, but by the time Reville was coming into her own in the film industry in the 1920s, the image of who could qualify to be director was quickly being reshaped in Hollywood.

When the medium was still young, it presented those willing to experiment with a new opportunity to take the artistic reins. Hollywood's French expat Alice Guy-Blaché directed more than 600 silent movies between 1896–1920, and created one of the very first narrative films *La Fée aux Choux* (The Cabbage Fairy).

Director Lois Weber (who had started out as an actress, appearing in a Guy-Blaché production) created films with her husband Phillips Smalley that dealt with abortion and birth control. Between 1912–1919, Universal had eleven female directors on its books. But by the 1920s, the commercialisation of the studios had put more men in boardrooms, edging women directors and editors out of positions of power. 'I would have embarrassed the men', Guy-Blaché wrote, 'who wanted to smoke their cigars and to spit at their ease while discussing business'[12]. When Weber died, her obituary in the *Los Angeles Times* concentrated on her career as an actress and 'star maker', rather than a director. 'It's almost as if no one could imagine such a thing any more', says Hutchinson.

One of the few to survive this cull was Paramount director Dorothy Arzner. In the early nineties Katharine Hepburn recalled working with Arzner on the film *Christopher Strong*, which was released in 1933, and said, 'It seems odd now, a woman director, but it didn't seem strange to me then … She wore pants. So did I'[13].

Reville must have been aware of names like Weber and Guy-Blaché, and it's possible that seeing their achievements diminished could have affected her perception of who was allowed, or 'capable' of being a director. But she was also a private person – not timid, as so many writers have suggested, just not gasping for fame. 'I thought I might like to write a novel', she said, 'because you can do that alone'[14].

Instead she focused on background filmmaking roles, becoming part of the Hitchcock 'brand', finding source material for scripts and working on scenarios and adaptations. The pair always said that their favourite Hitchcock film was *Shadow of a Doubt* – a vertebrae-stiffening thriller about a young girl from a small town who uncovers her murderous uncle's dirty secrets – on which Reville has a writing credit. Playwright Thornton Wilder was employed to draft the script as he had a knack for capturing the strange pathos of rural American life that they wanted for the film. Then short story writer Sally Benson (author of *Meet me in St Louis*) was brought on board to sass up the dialogue. It was Alma

Reville's job to merge the worlds of literature and film and somehow pipe-bag the script into something they could commit to celluloid.

When the Hitchcocks had settled in Bel Air, Reville's name began to disappear; her last official credit was on the screenplay adaptation of *Stage Fright* in 1950. We can only speculate as to why − maybe she wanted to focus on their home and raising their daughter, or perhaps it was pressure from the American studio systems, who liked the idea of the director as an icon, showboating the films as Hitchcock productions with a capital H. Brand managers always want a strong, simple message to sell a movie and unless the brand is officially a 'duo', partnerships are seen to dilute it. The fact that they were married put the kibosh on the 'duo' possibility, even though she had been the more successful one when they met. 'We are too comfortable with the myth of the lone male genius − so much so that we even apply it to film, which is entirely a collaborative art', says Hutchinson, 'So we need to recognise that the myth is wrong sometimes. Everyone needs a sounding board, and Hitchcock was a very private figure, so he needed to keep his sounding board close.'

Even if her name was nowhere near the official 'written by' credit of the final script, her notes would be all over the copy in Hitchcock's hands. And it was common for Reville to be seen lurking on set for the first week of any production, 'He always wants me to go and see the first week's shooting just to see if the characters are coming across, and so I always do that'[15]. In an interview with *Written By* magazine, their daughter Pat Hitchcock reinforced the idea that her mother was heavily involved in *Marnie*, a story of sexual repression and abuse, starring Tippi Hedren. 'Although it was pretty much kept between my parents, Mama was extremely involved in the development of the screenplay for *Marnie*. I found some of the notes she wrote on the different drafts. They were quite indicative of her story sense but also of the fact that she liked logic. Other times she would suggest changes to improve character development or make new suggestions for the plot'[16].

Screenwriter Joseph Stefano, who collaborated with Hitchcock on *Psycho* remembered that, after he gave Hitchcock a draft of the script to read, he came back and said 'Alma loved it'[17]. That meant no more changes needed to be made.

'Alma loved it' was the highest compliment he could have hoped to receive.

'The Hitchcock touch had four hands'

Much of the fascination around Reville has focused on the dynamics of her marriage. It is usually described as sexless, with Hitchcock portrayed like a Benny Hill character zig-zagging in pursuit of starlets before returning home to spend the night in a separate bed from Reville, both tucked under the covers in their PJs like platonic roommates on respite from a carehome. He would joke about his impotence, though Hitchcock loved to speak in dirty limericks, and it could be hard to separate the facts from the bawdy jokes.

Though Reville never spoke a word against Hitchcock to the press, he did appear to resent journalists who tried to centre her in the story. An old cutting from *Sight & Sound* in 1976 describes how he 'vetoed' the writer's attempts to interview his wife, and when he finally got some face time with her, the director would sit broodingly 'when she discusses something that doesn't concern him'[18].

When speaking to the *Sunday Express* in 1972, she dismissed any suggestion that she might be jealous of his leading ladies, or of him, 'He has never had any interest whatsoever except what performances they are giving ... Grace Kelly is our greatest friend ... I don't mind taking second place. I am just pleased for his success because I know what it means to him. You know I don't think he has any bad points. Even after fifty-two years of knowing him. I don't find anything irritating about him. I am very lucky.'[19]

In his acceptance speech for his Lifetime Achievement Award, Hitchcock did acknowledge the 'constant collaboration' of four important people in his life. 'The first of the four is a film editor, the second is a scriptwriter, the third is the mother of my daughter Pat, and the fourth is as fine a cook as ever performed miracles in a domestic kitchen – and their names are Alma Reville'. Had he never met all four, he went on, he might have been at the awards ceremony, but only as 'one of the slower waiters on the floor'.

Even if she did prefer to be in the shadows, we need to recognise Reville as something more than a second-division amanuensis. To fully understand her contribution, we need to rethink entirely how we see these movies today, to approach them as a wider collaboration, instead of projects that belong to individuals. Provenance is important – and the fact that Alma Reville was one of the most high-profile editors in the British film industry in the 1920s, that she was a writer on *Suspicion* and *Shadow of a Doubt* ought, most emphatically, to be common film knowledge. These are not facts we can afford to lose 'behind a great man', whom she always worked alongside. And it is not just about equal credit; these works are scrutinised in film courses across the globe. How can any Hitchcock study ever be considered exhaustive, unless it considers Reville? 'We'd be fools not to look at everything that contributed to their success', says Hutchinson.

As *The Los Angeles Times* arts editor Charles Champlin put it after her death in 1982, 'The Hitchcock touch had four hands, and two of them were Alma's'[20].

12
JOSEPHINE NIVISON HOPPER: THE RECOVERY

The lighthouse has always been a vessel for romantic ideas about solitude. For Virginia Woolf, it's the climax of her novel *To the Lighthouse*. For Edgar Allan Poe, the source of his final, unfinished short story about a paranoid keeper clinging to his sanity. And for artist Jo Nivison Hopper, it was a symbolic representation of her husband, Edward Hopper. Talking about the two granite seaside towers in his oil landscapes of *Two Lights at Cape Elizabeth* she said, 'Those lighthouses are self-portraits … It was pitiful to see all the poor dead birds that had run into them on a dark night', she went on, 'I know just how they felt. The bright light on top had deceived them – and in no way they could think of to wring its neck[1]'. It's a familiar analogy of Hopper; the solemn but enigmatic painter who found it difficult to articulate the meaning of famous paintings like *Nighthawks* or *Chop Suey* with more than a few words. He had what art critic Brian O'Doherty called 'a great stone face'[2], standing noble but saturnine while the storms of the art world broke around him. The descriptions of Jo Nivison Hopper weren't so generous. Where Ed was seen as quiet and introspective, in 1971, *The New York Times* described Jo like a nuisance who would set up 'a barrage of conversation around her usually resigned husband', she was 'an indefatigable tug piping around a somnolent gray cruiser … Hopper's relationship with his wife, it appears, was much like his relationship with his art: silent, patient, totally committed to the nagging problems involved'[3], says the writer.

When Jo died in 1968, she bequeathed 3,000 artworks, a mix of her own and Edward's, to the Whitney Museum of American Art, something *The New York Times* mocks her for, 'a painter herself, she was convinced of the value of her work'[4], implying arrogance on her part. With a nod between superlatives, the critic writes about her art much like he does her personality. Jo's painting is 'fussed over', her nature 'high spirited and difficult', they are 'lightweight' to Edward Hopper's heavyweight.

There's a moment in *To the Lighthouse* where character Lily Briscoe, a frustrated artist, is staring at an unfinished canvas covered in running lines. 'Can't paint, can't write'[5] she murmurs to herself. The gremlin is on her shoulder and will not leave. She is talking to herself. Why bother? She wants to give up, roll it away, hide it under the sofa. It's a mess of blues and umbers she can't control, 'a fountain spurting over that glaring, hideously difficult white space'[6]. 'Can't paint, can't write', the words are thrumming in her mind, a mantra. Where has she heard it before? She remembers. Charles Tansley, another guest in the house where she was staying, had said 'Women can't paint, can't write. Coming up behind her, he had stood close beside her, a thing she hated, as she painted here on this very spot'[7].

After receiving the gift in Jo's will, the Whitney rummaged for Edward Hoppers to include in its collection, while it seems an unknown number of her original oil paintings and watercolours were unceremoniously discarded. Others were reportedly 'loaned' and given away to hospital receptions. Somewhere in America, they may still be filling wall space and waiting time, associated with little else than the anxiety of waiting for the results of a blood test or a second job interview. They have still not been located. The more I read about Jo, the more I understand her affinity with those lighthouse-colliding birds.

'No trespassing'

Jo was portrayed by the media as a deluded opportunist trying to piggyback her legacy onto her husband's. But she had a successful career as an artist long before she married Edward. So much of women's art is left up to women to reclaim, and it's mainly through the archive-digging commitment of two art historians that we are able to see Jo's story from a different angle. In 1995, Gail Levin put together an intimate biography of Edward Hopper, and unearthed Jo's private diaries in the process. Through Jo's writings, we get to know a frustrated artist trying to find space for her painting, piqued with bitterness and anger towards her unsupportive husband.

It's easy to empathise with these feelings when you learn that, when their relationship first began, Jo's reputation as an artist exceeded Edward's. And there is a particular sting that comes with seeing Edward Hopper and Jo Nivison Hopper's names on the list of an annual exhibition of contemporary American painting at the Whitney Museum in 1953, years before they resigned 'some' of her works to who knows where.

Jo Nivison had originally trained under Robert Henri at the New York School of Art in 1905, finding her feet as a watercolourist. She supported herself day-to-day as a school teacher, with a brief interlude working in occupational therapy in France. Jo had rotten luck with her health – she got acute bronchitis – and faced one of the worst years of her life; her mother died, and she lost both her home and her job in rapid succession. When she recovered her position as a schoolteacher in 1920, she caught diphtheria from the kids. There was one good thing to come out of it: she won early retirement, and managed to secure enough government money to support herself as an artist, producing work at her 9th Street studio that she called 'Titmouse Terrace'.

In the early 1920s, her work was exhibited in a group show alongside Pablo Picasso, Amedeo Modigliani and William and Marguerite Zorach in the New Gallery in New York. And when she was invited to show six of her watercolours at the Brooklyn Museum, Jo went out of her way to ask the curators to consider including the paintings of her new partner, Edward Hopper, who at that stage in his career was mainly known as a commercial illustrator and etcher. 'I got over there and they liked the stuff and I started writing and talking about Edward Hopper, my neighbour'[8], she said. It was at that show Edward sold *The Mansard Roof*, his first sale in almost a decade. A *New York Times* critic complimented 'Josephine Nivison's far-away echoes of Mary Rodgers'[9], in a review in which John Singer Sargent and Georgia O'Keeffe were merely listed names, but it was Edward who got the real critical attention.

He didn't directly acknowledge Jo's intervention in interviews, but that exhibition launched his career, giving him the confidence to show his work to the Frank K.M. Rehn Gallery, who still represent him today.

The critics just weren't that fired up by the bright, cheerful watercolour landscapes Jo offered when they could have his back-street American bleakness. But his work being the better accomplished does not explain why her career – and her individual artistic identity – almost disappeared altogether after their marriage. Something more complicated was at play.

In 2000, art historian Elizabeth Thompson Colleary uncovered 200 pieces by Jo Nivison gathering dust in the Whitney Museum basement. Jo was returning to the world again and again, like a restless spectre. Colleary went further, and tracked down Reverend Sanborn, a family friend of the Hoppers who had lovingly preserved thousands of letters and personal documents belonging to the couple, as well as a number of Jo's watercolours and photographs of her lost works. It all culminates to give us a still incomplete, but more coherent picture of Jo's style. The resurrected paintings of her pre-Hopper years were among her best – usually American landscape and seaside scenes – but painted with vivid, almost unnatural colours of cherry reds, lime greens and hot licks of blue that flicker on the canvas like flames on a Bunsen burner. As Colleary pointed out, some of the most interesting are the technically unfinished, the small 'pochades' or sketchy oil portraits, that Jo marked self-consciously as 'all pre-Hopper influence'[10].

Their home lacked the room for two artists' egos, and soon the value of those cheerful, kinetic watercolours start to feel clear as a quagmire. Writing in her diary on the night of their eighteenth wedding anniversary, she says, 'There are several things I've been clean pushed out of by his strutting superiority … It's as though he had a no trespassing sign hung on them, which isn't his intention at all. But he came to feel sex, swimming, French – are his domain – Painting too – I've been slowly crowded out of that too – almost. But I'm ready to fight'[11].

'Living their tossed lives in the teeth of the east winds'

On the day of the Hopper wedding, the couple were wandering around New York City, trying to find a clergyman who would actually agree to do the ceremony. The engagement had been just as laid-back – they had been trying to decide on where to spend the summer; she wanted Cape Cod he wanted Gloucester. As a compromise, she would agree to go to Gloucester, if they could get married too. And so they did, when they were in their early forties (though her marriage certificate had her aged thirty-seven).

Edward was also unwittingly marrying Arthur, Jo's cat and personal muse, the subject of so many of her watercolours, the prince of Titmouse Terrace. 'I was taking out a maternity complex on a big warrior alley cat – the scourge of 9th Street'[12], she wrote. In one of Hopper's many teasing caricatures of Jo, he draws her seated haughtily at the dining room table sharing a silver service dinner with a human-sized Arthur, while he is subservient on all fours by the table leg.

Jo hated to cook. Really abhorred it. Dinners, as she described them were made up of 'cans of the friendly bean on the shelf … and the opening of the cans is just bad enough'. Edward made fun of her hatred of domesticity by drawing himself emaciated, on his knees, begging her for a meal while she sat reading on a cloud, as though he'd been unable to manage in the forty-three years he'd spent without a wife to feed him. They seemed to be constantly fighting against one another's expectations – and sex was just another disappointment. Jo had been a virgin when she married, and confided to her diaries under a passage named 'the matters of sex' what a shock it had been, to learn that it was 'entirely for him'. 'There was my body, let him take it – but I'd not consent to be hurt too much – only a certain amount – I'd not be the object of pure sadism. I was forbidden to consult with other women over the mysteries. If he had drawn a lemon, I needn't advertise his misfortune … !'[13]. She'd resigned herself to this idea that she was inherently abnormal, as though she were a faulty 'lemon' car that cannot be fixed – as though Edward had no part to play in her enjoyment.

Their relationship was fraught, and some of the worst fights sprang from Jo's deep unhappiness with his lack of encouragement. As Edward gained clout with museums and curators, he appeared on art-judging panels and was approached about what artists to include in certain catalogues. When he failed to recommend Jo, as she had done for him with the Brooklyn Museum show, the bitterness intensified. Things could and did get violent. During explosive rows, he hit her, and she hit back to defend herself, scratching and biting, as she told a friend sometimes 'to the bone'[14]. Writing about how frustrated she had become with his 'meanness' about her work, she wrote, 'I got cuffed and could I but have reached, he'd have been bitten'[15]. She once joked that they should have a 'croix de guerre – a medal for distinguished combat'[16], and Edward obliged by making her a little coat of arms made out of a rolling pin and a ladle, a disturbing badge of honour for the domestic abuse.

Edward did undermine her work at times, delivering dismissive barbs about flower painting. But friends of the couple say they could both be unbearably frank with each other; Edward once called Jo 'my best pal and severest critic'[17]. Like Jo's critics, he seemed to view floral subjects as lightweight. But that all depends on who is doing the interpreting. Who gets to decide the worth of a flower painting and make assumptions about the intent of the artist?

Instead of fighting against the derogatory feminine labels, Jo stepped into the stereotype, 'that is what is expected of a lady artist: to do flowers … but one day when at a loss for subject matter my skirt brushed against some lovely petunias, zinnias – most arresting creatures really … I marvelled at the exquisite tilt of the petals and the gesture of the long stems, so friendly, living their tossed lives in the teeth of the east winds and ocean spray … I felt they should be painted'[18].

It makes me think of a David Shrigley drawing, a squiggle of a beret-wearing artist at a canvas that reads: 'I am a painter, don't tell me what to paint, I will paint flowers if I want, I will paint dead bodies if I want, and you can all fuck off.'

'Reading Robert Frost'

The Hoppers loved to live frugally. Though they had the money to eat out they preferred to live on canned foods, stewed beef and pea soup. The one luxury they did splash out on was American travel, driving from Gloucester to Wyoming to Mexico, and to their holiday home in South Truro, Cape Cod, the site of so many Edward Hopper landscapes, where they would spend almost every summer from 1930–1967 overlooking Fisher Beach.

On their road trips, they would look out for decent painting subjects, probably getting into an argument about where to stop. Some of the recovered watercolours from Reverend Sanborn let us see how the two painted side-by-side, capturing the same subject from two entirely different viewpoints. When they paused to paint some circus tents in Gloucester, Jo produced a watercolour bursting with bright blues and greens. Her version of the stripy big top is flanked by two trees blotted with sonorous lemon yellow for the leaves. Meanwhile Edward went in search of the grit, painting the back ends of a rusty circus wagon and parked car; the scene feels smooth and still, with no trace of the wind. Their car was a joint mobile studio and can be seen in action thanks to Ed's *Jo in Wyoming*, where she is captured painting energetically from the passenger seat, while his long legs were squished up beside his own canvas in the back.

Jo was the model for every single woman that appeared in his paintings (with the exception of *South Carolina Morning*). Like Alec Guinness in *Kind Hearts and Coronets*, she adopted new characters for each one: the bored redhead at the diner, a blonde usherette at the movie theatre, and at the age of almost sixty, she modelled for *Girlie Show*, a painting of a lithe, young, completely naked burlesque dancer with impossibly red nipples strutting across the stage. The role had her 'posing without a stitch on in front of the stove – nothing but high heels in a lottery dance pose'[19]. She might have been the muse but from her own account, she was more his artistic collaborator than passive model.

For all their problems, Jo supported Edward with his work with as much energy as she spent chastising him in her diaries. She kept records of his paintings and sales that were used to inform gallery collections and categories, and cut out newspaper clippings of any article that so much as mentioned his name.

Her diary writings, according to some, should not always be taken at face value because Jo was an eccentric, 'mad, but gloriously mad'[20], as her friend the art historian Barbara Novak told *The Guardian*. There is no call for a hagiographic rewrite of history here – whether or not everything in Jo's diaries was accurate, nobody is denying she had flaws: while she put a huge amount of time into archiving Edward's documents, there were claims she burned a stack of his early works, watercolours and early nudes on wooden panels.

She felt bitter about the impact the marriage had on her career, and for that, she has great cause. Look at what happened to her artistic legacy. This is not about what kind of painter she was compared to him. The fact is they were individuals with a different painting style. And where they were similar – in their watercolour landscapes – she is denigrated as 'lightweight', while his are compiled for books that argue their greatness.

It's possible Jo really was this vindictive woman who spent the latter days of her marriage muttering curses about her bastard husband's paintings while angrily drying plates over the kitchen sink. Maybe she couldn't be bothered feeding him anything but canned beef for dinner because she so resented his success. And if she was, that only makes me want to see her paintings more, to look at these fuchsia-flecked, egregiously cheerful watercolours, and consider the complex mind that produced them.

As Levin points out, how can we expect to form an opinion about Jo when so little of her work survives? And with what does survive, what are we given the chance to see? It's like comparing a published novel to an unfinished manuscript. Even the physical work that has resurfaced is not her best. I have asked myself again and again: do I just want her to be good? But I don't even get to decide. The decision was already made for us when so much of her work was lost to hospital hallways or discarded.

I know of an oil painting by Jo, where she paints Edward Hopper in a saggy vest, reading Robert Frost. His 6ft-5in body is perched uncomfortably on an armchair, like a stick insect resting on a buttercup. I want to admire the way she painted the atrophied muscles of his arms and his drooping skin, to think about the strange elegance of this age, contained in his long frame. I want to analyse it, to investigate the perspective around the living room, to look for objects around him the same way I scrutinise the mugs and the salt shakers on the countertop of the diner in *Nighthawks*. I want to talk about how Jo approached the empty space and make far-reaching assumptions about what Frost passage he's reading based on his posture. I want to think about why Jo chose this quiet moment to paint him, and wonder on paper how Edward felt about playing the muse. But I can't. At least, not with any real conviction. Because that painting is gone. It only exists in name and through a poorly reproduced black-and-white photograph. I feel such frustration, as though I have suddenly become short-sighted, and someone is pushing my reading glasses just out of reach. It's the collective myopia towards art made by women, the kind that causes museums to throw work in bins or leave it untouched in a basement. The kind that, in 1984, caused MoMA to hold *An International Survey of Recent Painting and Sculpture* with just thirteen women on a list of 169 artists. The kind that caused the curator of said exhibition to claim that any artist who wasn't in the show should rethink *his* career.

Edward and Jo were travelling from New York to Maine looking for intriguing places to paint when he spotted the lighthouse at Two Lights at Cape Elizabeth. As usual, Edward was driving, because he didn't like to let Jo behind the wheel. He stopped the car and decided this was what he was going to paint. When Jo thought to do the same – she liked the solitude of the lighthouse too – he snapped: 'Then I won't'[21]. Edward eventually relaxed, and that day, they painted the lighthouse together, but separately, committing the sobering granite tower to canvas from their own perspectives. It was that day that Edward made one of his 'self-portraits' – *The Lighthouse at Two Lights*, along with three other works, an oil and two watercolours. Jo painted multiple versions of the lighthouse that day too, but only one watercolour survives. As for the rest, well, someone could be looking at it in a hospital reception room right now, anxiously tapping their foot on the linoleum floor, waiting to be called for the results of their blood test.

13
SHIRLEY GRAHAM DU BOIS: RENAISSANCE WOMAN

To describe Shirley Graham Du Bois' epic three-act opera *Tom-Tom* as ambitious would be a gross understatement. When the production opened in 1932, it was to an audience of 10,000, who eagerly lined the bleachers of Cleveland Stadium in Ohio. Through sixteen scenes, the narrative of the opera leapt from pre-colonial Africa to the streets of 1930s Harlem, and brought an evolving score of folk, jazz and blues along for the ride. Every moment was punctuated by the steady beat of the tom-tom drum. It was a blockbuster production; reports from the time mention a real waterfall and a live elephant stomping onto the stage. No spoken dialogue was used, instead the great historical passage from the Africa of 1619 to the twentieth-century US was told through the songs and complex compositions Graham bestowed upon a cast of around 500 actors. It was a style that musicologist Sarah Schnalenberger decades later described as 'reminiscent of the realism that permeates nineteenth-century Italian verismo operas and French renaissance verité literature'[1].

Three months before curtain-up, playwright Graham was sitting at an upright piano in a hotel room, staring down the line of her twelve-week deadline to transform *Tom-Tom* from a one-act play into the monumental opera seen by that Cleveland crowd.

She was a single mother at the time, on leave from her job as a music teacher, but somehow, she pulled the music and libretto together in time for opening night. *Tom-Tom* was the first opera composed by an African-American woman for a major institution, and was performed by an all-black cast. Graham is not generally considered a prominent figure of the Harlem Renaissance (the explosive black arts movement of the 1920s that encompassed the sculptures of Augusta Savage, the poetry of Langston Hughes and the novels of Zora Neale Hurston) but she was closely associated with members of the movement. Given *Tom-Tom*'s centring of Harlem in the African American story, and its defiant celebration of black cultural identity, the play is slowly being recognised as an important work of the era. As Graham's biographer Professor Gerald Horne put it to me in an interview, the movement is "so flexibly defined … it is hard to say who would be part of it and who would not be part of it"[2].

Tom-Tom was well received by critics; there was even talk of being staged at Madison Square Garden that same year. It never transpired. Perhaps if it had, you might have heard of it. The play's lifespan was cut short owing to lack of financing; it didn't help that it was written in the midst of The Great Depression. Like millions of others in the US, Lawrence Higgins, who'd commissioned it for the Cleveland Stadium Opera Company, ran into financial and legal difficulty. With its enormous cast and elaborate staging, the cost of bringing *Tom-Tom* to the stage became insurmountable. And things got worse: Higgins kept the copyright, so it could not be staged elsewhere, and there's evidence in Graham's letters to suggest she was not paid for her labour at all. After its colossal premiere, *Tom-Tom* was never seen by an audience in its entirety again.

As a black woman in the Depression era, Graham had nothing but obstacles in her path, but managed to navigate them all. She left Oberlin with two degrees, and when she took a job at what is now known as Tennessee State University in Nashville, she was pushed out by the mediocre pay, lack of resources and poor treatment from her colleagues. Later, she was fired from a post at Federal Theatre Project in Chicago, most likely for her socialist politics and assumed connections with the Communist Party. Still, she remained prolific as a playwright, producing script after script during a fellowship at Yale Drama School, putting on plays for interracial audiences. One of these little-known productions was *It's Morning*, a one-act tragedy that follows the story of an enslaved woman who contemplates infanticide to prevent her child from being subject to a life of slavery. A critic called it 'a major breakthrough in African-American drama'[3].

As she balanced motherhood with a hugely productive creative life, the money from composition ran dry, so Graham decided to find employment elsewhere as a journalist and author. Even with this career shift, the music was never far away; traces of her composer's mind can be found throughout her writings.

In 1946, she published the biography of actor Paul Robeson, whom she'd met while studying music at the Sorbonne in Paris. Robeson was too busy for a first-person account, but he reluctantly agreed to the project, allowing Graham to gather anecdotes from those close to him, and to assert in the book's introduction that 'woven together, I believe they make his song'[4].

The biography Graham produced through this magpie method takes strange, symphonic form: Robeson's moves from star athlete to *Ol' Man River* fame via chapters with names like 'Second Movement, Adagio'. Her words too, have a melodic tone; she describes the sound of Robeson playing 'the full-throated, fluid wail and plunk plunk of the cheap piano'[5] on a hot summer's day in Harlem. Just one year after the Robeson biography, Graham produced *There Once Was a Slave*, a novel about Frederick Douglass, which was awarded the title of 'Best Book Combating Intolerance' by American publisher Julian Messner. Between all this – motherhood, books, plays – she remained a respected figure in leftist politics. In 1948, Graham delivered the keynote address for the Progressive Party, urging support for Henry Wallace and Glen Taylor in the American presidential race.

By the time she'd reached her fifties, Graham had an established reputation as an Ivy League composer and playwright, as a major political activist, a scholar, journalist and award-winning biographer, but for decades after her death, these achievements fell under the radar. With a few exceptions, such as Graham's biography, *Race Woman*, authored by Professor Gerald Horne, most academic and media interest in Graham's life tends to weigh heavily on the events that occurred after 1951 – the year she married the renowned writer, scholar and civil-rights activist W.E.B. Du Bois.

Tom-Tom was a revolutionary production, but lack of inquiry meant its score was presumed lost. It was finally placed in an archive in 2001, when it was discovered among her documents by her son David Du Bois. There have been attempts at revivals, but *Tom-Tom*, the first large-scale opera composed by an African-American woman for a major institution, is only really known in specific American academic circles.

As her son David Du Bois put it in his oral history interview with the National Visionary Leadership Project, 'One of the important things to realise about my mother is that she had a lifetime of accomplishments before she married [W.E.B. Du Bois]. And this is not known. In the same way that the accomplishments of most black women are unknown in our society today'[6].

'The people do not forget'

Graham was just thirteen years old when she got her first big editorial piece published. Incensed by the racist swimming policies at her local YWCA, she wrote a piece about the discrimination that appeared in a Colorado Springs newspaper. Her father, a methodist minister and missionary, had introduced her to civil rights activism from an early age. He would read Graham passages from political magazine *The Crisis*, which was edited by W.E.B. Du Bois and founded by the National Association for the Advancement of Colored People. She was not long out of high school by the time *The Crisis* was publishing her work too, 'I found the courage to send a poem to the magazine ... I doubt if any publication can ever bring me the same pride with which I read my poem from the smooth, white page of *The Crisis*'[7].

Graham had met Du Bois as a child (he was an acquaintance of her father's, and came to visit the family home), but by the time they were married (after the death of Du Bois's first wife), she was fifty-four, and he was eighty-three. Graham had also married before, and had two sons; when asked about her first husband later on, she claimed he was dead, when he was in fact very much alive.

Graham and Du Bois had a supportive partnership bound by their political ideas as much as love, but the years of the marriage would be some of her least productive, 'I gave up all my own work: whatever I was doing seemed so insignificant compared to what he was doing that I let it all go so I could devote myself to him and his needs,'[8] she once said. For Graham, challenges came from all angles: racial, gender and political. The feminist movement of the 1960s America largely failed to recognise the intersection of persecutions faced by women of colour. 'Black women are persecuted for gender and race reasons … sometimes that complicated the ability of many black women to sign a blank cheque to feminism as it was evolving in its wave in the 1960s', says Professor Horne. The scenario was more complex than Graham being subject to stereotypical gender roles, 'Like many in this country, Shirley Graham Du Bois has been victimised by anti-communism, McCarthyism, The Red Scare and defaming of anyone who is perceived to be part of the radical left and perceived to be part of the Communist Party. That's part number one,' Horne explains, 'part number two, to a degree, she has been overshadowed by the towering accomplishments of W.E.B. Du Bois … they got married in the midst of the prosecution which had befallen him [Du Bois was accused of being an agent of the Soviet Union and arrested in 1951] and then that created momentum for her being an organiser on his behalf, to save him from prison'[9]. Graham addressed this last point herself in a special edition of W.E.B. Du Bois' book *In Battle for Peace*, which featured her commentary, 'With him in jail, only a wife could carry the case to the people. I must be in a position to stand at his side – this I felt was essential'[10].

Her gradual recasting as an obscured figure was caused not simply by her marriage to the 'towering' figure of Du Bois, but through the systemic racism that actively works against powerful black women to keep their achievements out of view.

Graham remained politically outspoken after their marriage; some have even painted her as a sort of socialist temptress, leading Du Bois down the red garden path into the Communist Party, as if a man as established as Du Bois could not make decisions of his own (Du Bois had spoken out against communism and communist regimes, but joined the Party in protest when the McCarran Act was passed, forcing communists to register with the government). The oppressive descent of McCarthyism on America left the couple dogged by the FBI, and so they fled to Ghana in 1961. He was personally invited by the

President of Ghana, Kwame Nkrumah to work on an *Encyclopedia Africana*, an encyclopaedia of the African diaspora, and she had yet another career change, working within government to implement Ghanian television. It was in Ghana where Graham and her husband evolved their ideas around Pan-Africanism, a movement supported by Malcolm X and Marcus Garvey.

They also co-founded a magazine called *Freedomways* in 1961, the leading political journal for the civil rights movement and African liberation movements. It was a siren call across the African diaspora with an anti-colonial message at its core. With Shirley Graham Du Bois as its inaugural editor (by then, she had changed her surname), it showcased the writing of James Baldwin, Angela Davis and Martin Luther King. As it moved into the 1970s, *Freedomways* became a celebration of black arts as well as politics, publishing early short stories by Alice Walker, poems by Audre Lorde, and cover art from Charles White.

When W.E.B Du Bois died in Ghana in 1963, Graham Du Bois committed herself fully to ironing out the reputation the US government had gone to such great lengths to tarnish, standing in the face of anyone or anything who tried to denigrate the Du Bois legacy. She reverted to being what her son David described as a '25-hour-a-day worker', speaking at university conferences, again becoming politically active, authoring books and articles (in 1971, she published *His Day is Marching On: A Memoir of W.E.B. Du Bois*, to mixed response – Graham was understandably fairly uncritical of her subject) and another biography, this time Julius Nyerere, the African nationalist, freedom fighter and first president of Tansania.

Her movements remained under close surveillance from the American government. Her FBI file was as big as a phone book, coming to a full 1,068 pages (some sources say it was closer to 2,000). When she spoke at UCLA in 1970, a speaker introduced her to the crowd with the line 'I want to welcome members of the FBI, the CIA'.

The speech she gave that night had the kind of evocative calls to action that usually end up edited into documentary montages, quoted in textbooks or pasted over black-and-white images that are circulated on social media, but

Graham Du Bois' reach into public consciousness has yet to unfold. She spoke of the pervading power of African music, extolling the day North Africans landed in Gibraltar and across Europe. It was as though she was trying to join the two most prominent themes of her life: activism, and composition, saying: '[North Africans] changed the music, the whole course of European music ... They had the Gregorian chants, the melodies, weaving in and out, but these forces from North Africa brought rhythm, they had never had rhythm before'. Moments later, she had the audience rapt with a message about the enduring evil of the colonisation of Africa, 'Over and above the crime of killing and enslaving its peoples, was the white man's robbing of black people of their past ... Bombs can be dropped on them, people can be tortured, great armies can march, and planes can fly, for a little while ... but the people do not forget'[11].

When Graham Du Bois died from breast cancer in 1977 in Beijing, her death was acknowledged by a *New York Times* obituary, with the headline 'Shirley Graham Du Bois, 69, writer and widow of civil rights leader'[12]. It's a theme that followed her entire career following W.E.B. Du Bois' death, the idea of the professional widow, a trope she castigated as 'the promotion which has been used so widely on me ... the widow of so and so'. By sewing up her identity with Du Bois' legacy, we lose the reality of Shirley Graham's life before it. She should be an icon, not a conduit for Du Bois. We need to see her operas studied and restaged, her compositions heard, her biographies and articles reprinted. Woven together, they make her song.

The first time I ever encountered a piece of Surrealist art was not in a book, a poster, or gallery, but on an episode of *The Simpsons*. It was one of those portmanteau 'Treehouse of Horror' specials, with one particular scene set in a spooky gallery hung with 'classic' paintings that had been elaborately Simpsonified. For just a few brief seconds, you can see a painting of Bart, his face obscured by a giant green apple, recognisable only through those distinctive triangles of yellow hair poking out the top. I remember asking the name of the real artwork, powering up the dial-up internet so I could search for it on AltaVista: *The Son of Man*, by René Magritte.

The image made total sense to me at the time, dramatically altering my perception of the world of adulthood as a drab and dreary, predictable old place into one of breathtakingly plausible, aggressive and challenging absurdities. A shock for a nine-year-old. To someone that age, the barrier between reality and fantasy is cigarette-paper thin, and Surrealism offered a way to tear through it. I was able to absorb the painting into my consciousness so early and so easily, simply because the works of male Surrealists are so ubiquitous. They are mainstream, mass market. A rip-off of Dalí's *Mae West Lips* sofa can readily be found in almost any major furniture outlet, with cartoon parodies of his congealed clocks as blithely accessible as the original source, his painting *The Persistence Of Memory*. René Magritte's mix of floating hats and cumulus clouds have been recruited to sell Volkswagens. And how many hundreds of models have had to sit patiently while the details of a violin are painted on their lower backs for a fashion shoot tribute to cabaret performer Kiki de Montparnasse in *Le Violon d'Ingres* by Man Ray?

Along winding arteries, they drip drip drip into our subconscious, situating these man-made images at the forefront of our minds. For most of us, they are what formed our understanding of Surrealism: the quixotic desire, the idealised feminine form, the woman represented by her red, disembodied lips. They are what we get when, instead of looking at the movement in any sort of depth, we limit ourselves to a mere glance.

When walking around the 2019 Tate retrospective of Surrealist artist Dorothea Tanning, something shifted in me. I peered into a perspex box at her sculpture, *Tweedy*, a lumpy, dog-like creature cast in cloth. Beside it, there was a tiny, curled brown slither, a tweed turd. For the first time in years, I burst out laughing in a gallery. And when I turned the corner to see Tanning's *Emma*, a round pink belly circled by a pelmet of perished lace, I clutched my stomach, feeling a jolt of awareness of my own potential for maternity. All those teenage nightmares featuring a floating pregnant belly, with a vivid impertinence presenting themselves at the forefront of my consciousness. I looked at her sculptures again and again. I looked until the gallery attendant was yawning and tapping his watch and politely edging me towards the door. I looked at them and thought, 'Where the hell have these been?'

Mad love ('L'Amour Fou')

In her encyclopedic study of women in Surrealism, writer and artist Penelope Rosemont pulled together the work of ninety-six women artists and writers associated with the movement spread across twenty-eight countries. Leonora Carrington, Dorothea Tanning, Remedios Varo, Lee Miller and Kay Sage all entered the Surrealist orbit (though a number of them rejected the title), while Meret Oppenheim, Jacqueline Lamba and Eileen Agar appeared in the original, and official *International Surrealist Exhibition* in London 1936. So why, in 1968, when critic William S. Rubin released his 525 page tome on *Dada & Surrealist Art*, did he not see fit to discuss a single Surrealist woman and instead, only mentioned them in passing? Before the 1980s, the women of Surrealism were dangerously underestimated and under-studied.

Surrealism began as a web of contradictions, most notably in respect of its attitude towards women. The movement was founded by poet André Breton, having grown out of a kind of handshake between the absurdist art of Dada and Freudian theory. Before becoming a writer, Breton had been a medical orderly working on a military psychiatric ward during World War One. There he would scribble feverishly on his notepad as a shell-shocked soldier told him that the war was not real, that the whole thing had been staged, insisting the bullets had been blank, the wounds nothing more than theatrical make-up. Breton became fixated on the philosophical potential of dreams and irrational states. Like the Dadaists, he thought that art might provide a means to make sense of trauma. He wanted to access the depths of the disordered mind, alchemising them, somehow, into art.

The idea of breaking away from the 'rational' world had appeal for women, bringing with it the promise of liberation from the 'rational' expectation of tawdry domesticity, from monogamy, from marriage. But it didn't quite live up to its promise.

Desire became a central part of the Surrealist theory; the accession of love was seen as one of the numerous keys central to the unlocking of the consciousness. This was 'Mad Love' or *L'Amour Fou*, based on the book of the same name by Breton, written about his first meeting with artist Jacqueline Lamba. *Mad Love* charted the journey of their relationship, and the birth of their first child, Aube. According to writer Mary Ann Caws it was 'an incandescent testimony to the love of the irrational and the irrational of love'[1].

Women were considered innately 'Surrealist' beings, but were simultaneously elevated and denigrated, defined in terms of beauty and male desire. They were expected to occupy fictitious roles of *femme-enfants*, nymphs and spiritual artistic guides, leaving precious little space for the 'self'. Feminine bodies were painted, sculpted and photographed in collaged fragments: an eye, a mouth, a headless and armless torso.

If it wasn't their bodies being objectified, it was the deterioration of their minds. In André Breton's novel *Nadja*, considered by some one of the most important texts of the twentieth century, he turns his real life meeting with a young woman named Léona Delcourt into an obsessive story romanticising her letters, drawings and her psychosis. It is most famous for its closing lines, a conception of beauty as an unstoppable force, 'Beauty, neither static nor dynamic. The human heart, beautiful as a seismograph... Beauty will be CONVULSIVE or will not be at all'[2]. Her mad love is the vantage point for his own artistic breakthrough, with Breton cast as the intellectual observer of her breakdown.

In Surrealism, the male gaze is significantly amplified by the lens of a magnifying glass. As Dorothea Tanning once put it to journalist Alain Jouffroy, 'I noticed with a certain consternation ... that the place of women in Surrealism was no different than her place in bourgeois society in general'[3]. Admittedly, not everyone sees it this way. In her anthology, Penelope Rosemont made it clear that she viewed Surrealism as 'one of the least sexist art movements'[4] pointing out Breton's support and inclusion of women from the very beginning. Dorothea Tanning, Meret Oppenheim, Leonora Carrington and others were opposed to the idea of separating 'women's art' for analysis, seeing it as another exile, 'Women artists. There is no such thing – or person', said Tanning, 'It's just as much a contradiction in terms as "man artist" or "elephant artist." You may be a woman and you may be an artist; but the one is a given and the other is you'[5].

For her book *Women Artists and the Surrealist Movement* in 1985, one of the first substantial explorations into the women of the movement, feminist art historian Whitney Chadwick (an expert in this area), received a letter from Meret Oppenheim, who requested that none of her work be reproduced in the text. Oppenheim categorically rejected the idea that there was a problem, stating that any 'male centredness'[6] was simply a byproduct of late-nineteenth century behaviour.

But the inclusiveness of the Surrealists' exhibitions, and the innate Surrealism of women didn't deter critics from concentrating their attention almost exclusively on the men of the movement. When Meret Oppenheim first showed her famous fur-lined tea cup, named *Object* many of them referred to her as 'Mr Oppenheim'[7], mistaking the hairy erotic vessel to be a man's creation. And if the often-contradictory Breton is a misunderstood feminist with a mind distracted by *L'Amour Fou*, not all were able to shift the weight of that nineteenth-century inheritance. When Chadwick interviewed artist and poet Roland Penrose (who was married to writer Valentine Penrose, then to writer and photographer Lee Miller) and explained how she planned to write a book on the women of Surrealism, he informed her, 'You shouldn't write a book about the women ... they weren't artists ... Of course the women were important ... But it was because they were our muses'[8].

Surrealism, with its emphasis on the pursuit of love and desire at all costs, had more notable couples than any other art movement. Leonora Carrington and Dorothea Tanning both had romantic relationships with Max Ernst, Kay Sage and Yves Tanguy were married, and Jacqueline Lamba's first marriage was to André Breton. And in almost every case except with Frida Kahlo and Diego Rivera, women in Surrealism have struggled for independent recognition. Though the reappraisal of their work began in earnest with Chadwick's book as far back as 1985, it was only in the 2000s that the commercial art world began to treat these names with real significance, acknowledging them as boundary-pushing artists who cultivated a new image of female sexuality in the 1930s and '40s. Recent high-profile gallery retrospectives have gone some way toward redressing the balance, and works by Dorothea Tanning, Leonora Carrington and Kay Sage are selling at auction for prices in the millions (Sage's painting *Le Passage* sold for $7 million in 2014). For others, such as Jacqueline Lamba, things have been more fragmented. She had the daunting task of escaping the association with the 'father' of Surrealism, an association that followed her for her entire career. And though the focus on visual artists of Surrealism obviously is a positive, the awareness of women writers influenced by the movement, such as Suzanne Césaire, lags behind.

Jacqueline Lamba

Uncovering the independent image of Jacqueline Lamba is no easy task; she was constantly being held up as a mirror for others, spoken about as though she were a piece of art, instead of a practitioner. Even as a child, she wasn't allowed to inhabit her own self comfortably; her parents had been hoping for a boy, so as a teen she cropped her hair, and called herself 'Jacko'. She was referred to by her family as *garçon manqué* (tomboy, though it translates as 'failed' boy). As an adult, when she was trying to support herself as a painter, Lamba had a job swimming naked at the aquarium in Coliséum dance hall in Montmartre to entertain punters. It was a side hustle that coincided with her first meeting with André Breton, her first husband, who then cast her in his mind in the role of ondine, the ethereal watersprite leading him through an opiate gulf to create *L'Amour Fou*. The expectation that came with being the queen to the 'king' of Surrealists, coupled with being a living 'character' in Breton's writing, wreaked havoc with Lamba's artistic subjectivity. Years later she would say, 'He saw in me what he wanted to see, but he didn't really see me'[9].

For all the posturing about Surrealism as a source of liberation for women, Lamba's place in its circle left her consumed with doubts about her work, to the point that she destroyed a significant amount of her own paintings. The early, fractal landscapes that did survive are jagged and unpredictable, like a mirror glass that's been smashed and reassembled.

'You know that she's a very good painter...'

It was Lamba's friendships with other women that would foster her early development as an artist. At the age of twelve, she met Marianne Clouzot, whose father happened to be a curator at Palais Galliera, introducing Lamba to Oceanic and African art that covered the walls of the Clouzot family home. And while she was studying at Ecole de L'Union Centrale des Arts Décoratifs, cobbling together designs for books and advertisements to pay the rent, it was her friend Dora Maar who helped her find cheap boarding in a home for young women run by nuns in the 1920s. Marianne Clouzot gave her a copy of *Orpheus* by Jean Cocteau and Maar introduced her to new ideas on photography (when they met, Maar was already developing her eye for Surrealist imagery). But it was Lamba's political disillusionment, and an evening spent reading Breton's *Les Vases Communicants*, that directed her towards Surrealism. The spirit of the October Revolution in Russia shifted her towards the radical left, but she didn't have the militant motivations of other young people in those circles. Lamba described how leftist meetings she attended felt 'utterly routine in character, elementary and grey ... they turned me off'[10]. Surrealism offered a more abstract response, a way to marry the poetic and artistic mind with the 'revolutionary consciousness ... All this fulfilled me, liberated me, and instilled in me a joy such as I suspect young people today can scarcely grasp,'[11] she wrote. Her eventual meeting with Breton has been romanticised and aggrandised so often that I feel no need to dress it up here; just know that in 1934, Lamba orchestrated a 'coincidence' that would have them at Café de la Place Blanche at the same time. They met. They married (with Alberto Giacometti as their best man) and had a daughter, Aube.

Lamba was immediately pitched into the Surrealist labyrinth. Two of her paintings were included in the *International Surrealist Exhibition* on the Canary Islands in 1935, along with artworks by Salvador Dalí and Joan Miró , but Lamba's work went unattributed, and did not appear in the catalogue. When the group made their way to London for the landmark show in Burlington Gardens in 1936, Lamba arrived with hair dyed green – a mirror to match Breton's suit. Dylan Thomas was moving through the crowds offering 'tea' brewed with string, Dalí almost suffocated whilst attempting to perform a lecture attired in a full-size diving suit. The pomp and absurdity of the aesthetic was all part of the game, but Eileen Agar, the only female British artist to exhibit at the show noticed there was something quite different about the treatment of Lamba, 'She was a very good painter, but you see, in those days, men thought of women simply as muses, they never thought that they could do something for themselves.' Agar suggested that Lamba had been 'too frightened' to show her work to Breton, 'she'd kept them in a cupboard or something, until somebody said, "You know that she's a very good painter." He said, "I've never seen anything she's painted".'[12] Lamba was not, as it turned out, 'too frightened' to share her art after all, she had three pieces in that 1936 show, two found objects and one oil painting, *Les Heures*, a vulvic shell submerged at the bottom of the ocean, topped with a little foot wearing heeled shoes which she painted while she was pregnant with Aube. It's possible Agar was making a point about Breton's detached attitude to Lamba's work, or that the conversation took place before the exhibition, but, as she would suggest to another interviewer, the muse culture of the European surrealists provoked a double standard where 'the women came off worst'[13].

'The line does not exist'

None of the efforts to cast Lamba as the shy, submissive muse or the reluctant painter fit with her. She knew the value of creative freedom, and she sought it out, sometimes leaving her family for months at a time to seek out work as an artist. When World War Two broke out, Lamba was supposedly on a beach with Picasso and Dora Maar. The war catapulted her and her family to the US. She and Breton were lucky enough to be on the list of intellectual elites that were plucked from Vichy France by the rescue network of American journalist Varian Fry after the Nazis had occupied Northern Paris. They were protected in a mansion in Marseille, which had become a safe house for the avant-garde, maintaining the lives of painters, personalities and poets like Wilfredo Lam, Tristan Tzara, Max Ernst and Remedios Varo. They called the house 'Villa Air-Bel'.

As Hitler unleashed the German Blitzkrieg on the UK, they sat around playing 'Exquisite Corpse', a Surrealist parlour game that had each member contribute words or images to a piece of paper to produce a collective work of art.

It's from the 'corpses' game that we still have access to some of Lamba's surviving pieces. In her collaborative collages with Breton and Yves Tanguy she produced steampunk-like totems of gramophone fish, grandfather clocks with flies' wings and bearded men with caterpillar hats. During the day, she passed time exercising on her trapeze, suspended beneath a tree like a chrysalis. This strange, dangling sabbatical from life came to an end after a sponsorship from Peggy Guggenheim allowed Lamba and her family to move to America in 1941, as she called it, 'the Christmas tree of the world'[14], settling in a Greenwich Village apartment.

It was a revelatory period for Lamba. With the concentrated forcefield of Surrealism punctured by the war, she found a new freedom with her landscape painting. She wrote to Dora Maar exclaiming, 'now I am working in a completely serious way, to such an extent that I can't possibly understand how I could have managed to avoid it before'[15]. These paintings are dark, sharp shapes that make the viewer feel like they are piloting a spacecraft travelling through alien terrain, but they possess a Lamba originality that's distinct from the desolate Surrealist landscapes of Dalí or Tanguy.

In one of the most incisive English language investigations into her work, Salomon Grimberg shares a note she wrote about her most well-known painting from this period: *In Spite of Everything, Spring* 'The line does not exist, it is already form. Shadow does not exist, it is already light'[16]. Peggy Guggenheim boosted her confidence by selecting her work for *Exhibition by 31 Women*, a now legendary show that took place at her The Art of this Century Gallery (one critic refused to review it on the grounds that 'there are no worthy women artists'). And she had her first one-woman show, at Norlyst Gallery, though media coverage continued to undermine her independence; a listing for the show in a 1944 issue of *The New Yorker* just read 'surrealist paintings by the wife of André Breton'. It is made all the more offensive by the fact that the marriage, by that point, was unravelling. In an attempt to piece her life together, Lamba escaped to Mexico to seek guidance and support from Frida Kahlo, spending seven months sleeping in her spare room at the Casa Azul with Aube. From this moment of crisis, Kahlo painted *The Bride Frightened at Seeing Life Opened*, a still-life platter of fresh split papaya and ageing bananas, where a small white doll peers out from behind the curve of a watermelon, troubled by this fleshy canyon of wounded fruit. If Mexico allowed Lamba cut her life open, what she observed inside convinced her to leave Breton. It's likely he lost or maybe even destroyed the pre-War work that she did not discard herself. When Lamba returned to retrieve them after his death, there was no evidence of them in the couple's old Parisian home. The artist dissociated herself from Surrealism completely; the label became irrelevant, tied to years of restriction and self-doubt. Now the line did not exist. Lamba scaled up her paintings, producing semi-abstract landscapes with thick daubs of paint that gathered in colourful storms across the canvas. As she reached her seventies, isolation itself became her muse. She wrote to a friend that 'being alone did not mean my lack of desire to meet neither beings nor friends, but to be inhabited by one's self"[17]. Her reflection was no longer distorted. She was not *L'Amour Fou*. Not Ondine. Just Lamba.

Suzanne Césaire

Seven articles. When revisiting the writing of Martiniquan scholar Suzanne Césaire, it is all we have to go on, seven articles that have only recently been republished. Seven articles which originally appeared in the journal *Tropiques*, a literary smokescreen for revolutionary voices that ran from 1941–1945, when Nazism was advancing into the Caribbean through Vichy Government rule. The volume of her surviving work might be sparse, but the rich originality of her ideas and rhapsodical tone of her writing have carried her out of obscurity. Her essays are dogmatic but poetic, and have what a translator of her work called a 'dissident lyricism' – exploring what it means to be Martiniquan in a colonised country that was in the midst of being colonised by a whole new oppressor. And in her search for answers to these difficult questions, she channelled the ideas of Surrealism, giving its theories new life beyond its white, eccentric European context.

The difference of Césaire's Surrealism can, emphatically, be noted in the title of her essay *1943: Surrealism and Us* – Césaire was conceiving the broader, ambitious and philosophical possibilities of the movement, maybe even more so than André Breton. While European Surrealists absorbed the individualistic 'Mad Love' doctrine by obsessively turning their lovers into artworks and penetrating deep into the black hole of sexual desire, Césaire harnessed its ideas about the subconscious and disordered society to unpack the irrationality of racism.

In her essays, she deconstructs the language of the Surrealist manifestos to reveal the complex veins of its fruit. In Césaire's hands, Surrealism is not an embarrassment of sexual riches or playful escapism. It is not a poetic courtship with madness. It is a call to action, a 'tightrope of our hope', on which Antillean people could tentatively walk, one foot in front of the other, to a better reality. 'Surrealism can claim the glory of being at the extreme point of the bow of life drawn to the breaking point'[18], she wrote. The writer did eventually meet André Breton when he came to visit Martinique in 1941 (he'd found a copy of the *Tropiques*, and been enthralled by the potency of the writing). The poet was so taken with her that he dedicated a poem to her *For Madame Césaire*. He also exoticised her looks, comparing her beauty to the flame of rum punch. Breton's Surrealism, at that point, seemed inward-looking and painfully aesthetic, but she had grander plans for the poet's own vision.

Césaire was convinced of Surrealism's potential, inspired by its message of freedom at a time when freedom was under its greatest threat. By unlocking the subconscious, it could lay bare the 'blind myths' that enforced the colonial mindset. 'It will be time finally to transcend the sordid contemporary antinomies: Whites-Blacks, Europeans-Africans, civilised-savage: the powerful magic of the mahoulis will be rediscovered, drawn directly from the very wellsprings of life. Colonial idiocies will be purified by the welding arch's blue flame. The mettle of our metal, our cutting edge of steel, our unique communications – all will be recovered.'[19]

'The great camouflage'

Suzanne Césaire died prematurely from brain cancer in 1966, but there is no record of a single piece from her written after 1945. Piecing together the reasons for this rapid evaporation soon descends into the realm of frustrating conjecture, for when it comes to detail, her biography is pretty porous. We know that she was born in Martinique, moved to Paris to study philosophy in the 1930s, and returned to her birthplace to work as a schoolteacher at the Lycée Schoelcher. But the one firm detail we have about her personal life is her marriage to the well-known poet, politician and father of the Négritude movement, Aimé Césaire.

Given his very public persona, and the scant nature of her surviving output, her work very nearly disappeared into his. The author of *Surrealist Women: An International Anthology* said of Suzanne Césaire that 'No important figure in the history of surrealism has been so overshadowed by a spouse,'[20] – and, regrettably, there has been some very real competition on that front. For two decades after her death, it was as if Suzanne's writing had never, in fact, existed; her name was almost totally absent from Surrealist literature, and on texts on Aimé Césaire.

A play she composed, *Dawn of Freedom*, adapted from folklorist Lafcadio Hearn's book *Youma: the Story of a West Indian Slave*, was staged but never published.

It's possible she became preoccupied by her home life, as she and Aimé had six children, or perhaps Aimé's career assumed precedence as he gained notoriety and political office (he was elected Mayor of Fort-de-France, Martinique). The couple separated in the 1960s, but there are limited details about the inner workings of their relationship and maybe this should be considered a positive. The lack of biographical detail has meant that in the slow rehabilitation of Suzanne Césaire's work, the focus has been on the depth and influence of her writing, instead of her personal life. If it was her marriage which obscured her writing during her lifetime, then at least we can allow her writing to stand alone unburdened by biographical gossip today.

Aimé Césaire is considered one of the leaders of Négritude, the radical Francophone literary movement of the 1930s that absorbed ideas from Pan-Africanism, the Harlem Renaissance and Surrealism to explore black identities beyond the boundaries of French colonialism. But both he and Suzanne were founders of *Tropiques*, the journal that helped spread Négritude's message.

The name Négritude was a reclamation of a racist slur. As their fellow Surrealist writer René Ménil said 'we gathered the insults to make diamonds of them'[21]. But *Tropiques* was born into an atmosphere of censorship. During the period when *Tropiques* was being published (1941–1945) the Pétainist regime had installed Admiral Georges Robert in Martinique as 'High Commissioner for the French West Indies', with practically dictatorial power. He was in charge of enforcing all laws issued by the Vichy Government.

To get the political messaging of *Tropiques* past the officials, Suzanne Césaire and her editorial team covertly presented it as a literary journal concerned with folklore and Antillean poetry. Some of her articles began with wilfully and intentionally obtuse language, crowding her opening paragraphs with broad, rhetorical questions or lines of poetry to throw the censors off the scent. In one of her most famous essays, 'The Malaise of a Civilization', she elegantly unravels the impact of the colonial violence on Martiniquan history, how it has denied people their own sense of self. She takes aim at the illusion of liberation through assimilation into white society, and the creation of undignified work laws that gave little option but to choose such assimilation. In 'Poetic Destitution', Césaire calls for a new Caribbean poetry, free from the white, exoticised gaze and limp visual sentimentality, 'To hell with hibiscus, frangipani, and bougainvillea. Martinican poetry will be cannibal or it will not be'[22].

Suzanne's essays adopt this very imagery for her verbose intros and interludes, but it was all a poetic ruse, a camouflage that would enable her anti-colonial ideas to hide in plain sight. In her essay, which actually takes the title of *The Great Camouflage*, her opening lines uncoil with a lyrical description of the Caribbean: 'There are, melded into the isles, beautiful green waves of water and of silence', then descend into a criticism of the hypocrisy of the Vichy Government and the French colonists, 'the new arrival are hardly adapting to our "old French territories". When they lean over the malefic mirror of the Caribbean, they see therein the delirious reflection of themselves. They dare not recognise themselves in this ambiguous being, the Antillean'[23]. Her essays were searing criticisms of the very people who were signing off the magazine for publication, carefully concealed beneath the petals of a hibiscus flower.

'Expect from us neither a plea, nor vain recriminations'

Tropiques was closed for good by Vichy Government officials in 1945. Suzanne and her team sent a letter in response, making no effort to occlude their real feelings through the use of romantic imagery of hibiscus petals or sea breeze for the censors. Instead, she and her colleagues co-signed the message: 'Expect from us neither a plea, nor vain recriminations, not even a debate. We do not speak the same language'[24]. *Tropiques* did go on to produce more issues, but the closure marked the end of Suzanne Césaire's published works. Thanks to the efforts of academics, and in particular the novelist David Maximin (who edited the first ever published volume of Suzanne Césaire's collected works,

The Great Camouflage) her essays are gradually being absorbed into the canon of Caribbean literature. In her theories on Surrealism, she set the wheels in motion for the explosive genealogy of Afro-Surrealism, which was further defined as an arts movement in 'The Afrosurreal Manifesto' by D. Scot Miller for the *San Francisco Bay Guardian* in 2009. The manifesto placed works by artists like Kara Walker and Kehinde Wiley in the Afro-Surrealist realm. So when you see Walker's breathtaking and elaborate sculptures, be mindful that Suzanne Césaire might have played some small part. When you watch Boots Riley's film *Sorry to Bother You* or even, as Miller pointed out later, Marvel's *Black Panther*, know that she was one of the first to see Surrealism as a creative power-source for black people to access the painful, irrational world of the disordered, racist colonial mindset. We may not know much about what happened to Suzanne Césaire after 1945, when she wrote her last essay *The Great Camouflage*, but happily, we do have these consoling words from her daughter, the playwright Ina Césaire:

'My mother who believed more in struggles than in tears
my mother with the explosive humor
with the gaiety tinged with melancholy, with the fragile health, but
    indefatigable tenacity
My unforgettable mother, who was not able to grow old
Suzanne Césaire, born Roussi'[25].

15
DORA MAAR: RADICAL PHOTOGRAPHY

It's hard to be a woman of mystery when everyone is rooting around in the back of your closet. Surrealist photographer, photojournalist and painter Dora Maar spent the last fifty years of her life living as a fairweather recluse in Paris and in Ménerbes refusing enquiries from the press, publishers and gallery owners. Maar enjoyed huge success in the 1930s and '40s, creating oneiric black-and-white images that swept into the upside-down world of the Surrealists. By the time of her death in 1997, however, her photography was forgotten by the public at large, but celebrated among a few loyal followers. And at the same time, she was one of the most visible figures in Modern art, as the *Weeping Woman* in Pablo Picasso's paintings, artworks created during their relationship, before he unceremoniously left her for the younger Françoise Gilot. With her image, he forged a symbol of mourning for the atrocities of the Spanish Civil War. The insatiable hunger for detail about Picasso's personal life resulted in those paintings being treated as a biographical storyboard of their time together. The realities held in the pigment became wrapped up with Maar's own, at least in the eyes of the public. Proximity to him had opened the door to Dora Maar's art immortality, but slammed the window of autonomy shut.

When the photographer died, she had no definitive beneficiary in her will, leaving the State to step in. Somewhere along the line, the Musée Picasso was given permission to photograph her Paris apartment at 6 rue de Savoie. It appeared her link to the artist (who had bought her the property) gave it historical importance, prompting urgent calls for archive and inventory. It was the most anyone outside her friendship circle had seen of Maar's life for almost fifty years – each *click* capturing some small detritus of biographical evidence to be stitched together. A bed, still unmade. Stacks of battered luggage tagged with labels from her travels as a photojournalist in the 1930s. A Rolleiflex camera still in its brown case. A crucifix on its side. A bathroom wall, covered in tiny *trompe l'oeil* spiders and millipedes Picasso had painted onto the plaster. A reproduction of a human skull on the shelf, being used as a morbid book end.

The books that rested on the nose of that skull, are, as books tend to be, the most revealing of the Maar chattels. She was a voracious reader right up until the end of her life, and had a collection fat with texts on Minoan art, Tintoretto, Goya, El Greco. She had *The Complete Works of Saint Augustine*, a copy of introductory Buddhist guide *The Spirit of Zen* – their pages dog-eared and covered in her notes.

For this photographic inventory, the gaze might have been fixed on Maar, but travelled through her to reach Picasso, the biggest fish in the pond of twentieth century art. It's a paradox that has always followed the photographer's work. After her death, she was written about extensively, in memoirs, in articles, even in novels, but the quest for juicy anecdotes about their relationship has far exceeded examination of her photography, and paintings.

Picasso's paintings responded to his ever-changing and destructive relationships with the women in his life. As a result, his biography has been skinned, flayed and picked to the marrow to get closer to the meaning of what was happening in his studio. Maar's story offered a different route, but the road, more often than not, would lead straight back into the Spaniard's bullring. That valorisation is a trap we set for ourselves and repeatedly fall into, and I absolutely include myself in that 'we'. I once ran an interview in *Artists & Illustrators* magazine with painter Lydia Corbett, a painter who also modelled for multiple Picasso portraits in the mid-1950s. When finalising the article, I placed interesting stories she'd told about him in the pullquote, and worked his name into a coverline, believing his name was more likely to catch a reader's eye, knowing the link would help shift copies of the magazine. It was an obvious, cynical approach I was complicit in, offering an illusion of change while using the same guile. Not centring him in the story didn't feel like an option. The shadow was always there.

Before she passed away, one of Maar's close friends James Lord, an affluent American who'd used his family money to deposit himself among the Paris art intelligentsia of the 1940s, wrote a memoir called *Picasso and Dora* (against Maar's admonition that she didn't want to be written about because she believed writers could not be trusted). Lord's book is one of the most extensive sources of information about Maar (if unquantifiable – its authority depends how much trust we place in Lord's memories) but he too sometimes speaks about her as though she were a living portrait. Writing on her solitude in the years after her relationship with Picasso had ended, he rejects the idea that Maar should be pitied, because she had been immortalised. Her loneliness was itself like a piece of art because 'the solitude was likewise his creation, his largesse, bearing all the imperishable imprint of his genius'[1]. He seemed to view her second identity of the *Weeping Woman* as a badge of honour from the supposed artist untouchable.

It's a badge that overwhelmed her artistic identity, and one she wore with a changeable mix of pride and frustration, 'I have to talk about Picasso, because people expect it, because nobody knows as much about him as I do'[2]. Before he came into her life, Maar's reputation was one of a daring, experimental Surrealist photographer. And after, she was the verklempt, abandoned muse. When she died, a re-examination began. Her prints were revisited for small shows and auctions, revealing that incandescent oddness of her photographer's eye. A slow divorce began, severing Maar as artist from Maar as two-dimensional painting. If she was going to be immortalised, could it finally be through her own work?

Double negative

Maar learned early on that privacy, for her, was a privilege. As a child, growing up in Buenos Aires (though she was born in Paris) her bedroom door was made of glass, covered by a curtain, so she could never escape the outside gaze. According to Lord's memoir, her relationship with her parents was strained, usually leaving her as a confidante to her French Catholic mother over different flavours of parental warfare. Her father was an architect, who Maar joked was the only one 'who failed to make a fortune in Buenos Aires'[3].

Whatever he earned, it was enough to send his daughter to study at various art institutions, as well as under Cubist painter André Lhote and help fund her life in Paris. It was here she met artist Jacqueline Lamba, a lifelong friend and fellow member of the Surrealists. This was also around the time she stopped going by her birth name of Henriette Theodora Markovitch and became known as Dora Maar, putting distance between her youth in Buenos Aires and rebranding her life on the Paris café scene.

At nineteen, Maar was vacillating between painting and photography, and struggling under Lhote's teachings. Through encouragement from Henri Cartier-Bresson (one of the founders of Magnum Photos) she decided to focus her artistic efforts on her Rolleiflex camera. 'She was a remarkable photographer', Cartier-Bresson said of her in 1994, 'striking and mysterious'[4].

Even in her earliest pictures, there is an unmistakable signature on Maar's photographs. In a self-portrait captured in her mirror in 1930, she frames her face with the blades of a fan. Like many of the Surrealists she would go on to exhibit with, Maar danced with the 'exquisite corpse', producing photomontages that saw the feminine body segmented into legs and torsos. But there is something different about Maar's vision; her images of women in particular possess an internal ferocity that is often absent from the photographic portraits by Surrealist men. Assia Granatouroff, the Ukrainian-born textile designer who became an avant-garde supermodel for photographers of the 1930s, was a favourite subject of Dora Maar. Posing for Emmanuel Sougez and Roger Schall, Granatouroff helped create new possibilities for the photographic nude.

Typically, the men would focus on her breasts and torso, using lighting that made her curves glow. They captured Granatouroff as faceless and contorted, like a sculpture. And when her face was photographed, it was usually in close-up, her expression passive and bored.

But Maar often took a different approach. In a portrait of Assia, taken in 1935, she had Granatouroff hold a delicate flower to her mouth, not to silence her, but to distract from the harshness of her gaze. Her eyes are fixed upward and wide, sensual but menacing, like Lauren Bacall sizing up a hardboiled Humphrey Bogart in her bedroom with one gloved hand on the pistol concealed in her purse. Maar dangles a symbol of vulnerability to mock those who fail to see the danger that lies beneath. It's ironic that poet Jean Cocteau would later describe Maar as having a 'mouth like a torn flower'[5]. While the male photographers envisioned Granatouroff like a gorgeous Galatea, a beautiful object to be admired, Maar's depiction of her was strong, sexual and a little dangerous.

Even when Maar began making studio-based commercial photography with the set designer Pierre Kefer, she redefined what it meant to create 'feminine' imagery. In her hands, ideas for an advert for hair oil became a dark, Turner-like dreamscape where a sail boat cut through choppy, undulating waters made up of a woman's wavy locks. Her street scenes from the early 1930s have distinctive Maar 'tells' like her love for nose-diving perspective or her recurring themes of abandoned mannequins, blindness and women staring out of windows.

Early in her career, Maar had asked Man Ray if she could work as his assistant, a request he refused, saying there was nothing he could teach her. He did, however, ask her to model for him, photographing her with her painted nails visible above her eyes like jewellery adorning her forehead, with two tiny doll hands perched beneath her chin. Picasso and Man Ray were both said to love the erotic aura of her manicured fingernails. In her own photo, *Untitled (Hand-Shell)* a set of manicured nails are seen on a dead, dismembered hand, emerging from a conch shell beneath a nebulous sky.

There's a quote from Picasso that appears in Françoise Gilot's book *Life with Picasso* that goes, 'Every time I change wives I should burn the last one. That way I'd be rid of them. They wouldn't be around to complicate my existence. Maybe, that would bring back my youth, too. You kill the woman and you wipe out the past she represents'[6].

The violent overtones of his words evoke an old story about American author Norman Mailer, who once stabbed his wife at a party, a crime one of his literary hangers-on would call a 'Dostoevskian ploy'[7], as though he were doing a piece of Manhattan performance art. Whenever Mailer referred to the night in question for interviews, instead of showing deep remorse, he would treat it as a primal moment of epiphany. When men reach a certain level of idolatry, the blood of women spilled in the name of self-realisation (whether real, or emotional) is treated as collateral damage; they are considered mere road-blocks on the path of ambition.

Looking at Maar's images of spliced female faces, faces threatened by fan blades and overlaid with spiders' webs to give the illusion of shattered glass, there is a glimmer of her own appetite for destruction, as though she were reflecting that macho obliteration back out into the world. We have to wonder if she felt the desire at once to consume, to own, and to destroy female beauty, and all it represented. Maybe she too wanted to wipe things out, to burn them, to tear the world apart, at least, through her art.

At the *International Surrealist Exhibition* at the New Burlington Galleries in London in 1936, Maar exhibited three works including *Portrait of Ubu (Père Ubu)*, a larval creature, thought to be an armadillo foetus floating in a jar, arrested in failed parturition. Named after the 'scatological' character from an Alfred Jarry play *Ubu Roi*, Maar's Ubu became something of a mascot for the Surrealists, who reproduced and circulated the image on a postcard. Maar bought into their love of the claustrophobic grotesque, which can be seen again in *Le Simulateur*, her Escher-like contortion of a child abandoned in a vault. The image has been flipped, but no matter how you spin it, he remains trapped, suspended from the damp brick ceiling.

One of her best-known images, her photomontage *29 Rue d'Astorg*, an image that takes its name from the address of her first proper photography studio, continues this trend. In the foreground of some very grand architecture (thought to be from an old photograph taken of the Palace of Versailles) Maar places a female figure, thick and curvaceous, with a silky purple dress falling about her shoulders. Immediately, the viewer sees that something is not right. The figure is a found object, a 15cm headless statuette of a woman. In place of her mouth is a small, useless V which cannot speak. With two fissures for eyes, she sits upright, like a femur bone.

In her memoir, Françoise Gilot described how Picasso always kept his exes Dora Maar and Marie-Thérèse Walter in view, and hypothesised that he had a kind of Bluebeard complex. But instead of cutting women's heads off, 'he preferred to have life go on and to have all those women who he had shared his life at one moment or another still letting out little peeps and cries of pain and making a few gestures like disjointed dolls'[8].

Dora Maar just ripped that head right off, but made sure to leave a little V, to help her smile through it.

'Not one is Dora Maar'

The story of Maar's first real meeting with Picasso is so extreme a legend that it has entered the world of parody, particularly when it appears in the film *Surviving Picasso*, a 1996 biopic about the Spanish painter's monstrous approach to love so cringeworthy and ham-fisted it makes you want to chew on your own. Maar is played by Julianne Moore, who darkened her ginger hair and had her face powdered white for an image that more closely resembled Wednesday Addams than the photographer. For the scene, taken from author Jean Paul Crespelle's version of how the two met, Moore-Maar picks up a knife in a beautiful Paris café and begins weaving the blade quickly between her fingers to stab its tip into the tablecloth. In the 'real' version of events, Maar was allegedly using the game to try and attract Picasso's attention. She nicked the web of her skin, causing droplets of blood to appear on the roses embroidered into the back gloves she was wearing. It sounds as though it were plucked right out of an episode of *Twin Peaks*, and whether it really unfolded with such high drama is uncertain, but in any case, the real Picasso always kept the blood-stained gloves.

Some writers have described Maar's knife game as a kind of Surrealist theatre, painting her as a wicca seductress, luring him in with what Maar's biographer Mary Ann Caws called a 'gratuitous act of self-mutilation'[9] to court his attraction to danger. Just as Jacqueline Lamba had with André Breton, Maar sought Picasso out, but it's not certain this micro blood sport had anything to do with her showing a side of submission.

Both Lamba and Maar, at least, in the beginning, knew how to play these older avant-garde men to their advantage. When I imagine them tearing through Paris in the years before the war, I can't help but think of the two Maries from Věra Chytilová's 1966 film *Sedmikrásky* (or Daisies), two young women who wreak brilliant havoc through Prague, getting hiccup-drunk, finding rich men to pay for their meals, and asking 'who cares about that old man?'. Maar harnessed Picasso's appetite for destruction, and sometimes used it to her benefit. He played the 'muse' almost as much as she, posing for her photographs, acting as the subject for her gaze.

Early on in their relationship, Maar and Picasso were collaborators too. They experimented together with cliché-verre, a mix of painting or etching using photographic paper, in which Maar took the lead. Most famously, Maar photographed the creation of Picasso's *Guernica* for French magazine *Cahiers d'Art* in May and June 1937 (some have speculated that it was Maar who first showed Picasso images of the bombed Spanish city) and she added grey brushstrokes of her own to the body of the dying horse at the centre of the painting. Until the 1990s, these in-progress images of someone else's work, were among Maar's most famous photographs. And soon after came the *Weeping Woman* artworks, said to be a wartime symbol of mourning. However, Picasso was projecting his view of Maar onto them. Not only that, but he was using his paintings to contrast his concurrent relationships with Maar and Marie-Thérèse Walter (who he began sleeping with when she was seventeen, and he was forty-five), even painting them on the same day. He portrayed Walter with soft, unthreatening curved shapes, Maar with sharp angles that looked as if they'd been carved with a hacksaw, rendered in heavy greens, yellows and reds. But it doesn't matter how long, and how often we look at these paintings, we will not find these women. Only his version of them. As the photographer herself said, 'They're Picassos. Not one is Dora Maar'[10].

'You'll have everything when I'm gone'

Maar drifted away from photography at Picasso's behest. He saw it as a lowly artform, and encouraged her to focus on her painting, which she did, producing moody portraits (like that of cookbook writer and member of the American avant-garde Alice B. Toklas), and dark semi-abstract landscapes. When their relationship ended with another of Picasso's ritual humiliations – he left her for Françoise Gilot, and had Maar meet them for lunch so he could parade his new lover in her face – Maar's mental health suffered. Her behaviour became volatile. She was brought to Jacques Lacan, a psychoanalyst who was a favourite of the Surrealists, for treatment. He encouraged Maar's descent into mysticism, and she began, as her mother had, to devote herself to Catholicism. When asked why he'd pursued this line of treatment, Lacan reportedly said it was 'something to crystallise upon. It came to a choice between the confessional and the straitjacket'[11].

This narrative of Maar going direct from this destructive relationship to breakdown to reclusive nun feeds neatly into the Picasso myth, but it's not exactly true. She is frequently quoted as having said 'After Picasso, only God'[12], as though it were part of some deathbed confession, uttered from her lips like *Citizen Kane*'s 'Rosebud'. But this was a self-aware response to a proposal from her friend, the Surrealist poet Paul Éluard – and for all we know, it was a dark joke.

Maar did enter into a reclusive lifestyle, and her paintings do veer towards a desperate bleakness, just as her photographs did in the 1930s. While she lived a quiet life, she was never short of a milieu. The treatment of Maar and Gilot has shown that when it comes to shaping an artistic identity in the shadow of a manipulative, world-famous ex, you enter something of a zero-sum game. Leave him on your terms, as Gilot did, and he will attempt to destroy your career, and your artwork, while muddying your name with the art collectors and gallery owners at the top. Try to redress the balance with a book describing your experience and be lacerated in a review that emphasises his brilliance. When Gilot released *Life with Picasso* critic John Richardson opened his review with the line 'Everything about Picasso is interesting' and then proceeded to tear it to shreds, claiming that she 'mercilessly rattles the skeletons in any closet to which she has the key'[13]. And then there was Maar, who never denounced him publicly and preserved the residue of their time together everywhere in their home. She worked away from the public eye, rarely speaking to the media, allowing others to make assumptions and comparisons. And still, the world reached her through Picasso's portraits of the weeping women and defined her by them. Avoid, deny, explain, reform – it didn't seem to matter.

Maar was aware of this contradiction. Maybe that's why she kept at a distance. When Anne Baldassari at the Musée Picasso in Paris sought the artist's negatives to exhibit her photographs shortly before she died, Maar told her, 'What's the point of trying to buy those glass plate negatives? You'll have everything once I'm gone'[14].

James Lord wrote of Maar that 'several times she remarked she was absolutely sure of herself as far as the future was concerned, it would recognise the enduring quality and the unique accomplishment of her work ... and there was a bizarre contradiction ... she refuses to be written about, to allow the world to see her, and yet she yearns for recognition and acclaim'[15].

As I write this, a huge retrospective of her photographs and rarely seen paintings is in progress at London's Tate Modern, imported from a highly acclaimed run at the Centre Pompidou in Paris. It's becoming abundantly clear that Dora Maar was right about her impending fame all along.

16
LEE KRASNER: RIP IT UP, START AGAIN

When the Royal Academy of Arts in London opened its big, bolshy exhibition of Abstract Expressionism in 2016, I was working as the editor of an art magazine. My desk was always a catastrophe of scattered papers and orange peel, lined by a wobbly barrier of exhibition catalogues. At least once a day, someone's chin would appear at the side of my head as they stopped to peer at images of paintings on my computer screen. This time, it was a jagged black and yellow abstract by Clyfford Still that caught a colleague's eye, the artwork the Academy had chosen to promote its *Abstract Expressionism* show. 'I've seen a lot of reviews complaining that there aren't enough women artists in this,' she said, while authoritatively tapping my screen, 'but there were no women in Abstract Expressionism, it was a masculine movement, you can't just create them out of thin air, can you?' I gathered the names of artists Lee Krasner, Elaine de Kooning, Joan Mitchell, Helen Frankenthaler and Grace Hartigan in my mind and swivelled my office chair around, all fired up with my 'Actually …' She was already halfway out the door on her way to lunch. I saw the same ideas reiterated in an op-ed about the exhibition in the *The Guardian* a few days later. Decrying 'these hypersensitive times'[1], the writer claimed the question, 'where are the women?' made no sense in relation to that show, because Abstract Expressionism was, as poet Frank O'Hara said 'the art of serious men'[2]. With a 'whatyagonnado' shrug the subtitle of the article read 'well, you can't change history'.

Such is the overarching perception of Abstract Expressionism, as the all-macho, all-American movement led by heavy-drinking men who painted intuitively and lived dangerously, in pursuit of an aesthetic truth. It was a major moment in twentieth-century art; instead of looking to Paris, they sent the contents of a paint tin crashing through European Modernism to create a New York School of Painting. But the 'full' story of Abstract Expressionism being led entirely by men depends on who you choose to listen to. If you only trust the account of American art critic Clement Greenberg, your view will be skewed: in more than 1,000 pages of his writings, Joan Mitchell is the only female artist of the movement who he discusses in any depth. Mitchell is one of the more successful women of Abstract Expressionism, who managed to establish a reputation for her work in Europe during her lifetime. If you look at, say, a copy of Mary Gabriel's *Ninth Street Women*, you'll find an account of the interweaving lives of Elaine de Kooning, Lee Krasner, Helen Frankenthaler and Grace Hartigan, who were all part of this gang of paint slingers, and all exhibitors in the historic *Ninth Street* exhibition that firmed up the reputation of the post-war New York avant-garde. Women were involved in the evolution of Abstract Expressionism from the very beginning, even in 'the heroic first generation'[3] that was for so long defined by gatekeeping art critics. The macho image has been so carefully etched into people's minds that any attempt to deviate from it is accused of attempting to at worst rewrite history, or at best indulge in tokenism.

That Royal Academy show did feature works by some of these women, including a huge abstract painting by Joan Mitchell, but overall, did little to dilute the perception of Abstract Expressionism as a boys' club. Whole rooms were dedicated to artists like Rothko and Pollock, cementing their already-established status as the doyens while paintings by the women (with the exception of Mitchell) were sprinkled in.

A large piece by Lee Krasner *The Eye is the First Circle* took up a whole wall in the Pollock room. Why? Because they were married. It was a curatorial choice that only reinforced a label that had stuck to Krasner like the scent of spilled turpentine for most of her career: first the 'wife of', then the 'widow of' the painter Jackson Pollock. Even though she was an established part of the New York avant-garde since the 1930s, before anyone had even heard his name, her career is constantly being defined by their shared biography.

Installing her work into the cathedral of Pollock's only skewed perception about her standing as an Abstract Expressionist and *The Eye is the First Circle* was poorly received in reviews of the show. As one *Evening Standard* critic pointed out the 'gender tokenism that the placement of her work in this position in the exhibition suggests doesn't do her or women artists generally any favours'[4].

Krasner and Pollock were one of the more prominent couples in Abstract Expressionism, but they weren't alone. Elaine and Willem de Kooning were married for almost fifty years, in an on-again-off-again open marriage. Dutch-American painter Willem was one of the artists who had a whole room to himself at the Royal Academy show, with his aggressive – and slightly monstrous – abstract portraits of women. Elaine created the closest thing the Abstract Expressionists had to the Paris Salons by inviting the New York School of Poets into their circle, poets like Frank O'Hara, who became a kind of literary hype-man for the movement. In her own practice, she produced expressive and sometimes erotic portraits of men, explaining that, 'women painted women: [Élisabeth] Vigée Lebrun, Mary Cassatt, and so forth. And I thought, men always painted the opposite sex, and I wanted to paint men as sex objects'[5]. It wasn't until the 1980s that she began to receive serious attention for her paintings.

Helen Frankenthaler's post-Abstract Expressionist stain-painting style was adopted by artists like Kenneth Noland, and received praise from her ex-boyfriend Clement Greenberg for the technique she pioneered. Frankenthaler was established as an artist by the time she married Robert Motherwell but it didn't stop critics from comparing her work to his.

All of these artists have struggled to receive recognition at some stage in their careers, but there was something more complex and lingering about the impact of Pollock's legacy on the perception of Lee Krasner.

Public awareness of painters like Krasner can only be changed with significant institutional support, otherwise the collective gaze stays fixed on 'kings' of the movement. The cycle is, if not quite vicious, completely lacklustre. Whatever is fed into institutions, is what will reach the media, and only then the public. If the work is treated as an extension of another artist's corpus, as it was in that Royal Academy show, whoever is relegated to the sidecar will be received as a dilettante.

When the news was announced in 2018 that Krasner's first large-scale European show in fifty-four years would take place in London, one paper ran with the headline 'Jackson Pollock's artist wife Lee Krasner to get major Barbican exhibition'. The tone seemed to have regressed since 1965, when Krasner held her first ever retrospective at the Whitechapel Gallery. Back then, *The Observer* wrote in its review that 'Mrs Krasner is a worthy portent of a movement that will go down in painting history'[6]. The movement, sure. Krasner? Not quite. With every new generation, every new solo show, she is supposedly 'retrieved' from his shadow, but the extraction is temporary. She said herself that all painting is biographical, but many critics continue to fish for the Pollock-heavy pages of her biography in the work.

After the UK retrospective opened at the Barbican in 2019, finally, there was a shift. It was covered by every broadsheet, with five-star reviews in *The Times*, *Time Out* and the *Evening Standard*. When given the necessary scope to show the full evolution of her work, instead of being included like some Pollock sidekick, Krasner blew the doors off. 'Painting, for me, when it really happens is as miraculous as any natural phenomenon – as say a lettuce leaf. By "happens" I mean the painting in which the inner aspect of man and his outer aspects interlock ... the painting I have in mind, painting in which inner and outer are inseparable, transcends technique, transcends subject and moves into the realm of the inevitable – then you have the lettuce leaf.'[7] These are some of Lee Krasner's most frequently quoted words on painting. When given the chance to see the work she was talking about, we too enter the realm of the inevitable.

'A cold shower'

Krasner never had much time for the arbitrary parameters people placed around her art. When studying at the National Academy of Design in the 1920s, she was suspended twice. Once for sneaking into a classroom reserved for men, and another for venturing into the basement with her friend Eda

Mirsky Mann to commit the sordid act of painting a still-life of a fish, a subject that was out of bounds for the women of the school. And when she decided she had to study under artist Hans Hofmann, she just turned up to his art school with her life drawings under her arm and what the registrar called an 'arrogance that blinds'[8]. The Academy had only taken her so far, working on representational portraits and *plein air* landscapes, but Krasner had no interest in being a 'good' painter, she wanted to be a 'great' one who could sit among the changemaking artists she would visit at MoMA: Picasso, Miró, de Chirico.

In one of her first classes with Hofmann, he circled the students to offer his critiques. He stopped at Krasner's easel, picked up her work, and ripped it to shreds, letting the pieces fall to the floor like confetti. It must have hurt to see her drawing reduced to smithereens, but the image stayed with her – ripping things up and starting over would become a cornerstone of the Krasner style. But there was another Hofmann sentiment that followed her, one that wasn't so easy to stomach: 'I can remember very clearly his criticism one day when he came in and said about the painting up in front of him, "This is so good you would not believe it was done by a woman." Well, that's pretty difficult to understand … You know, you get a cold shower before you've had a chance to receive the warmth of the compliment'[9].

Coming up as an artist during the Great Depression was a crippling financial struggle for Krasner, as she came from a working class background, there was no family money to fall back on. Even if she could get a gallery show, people could barely afford to buy bread, let alone an oil painting. Her hours as a nightclub waitress and model didn't provide enough to get by, so she took a job with the Federal Art Project, part of the United States Government's New Deal. When Roosevelt put people's jobs on the line by slashing funding, Krasner would be out protesting with her fellow artists and models, calling for justice. 'I was practically in every jail in New York City', she said. 'Each time we were fired, or threatened with being fired, we'd go out and picket. On many occasions we'd be taken off in a Black Maria [police van] and locked in a cell'[10].

Nobody could afford to buy paintings, but the New York avant-garde was coming into its own. At this time, Krasner was pinballing from one style to another. Initially she took her lead from the European modernists, and crowded her canvases with colourful Miró-esque shapes. After a visit to MoMA's *Fantastic Art, Dada, Surrealism* show in 1936, she experimented with a desolate Kay-Sage-like landscape that feels so far removed from her later abstract works. Artistically, she simply didn't like to stay in one place. She loved the poetry of Arthur Rimbaud, and scrawled his words on the wall of her Greenwich Village studio: 'Finally I came to consider my mind's disorder as sacred'.

Krasner was a respected figure in the New York art world, not just for her position in the Federal Art Project, but for the reputation she'd developed for her 'strict eye' for art. By the late 1930s, she was already friendly with Willem de Kooning and Arshile Gorky; at one point, she and her ex-boyfriend Igor Pantuhoff had shared a flat with Harold Rosenberg, a powerful American art critic. Krasner became a part of the American Abstract Artists group (AAA). At their group exhibition in 1941, she began talking with Piet Mondrian. The two hit it off so well, they met up again to spend the night dancing to jazz at Café Uptown. It's probably not much of a surprise that, Mondrian, the man who painted *Broadway Boogie-Woogie*, could cut some serious rug, 'I loved jazz and he loved jazz, so I saw him several times and we went dancing like crazy'[11] said Krasner. Mondrian was a hero figure to her. In her experiments with abstraction in the 1930s she would sometimes limit herself to his signature palette of just primary colours plus black and white in a kind of Mondrian homage, so she was understandably anxious as he approached her painting at the AAA exhibition that night. He told her she had a 'very strong inner rhythm; stay with it'[12].

It's clear that by the 1940s, Krasner was an established part of the city's Abstract art scene. If they were in secondary school, she'd be sitting at the back of the bus sharing Lucky Strikes with de Kooning. And Pollock? He'd be carving his initials into a table in the common room, taking slugs from the whisky flask tucked under his school jumper.

Soon after their relationship began, there was a shift in her work. Krasner, convinced of Pollock's ability, began introducing him to friends in the art world in an effort to boost his career. And at the same time, Krasner entered a battle with her own painting, producing what she called 'grey slabs'[13]. Much has been made of this 'dead' period in her work, as it fits neatly into the narrative of the all-consuming Pollock, with a painting style so original it could overwhelm a talent like Krasner's. The year after they'd married, she wrote to her friend, the artist Mercedes Matter, saying, 'I'm painting and nothing happens. It's maddening. I showed [gallery owner Sidney] Janis my last three paintings. He said they were too much Pollock – it's completely idiotic, but I have a feeling from now on that's going to be the story'[14]. What's rarely mentioned is that, around this time, Krasner lost her father and was in a state of grief, 'in spite of his age, he was 81, it pretty well tears you to pieces and is like some terrific eruption with everything being torn up … I must wait until spaces are closer and time changes feeling'[15]. When speaking about her process, Krasner reiterated again and again the importance of waiting, of taking a deep breath, and sitting through the 'dead' periods. She would never force it, no matter how painful the experience might be. When an interviewer asked Krasner what her husband had been working on during those years, she clipped back, 'I don't know, I had my own problems'[16].

'A very destructive act'

In an attempt to break away from Manhattan, Krasner managed to convince art collector Peggy Guggenheim to lend her the down payment on a house in the isolated hamlet of Springs, Long Island. Out there, in nature, she and Pollock made their entire lives about the work, surviving on very little cash, eating whatever clams they could dig out of the sand. But structurally, the balance was off. While he took over the famous 'barn' – a factory for drip painting where he had space to splash, pour and slash the canvas with paint, Krasner took on the bedroom as a studio, a smaller space, that resulted in smaller pieces, her 'Little Images'. They were her moments of controlled chaos, rectangles of white noise, sometimes featuring a pattern of swirling glyphs that Krasner called 'a kind of crazy writing of my own'[17]. The critics weren't speaking her language. When she showed her 'Little Images' alongside Pollock's works at *Artists: Man and Wife*, an exhibition at Sidney Janis Gallery, they were dismissed as tight, tidy imitations of his. It's a theme that would follow her for a large part of her career. It's true that she was no Jackson Pollock, but only in the sense that he was no Lee Krasner.

Her work spoke for itself at a solo show in Betty Parsons Gallery in 1951, and was better received, but still the paintings didn't sell. Frustrated by her lukewarm reception and with Pollock's aggressive drinking, in 1953, she grabbed the drawings that hung from the walls and ceiling of her studio – and started ripping them to shreds. 'Walked in one day, hated it all, took it down, tore everything and threw it on the floor, and when I went back ... it was seemingly a very destructive act. I don't know why I did it, except I certainly did it'[18]. After cannibalising her creations, she started reassembling them into a series of collages made up of old drawings, rough shards of paintings and bits of old burlap sack. When these trophies of iconoclasm went on display at the Stable Gallery in 1955, the same reviewer who had bashed her 'Little Images', Stuart Preston, said 'The eye is fenced in by the myriad scraps of paper, burlap and canvas swobbed [*sic*] with colour that she pastes up so energetically. She is a good noisy colourist'[19]. The destruction was the catalyst she needed to make her Frankensteinian pieces. Even Pollock's drawings got hoovered up in the frenzy for *Bald Eagle*, a piece that contains both of their DNA. When you look at it, you can hear the paper being ripped in two.

'Painting is not separate from life. It is one'

Lee Krasner had two jobs. A full-time artist and crisis manager. Living with a heavy-drinking, quick-tempered Pollock was not easy. When he began an affair with Ruth Kligman, and made no effort to hide the betrayal from her or their friends, Krasner had enough, deciding to take a break from the destruction to travel to Europe. Before she left, she made a start on the painting *Prophecy*, pink and menacing, like a liquid cadaver; even she admitted to being frightened by it.

Krasner was in Paris when she got the call from Clement Greenberg that Pollock had died in a car crash along with one of Ruth Kligman's friends. When she returned home, she had to face that painting: *Prophecy*. Within months, Krasner had taken over the barn as her studio, filling the negative space he had left behind. Her grief became a vehicle, and its scale can be seen in the enormous, rectangular paintings she produced after his death.

Plagued by insomnia and a hatred of working in colour without natural light, she began to use umber so she could cope with working at night. These are the paintings that move me most: stripped back to reveal Krasner's exhausted, emotionally charged gestures as she jumped to mark her canvas, paintings like *The Eye is the First Circle*, which, in my opinion, was unjustly ridiculed when it was presented without proper context in 2016.

When asked how she managed to face the canvas again, she said, 'Painting is not separate from life. It is one. It is like asking – do I want to live? My answer is yes – and I paint'[20]. With Krasner, there is never a singular style, even if she wanted one, 'My own image of my work is that I no sooner settle into something than a break occurs. These breaks are always painful and depressing but despite them I see that there's a consistency that holds out, but is hard to define'[21].

By the 1960s, she was working in full colour, monumental paintings with a flux of oranges and pinks and a dark arc peeking out from underneath. Sometimes her marks are bulbous and awkward; other times, diffused into concentrated splatters of paint. To see them together in one room is like experiencing an abstract expressionism group show.

In the 1970s, Krasner expressed regret that she had not yet been offered a retrospective in America, only in London. The opportunity to see a real period of work was something she considered important for a painter. When Pollock died, and she became the executor of his estate, she had a clear vision for how she wanted his art to be handled; she was generous with the work, lending it out to museum and gallery collections. If Krasner had only served her own interests, she could have taken advantage of certain connections to boost her own reputation, but she was a pugnacious character that had no interest in filling the pockets of art collectors, 'I behaved with the paintings as I saw fit. I stepped on a lot of toes. And I think even today it's difficult for people to see me, or to speak to me, or observe my work, and not connect it with Pollock. They cannot free themselves'[22].

For a long time, she was correct. Plenty of art critics could not be trusted to assess her work without bias. The Whitechapel show received dozens of reviews that painted her as the second fiddle widow, even in their veiled compliments. *The Observer* turned on the tap of that cold shower compliment issued by Hofmann in the 1930s: 'I doubt whether anybody would guess from the paintings that they are by a woman. On the other hand, they are unmistakably American'[23].

Things began to look brighter when, in 1984, MoMA honoured Krasner with the retrospective that had been her goal to secure. Although the term 'woman artist' never sat well with her, and she never really identified as a feminist, Krasner recognised the importance of the women's movement. Just over ten years before she got the news of the MoMA show, she was on the steps of the same gallery, protesting the dearth of female artists in its collection. She passed away months before the MoMA retrospective was due to open.

'When it really happens'

After the Barbican show in 2019, there was an outpouring of appreciation for Krasner, tinged with a kind of shame that it hadn't been there the entire time. She was referred to as one of the greats. Her work exists on a continuum from European Modernism to Abstract Expressionism, and in the latter, she deserves a whole lot more than a couple of paintings shoved into 'Pollock's room'. Though it's arrived late, her reputation as an artist has begun to match the quality of her work. The inner and outer aspects have finally begun to interlock, bringing Krasner into the realm of the inevitable. One day, very soon, we will have the lettuce leaf.

17
MARGARET KEANE:
BIG EYES

Margaret Keane was eighty-seven years old when she first saw her work inside the New York Museum of Modern Art in 2014. But this was no exhibition opening. She'd arrived for the US film premiere of *Big Eyes*, a film biopic about her life. Peering at the press on the red carpet through enormous, black-rimmed glasses she beamed, 'This whole thing is bizarre. I never in my life thought that my paintings would make it to the Museum of Modern Art; even if it is a Tim Burton movie'[1]. Margaret had come a long way since 1972, the year she broke one of the twentieth century's biggest and most peculiar stories of art fraud. Margaret finally got the courage to reveal that, for around fifteen years, her husband, Walter Keane, had been taking credit for her 'Big Eye' paintings, a style of art that was devoured by the public in the 1960s, but lampooned by art critics.

It was so popular, it went into mass production; Keane paintings were reproduced as affordable posters, postcards, plates, even coffee tables, making Walter millions, while Margaret was hidden away in a studio, churning out one 'eye' after another, feeding her husband's insatiable need for attention. Tim Burton had grown up around Keane's paintings, and spent a decade trying to get a film about her off the ground. She was played by Amy Adams, but in the beginning, the actress had turned the project down, believing Margaret was a 'weak' character who had allowed her husband to steal the credit. Adams had a change of heart, telling *The New York Times* that, when she became a mother, she began to see Margaret in a different light, 'She had a steely strength. Yes, she was manipulated. But I didn't see her as weak. I saw her as complicit'[2].

Why would a person like Margaret hand over her paintings, only to sit in the corner of a gallery watching her partner claim the accolades? She is the only woman to appear in this book who could offer the answers – at least in her case – first hand. When we spoke, in 2019, the excitement of the *Big Eyes* biopic had long faded; by then, Margaret was ninety-two and living in hospice care, still painting and drawing every day.

Her hearing had deteriorated, and the only way we could communicate was for me to deliver my questions one by one, to a speakerphone in Napa California, which were then carefully repeated to Margaret by her son-in-law. Religion is steeped into every moment of our conversation; Margaret, a devout Jehovah's Witness, never misses an opportunity to quote Paul the Apostle or praise Jehovah. But when speaking about her art, and the years spent living in near-imprisonment with Walter, she is surprisingly open, and filled with forgiveness. When I ask about the moment she broke the news on that talk show, it's recalled as though it had happened weeks before, 'I had come to realise that I could not live with myself any longer and I had to reveal it to survive and have any kind of self-respect. And also I couldn't expect my daughter to have any respect for me either. So I had no other choice'[3]. Margaret came clean because she could not cope with the guilt of her complicity; it wasn't just about reclaiming her rightful authorship, but righting the wrong of the lie itself. The reality was much darker, and more complex than some Faustian pact of husband and wife, something Margaret did not fully comprehend about her own memories, until she saw them projected onto a cinema screen inside MoMA. 'It made me respect myself more to see the whole thing portrayed. And the way the social and religious forces that were acceptable in the 1960s was portrayed so vividly … It was not a favourable time for a woman to be a creative artist and when I saw the movie it really had an emotional effect on me. I have forgiven Walter, I felt pity for him … I had to forgive myself that in fact I took the blame for it. I felt it was a totally hopeless situation.'[4]

Even if you think you have never seen 'a Keane painting' the chances are you have, or at least, a version of one. These sorrowful motifs of children with eyes the size of manhole covers, sometimes leaking a single tear, were once such a ubiquitous part of American culture that if you stepped into a gas station in the 1960s, you'd likely find hundreds of them staring out at you from posters and postcards, splashed with a big red 'sale' sign.

It was a time of booms – baby, financial, commercial. Post-war money was being made, quiet suburban streets were flanked by miles of 'white flight' family homes and even whiter picket fences. People were putting conversation pits in their living rooms, pastel-coloured electric mixers in their kitchens, and wondering what would fill the big empty expanse of wall above the mantelpieces. 'Keanes' became the suburban painting of choice. They were the first real form of populist, suburban art, causing *Life* magazine to declare in 1965 'Big Eyed paintings are the most popular art now being produced in the free world'[5].

In a TV appearance, the 'artist' Walter Keane, stood po-faced as he told an interviewer the inspiration for the paintings came from the poor, emaciated war orphans he encountered while traipsing through France and Germany in 1946: 'I came upon these frightened, waif-type children and they actually looked like rats running around and they acted like it … These children didn't even know how to talk; they couldn't even pray. And it's sort of like an artist's work – you don't know how to talk about it, but the painting can talk for you'[6].

The irony was Walter never stopped talking about 'his' work, and almost every word of it was a lie. The tearjerker backstory was fabricated to match Margaret's doe-eyed waifs. Obsessed with becoming known as a 'great artist'; he would speak about himself in the third person, mentioning his own name in the same breath as Michelangelo and El Greco.

In reality, the origin of the 'Big Eyes' could be traced back to the margins of Margaret's school notebooks. As a child in Tennessee, she had a mastoid operation that damaged her eardrum, leaving her hearing impaired. With one of her senses dulled, Margaret became fixated on connecting with people through the eyes. 'The eye is the only visible part of the human brain', she tells me down the phone line, 'Our struggle is communicated through our eyes. We can reveal the person's inner self. It offers direct insight into our heart and that's where our motivation comes from, there's a war going on between our minds and our heart, our feelings'.

From the age of ten, she was doodling eyes at every opportunity; her family recognised her talent for drawing, and she was sent to the Watkins Institute, where she learned to sketch in charcoal. Margaret was a quiet, fairly conservative young girl, raised as a Methodist, with a strong connection to the Bible that she inherited from her grandmother.

The bohemian life didn't interest her, even later on, when she was at the centre of it, living in California in the 1960s with members of the Beach Boys calling over to her house; she would tell interviewers how she watched from the side lines. The label of 'artist' was for adventurous people, 'crazy'[7] people. She was a traditionalist, in her art, and in her values.

At eighteen, Margaret attended the Traphagen School of Fashion in New York, where she developed a style that had shades of fashion illustration, and found odd-jobs hand-painting clothes and cribs for a furniture company. She married a man named Frank Ulbrich, and gave birth to her daughter, Jane, who inspired her to return to painting.

In the early years of Jane's life, she would star in dozens of Keane's 'Big Eyes'. The marriage to Ulbrich deteriorated, and in a move at odds with the norm for American women in the early 1950s, Margaret left him, taking Jane with her. Suddenly she was a single woman alone in San Francisco, with a young daughter to support. To try and keep her family afloat, Margaret sold her work at small art fairs and made portraits of children to try and earn a little extra money. Even then, her oils of saucer-eyed children violently polarised the opinions of everyone who saw them. 'People liked my paintings, they bought them then. Some people couldn't stand them', Margaret explains, 'They couldn't even stand to be in the room with them. But other people loved them and there wasn't much in-between.'

The same year her marriage had unravelled, she met Walter at a San Francisco art fair, where she was selling her 'waifs' of Jane, and he was flogging Parisian street scenes conceived with a palette knife (there are doubts about whether he really painted those, too). Things snowballed, and they married in 1955, not long after they'd met.

Living together in San Francisco, Walter tried to usher Margaret into the beatnik art scene he so desperately wanted to play a part in, taking her to the hip North Beach club, The Hungry I. It was Walter who convinced the club's owner, Enrico Banducci, to hang an exhibition of Margaret's paintings, but when she started making sales, he saw an opportunity. While Margaret sat nursing a drink in the club, he was working the crowds, lauding them with stories about his artistic process as he tried to flog her work as his own. For Walter, it was all about embodying the 'persona' of an artist to shift the work. She only realised what was happening when someone came over and asked 'Do you paint too?' At first, she was angry. But Walter had her cornered. We've made sales, he'd tell her; if we tell the truth now, we could get sued. And anyway – would anyone really buy the work of a woman painter? They were in it together, a fraudulent, artistic unit.

As well as manipulating Margaret, Walter had a gift for working the press, turning himself into fodder for gossip columns. Everything became about 'spin' – he wheedled his way into television spots. Like an early reality TV star, he would contrive moments in his life to be 'papped' by the papers. Walter invented feuds with people from the San Francisco social set, and gave paintings away for free to visiting politicians and celebrities like Joan Crawford, always making sure there was a press photographer booked to capture the exchange. It was all aided, as he said in a *Life* magazine interview, by living in the age of 'transportation and communication'[8].

Eventually, he opened a 'Walter Keane' gallery where he could sell the works himself. All the while, Margaret was working in secret, concealed in her studio. Walter pushed her friends away so he could commandeer all her time to focus on painting, adding to his growing mountain of Keanes. He would bark orders at her to try out different subjects; if he went out, he would call to check in and make sure she was staying on task. Sure, they'd earned enough money to move to an impressive home with a kidney-shaped pool, but the coercive control he had over Margaret was crippling. She became isolated, painting under pressure, weighed down by the guilt of their shared secret. Margaret attempted to teach him how to reproduce the style himself, and when he couldn't deliver, that was her fault, too. 'He practised and practised and he finally learned how to draw an eye and he could do a pretty good job of it and he would do that when he would sign an autograph, he would do this crude little eye. But he never painted eyes on a face, it was only a quick sketch. He only completed two paintings, they were both Paris street scenes that he did with a palette knife … he didn't do any faces', she says.

The tones in her paintings darkened, and the sad poppets of her canvas grew desperate. Smiles were replaced with downturned mouths, the round pupils always welling up with tears, 'It was my way of expressing what I was feeling. I felt it was a totally hopeless situation and I couldn't understand. It felt like being in a trap and I didn't know how to get out of the nightmare … The children reflected my inner feelings. They were searching and they were hopeful, but they were lost', Margaret tells me.

Then came the posters: suddenly one painting was turned into tens of thousands, and sold in the Keane gallery for a couple of dollars. Copycat 'Big Eyes' began sprouting: cartoonish paintings of dancing mod children by an artist named Lee, moon-eyed puppies by another called Gig. There's a moment in the Tim Burton film where Jason Schwartzman (a snooty gallery owner) stares aghast into a display of 'Big Eye' reproductions and says, in disgust 'dear God: it's a movement'. And in a way, it was – these children, with pupils, as Schwartzman's character put it 'like stale jelly beans' could be found in thousands of average American homes, staring out over a freshly set dinner table. This eruption was happening at exactly the same moment that the abject nihilism of Pop Art had entered public consciousness. With its use of print reproductions, and satirical take on American commerce, Pop Art sometimes got wrapped up in the perception of what was happening with the mass-produced approach of Walter Keane. They were seen as the sort of Peyton Place version of Andy Warhol's factory. Warhol himself added to the confusion with his frequently quoted endorsement of the 'Big Eyes': 'I think what Keane has done is just terrific. It has to be good. If it were bad, so many people wouldn't like it'[9]. But they weren't nihilistic, or a comment on commerce. The actual paintings were made with the most intense, earnest sincerity by Margaret, then shamelessly flogged by Walter.

'He couldn't accept reality'

When *Life* magazine ran its six-page article on Walter in 1965, the couple had already separated. Afraid for her and her daughter's safety, Margaret took Jane and relocated to Honolulu, Hawaii. By then, Margaret had adapted to another style of painting, one that she could sign her own name to, flat portraits of 'nubile girls', loosely inspired by Modgliani. Margaret 'paints eyes a little like those for which her husband is famous' the *Life* writer said. 'But hers are not so big'[10]. When pushed to defend the repetitive nature of his art, Walter would reach for the masters 'Rembrandt painted old men until they came out of his ears', he said, 'El Greco was always painting elongated saints … Why criticise Walter Keane because his symbol of humanity is a child?'[11]. He named his four poodles Rembrandt, Gauguin, Degas and Matisse; it was as though he thought, if he said the names often enough, his position among the Old Masters was inevitable.

Walter, by that point, had descended into heavy drinking. The article describes him like an Oliver Reed hellraiser, throwing women over his shoulder as he marched up a San Francisco hill to the next club. If the rogue wasn't lovable, a despicable one would do.

Margaret, however, was cleansing herself of life with him in Honolulu by following the guidance of Jehovah's Witnesses. She happily remarried, to a sports writer called Dan McGuire. The moment she broke the story, in 1972, a weight was lifted, something that was reflected in her paintings, 'I started using brighter colours and the greys and blacks and stormy clouds were gone. Immediately the colours changed, but it took about five years for the faces to be really smiling and happy.'

The clouds had momentarily parted, but the revelation had brought Walter's darkness back into her life. He derided her in the press, denouncing her as a greedy liar who'd lost the plot and claiming she'd been brainwashed by a religious cult. To protect her reputation, Margaret challenged Walter to a high-noon paint off in San Francisco Union Square. Walter never materialised. A decade-and-a-half after the big reveal, when he was almost seventy, Walter appeared in the press again (this time in *USA Today*) claiming authorship of the 'Big Eyes', and Margaret had enough, so she took the case to court. Walter decided to represent himself.

Margaret told the jury how Walter had ranted, raved and screamed at her during their marriage, how he had made her afraid to tell the truth, and even threatened her life. When the judge admonished Walter for interrupting Margaret's answers, he threw his arms up and said 'I'm sorry, I am an artist'[12]. 'The judge was very um, mean', Margaret tells me, 'He refused to let me paint, he said it was a domestic quarrel and it was wasting his time.' But as the trial rolled into a third week, the judge agreed to an in-courtroom paint-off, where each would have one hour to produce a 'Big Eye' piece. In front of the jury, the judge and the media, Margaret finished her piece in fifty-three minutes. Walter's canvas stayed blank. He protested that he had an acute shoulder pain, and could not possibly produce the painting. The judge ruled in Margaret's favour, ordering Walter to pay $4million dollars, but he'd drunk the 'Big Eye' earnings dry. She never saw a penny, but won the right to reclaim authorship of the work, and sell the 'Keanes' under her name. 'I loved the painting I did in the courtroom and I have never parted with it. I have it displayed in my living room', says Margaret. It's still marked 'exhibit 224' on the back.

After a psychiatric evaluation, Walter was diagnosed with delusional disorder, a form of psychosis that can cause a person to misinterpret personal experiences and while functioning quite normally, have an unshakeable belief in something untrue. It's one of the reasons Margaret has always expressed her forgiveness. 'I think we reap what we sow', she says, 'and I don't want to blame a sick person for being born that way. I think Walter was mentally ill and he couldn't accept reality.'

Right up until his death in December 2000, Walter Keane maintained he was the real creator of the 'Big Eye' paintings.

For over ten years Margaret had been painting in plain sight, and still nobody – not the media, not the art critics who made an enemy of Walter, not their celebrity friends – realised what was happening, even though, when you look at Margaret's work from that period in their 'different style', you can tell they are made by the same person. Walter was a mastermind when it came to marketing her work, and it's true, that, without his braggadocio and shrewd media manipulation, they might never have seen the light of day. But just think: if a woman had tried to sell that work with the same 'El Greco'-comparing arrogance of Walter, how would she have been received? The art 'Walter' produced did not fit the persona of this brouhaha-chasing egoist, because it wasn't his. He was laughed at for his arrogance, but he was lauded for it, too. The use of enlarged black pupils to provoke a viewer's emotional response was described as 'a cheap psychological trick'[13], but unlike Walter, Margaret hadn't set out to trick anyone. She was just painting her feelings.

'Big Eyes' are not high art, but they were never intended as such. And regardless of what the critics thought, they were eagerly taken up by popular culture. From the 1960s onwards, 'Keane-like' became a clichéd analogy for anything with big eyes. The Keane portrait of Joan Crawford appeared on the cover of the actress's memoir. 'Big Eyes' are namechecked in John Waters' book *Carsick*. The reference trickled right down to 1990s cartoons – if the humongous peepers of The Powerpuff Girls weren't enough of an homage, their teacher was called 'Mrs Keane'. The waifs haven't received the kind of lasting love and absorption into personal style required to earn the Susan Sontag-approved stamp of camp, but even if they are just 'kitsch', they are timelessly so.

Whether you like them, or despise them, (as Margaret says there is no in-between) those paintings are a portal to a very specific period in American culture. And that portal belongs to Margaret Keane.

18
SHIGEKO KUBOTA: THE MOTHER OF VIDEO ART

For Shigeko Kubota, death and videotape were inseparable. In the 1970s, Kubota was light-years ahead, prophesying, with terrifying clarity, how the permanence of video would come to define our lives. The way she saw it, video was not just a new artistic technology – the twentieth century's answer to paintbrush and canvas – it was an entry point into a new, 'liquid reality' that offered infinite possibilities to reshape our view of the world, even after we'd ceased to be a part of it. 'Videotape acts as an extension of the brain's memory cells,' Kubota wrote in an exhibition statement in 1981, 'life with video is like living with two brains, one plastic brain and one organic brain. One's life is inevitably altered. Change will affect even our relationship with death, as video is a living altar. Yes, videotaped death negates death as a simple terminal'[1].

Kubota began her life in the Japanese town of Niigata; her father's family came from a line of Buddhist monks, and owned a monastery in the 'hinterlands of Japan'. As a child, she would spend hours doing homework inside a temple room where 'fresh bones' were stored.

In this temple, she would stare at the images on the walls, looking at what she called, 'paintings of hell and paradise' and see them 'unfolding … like a film script'[2]. As an adult, she would learn her birthplace, Niigata, was one of the USA's potential targets for the atomic bomb. Funerals, and the presence of 'ghosts', had always been at the forefront of her mind. Video was a means of paying tribute, like leaving cookies and rice on a dead ancestor's grave; but more than that, it offered a new way to encapsulate the 'ghosts' by giving them a second, plastic life.

When the Sony Portapak recorder was introduced in the late 1960s, it allowed Kubota to integrate video into her art in a deeply personal way; she used it to create video diaries that would later be transformed into sculpture. Within years of this technological arrival, there was an upswing in video art made by women, a shift that coincided with the feminist art movement. A new medium, unburdened by centuries of association with great male artists, provided a new opportunity for women to take the lead. As Kubota explained, in an interview with *The Brooklyn Rail*, 'It was equal to both men and women because it was new and fairly inexpensive and we all had the same access to it'[3]. But equal access, did not necessarily translate to equal representation.

In 1977, Kubota married Korean artist Nam June Paik, considered the 'father' of video art, given that he was the first to exhibit it. Though Paik was fully behind Kubota's work from the beginning, acting as, what Kubota called her 'comrade' in art as well as in life, the long shadow of his reputation followed hers.

When reviewing Kubota's retrospective at the Museum of the Moving Image in 1991, *New York Times* critic Roberta Smith wrote, 'she was, with Mr. Paik, one of the first to appreciate the artistic possibilities of the new technology. In the case of Mr. Paik, the rest is, as they say, history. But in the case of Ms. Kubota it is a history that has been largely unexamined'[4]. It was a reality of which Kubota was acutely aware. 'We are very different, like water and oil', she said in her oral history interview, 'Even when I did my own stuff, people said, "She imitates Nam June". I found it infuriating. So I headed further in the direction of [Marcel] Duchamp. When Nam June went populist, I went for high art'[5].

'We were poor and crazy'

Kubota might have ventured further into 'high art' to carve out a path of her own in video, but she had always belonged to the avant-garde. When she was twenty-six, she left her life in Tokyo for New York, on the invitation of George Maciunas, leader of the wacky neo-Dadaist art group, Fluxus. Two key moments had led her to this point: one was witnessing experimental composer John Cage 'destroy' conventional music at a concert in Bunka Kaikan Hall in Tokyo in 1962; the other, was meeting Yoko Ono, who was already an active member of Fluxus. Ono would stage subversive events in New York like *Painting to be Stepped On*, encouraging visitors to add to her canvas by trampling all over it. These 'happenings' usually came with instructions, written in their own poetic form. Maciunas and the other Fluxus artists wanted art to be free and living, embodied by public performances in the absurdist Dada tradition. They sampled sounds of toilets flushing and dogs barking, they smashed up old LPs, pieced them back together and played the discordant 'music' to a tiny audience. They made giant salads and asked people to tell stories about their shoes. Kubota was pushing boundaries in her home country too, but it wasn't enough. New York was the centre of unpredictable anti-art art, and Kubota wanted a slice of the apple.

For her first solo show in Japan, Kubota staged her own Fluxus-style exhibition, by filling a gallery with a crumpled pile of newspaper that had a metal sculpture at the centre. At the same time, she was financially supporting herself and her boyfriend, a composer named Takehisa Kosugi, by working as an art teacher. Something had to give. 'I felt that I needed to go to New York, so I called my union friends, to say goodbye, and they were all very disappointed. They said, "Oh, why would you want to go to a capitalist city?" and I said, "You know, for art you have to go to New York"'[6].

She boarded a Boeing with her friend, composer Mieko Shiomi, to this 'glittering Pop Art world', where they were collected at JFK airport by George Maciunas. He whisked them straight to the 'Fluxus Centre' to join his raggle-taggle colony of electrified art hippies. 'That's where I met everybody: Nam June Paik [she had also met Paik previously, in Japan], Dick Higgins, George Brecht ... All of us were poor and crazy. It was a most exciting time'[7], she said. Kubota went all-in with the group, helping Maciunas organise events, designing her own Fluxus 'objects' (such as napkins covered in female lips snipped from magazines). He christened her 'the vice president of Fluxus', but the honorary role obviously didn't pay.

Vagina Painting

At the 1965 summer Perpetual Fluxus Festival, a year after she'd arrived in New York, Kubota secured a paintbrush to her underwear and stepped in front of the crowd to enact her most famous (in fact, her only) Fluxus performance piece. As she leapt around and swung the bristled phallus from her crotch, she allowed the paintbrush to lash calligraphic smears of red paint on the paper beneath her feet. The moment was captured in black and white camera photographs by Maciunas, showing Kubota's crouched body illuminated under a spotlight. *Vagina Painting* entered the lore of feminist performance. It was analysed for its menstrual imagery, the overt sexuality, and as a 'female' response to the machismo of Action Painting – but what many missed was the humour. Like Yoko Ono's 'Cut Piece', it was read as a baroque, political staging of the 'female' experience. Kubota later shared with interviewers that her 'colleagues' hated the performance at the time.

It's hard to imagine shock was a factor in the rejection of Kubota's *Vagina Painting*; it had all taken place three years after Yayoi Kusama debuted an *Accumulation no.1* sculpture comprised of hundreds of stuffed penises. But this was the paradox of Fluxus: while women were welcomed into the circle and encouraged to push limits, the sight of them being raw and political with their bodies before a crowd became 'too much' for some when it played out. It was something Yoko Ono spoke about openly, 'I was not well accepted even in the avant-garde … Because the New York avant-garde was into cool art … what I do was too emotional in a way they thought it was too animalistic'[8]. The irony of the whole thing, is that Kubota didn't even want to do it, later admitting, 'I was not so interested in performance. I did that piece because I was begged to do it … Begged by Maciunas and Nam June'[9]. *Vagina Painting* followed Kubota for her entire career, and is often treated with greater importance than the extensive body of video art that followed. It is one of the reasons she is regularly contextualised as an important figure in the Second Wave feminist art movement, despite her own belief that she hadn't made a direct contribution to it.

Midori Yoshimoto, associate professor of art history and gallery director at New Jersey City University, explored Kubota's career in her book *Into Performance: Japanese Women Artists* in New York. Speaking about the feminist relevance of *Vagina Painting*, she told me, 'It is kind of an oddity in her body of work ... It might be exaggerated maybe, to the extent that her other body of work became overshadowed by *Vagina Painting*. I think she didn't like that. So that's why she rarely talked about it ... she did not really do feminist performance after that'[10].

Kubota began to outgrow Fluxus, frustrated by the ephemerality of the work it produced, 'Fluxus is about destruction, and their work disappears. Their work vanishes after the fact ... Their work was fleeting ... I wanted to envision some shape. With video, then, I thought of the unity of moving images and non-moving images ... I was so disappointed ... Fluxus was too concerned about the small things'[11].

Kubota took a job with Japanese art magazine *Bijutsu Techo* (Art Notebook), which allowed her to cast a wider net across the New York art scene. She even interviewed Andy Warhol. Then, there was the chance meeting that would change the direction of her career: on her flight to Buffalo on her way to see a show by choreographer Merce Cunningham, she saw Duchamp sitting just a few seats away. By another coincidence, she had a copy of *Bijutsu Techo* with her, which included a freshly printed article on Duchamp by one of her fellow writers. She showed him the piece, presumably relieved he liked it. A blizzard grounded their flight, and so Kubota spent a long bus ride deep in conversation with Duchamp, sharing their thoughts on art.

Months after the fateful encounter, she photographed him playing chess against John Cage at a famous concert in Toronto. The photographs would later be found beaming out from the monitor of her installation *Video Chess*, where viewers could witness 'two great masters playing from the otherside of this world'[12]. It would be one of many video eulogies she would create for Duchamp. Within a year of their meeting on that Buffalo flight that never left the runway, the artist passed away, sending him into a new realm of idolatry for Kubota. In a move that flipped the conventionally held notion of the muse,

Duchamp became hers. Through video, she would create his 'living altar' in her *Duchampiana* series. The fruition of this obsession can be traced back to 1970, when a collaborator of Nam June Paik gave her a Sony Portapak camera that she would use to film a journey across Europe. Kubota's camera travelled with her to Duchamp's gravestone in Rouen, which was engraved with the epitaph 'Besides, It is Always the Others Who Die'. For her video sculpture, *Marcel Duchamp's Grave*, Kubota housed an edit of this footage inside a plywood structure, letting recorded sound of the wind from the cemetery whistle through the gallery. Through Duchamp's spirit, she would manifest a dialogue with death. Kubota, like a conceptual vlogger, had used the Portapak to capture personal grief on videotape, and translated it into sculpture.

'Portapak tears down my shoulder, backbone and waist'

In her desire to find new comrades in video, Kubota co-founded the short-lived collective *White, Black, Red & Yellow*, 'a multiracial group of four women artists'[13], satirically divided by race. For their first show, they had a poster with each artist in side profile, like a criminal mugshot. The message was clear: these were the new outlaws of video. At their show at The Kitchen gallery in New York, Shigeko Kubota debuted *Riverrun*, a multi-channel video sculpture that played excerpts from James Joyce's *Finnegans Wake*, with a live colourised fountain made of orange juice. According to Yoshimoto, she was the first artist to use multi-channel video in this way. 'She was the first to give sculptural form [to video], like wooden frame work to cover the monitors', says Yoshimoto, 'Within that, [there was her] use of natural elements such as water, and also kinetic movement. Many of her works rotate or are supposed to move like wheels, which was not really done at the time. Those were her inventions'[14].

Kubota connected with the physicality of the equipment, but the technology was so cumbersome that working under the weight of it, at one point, caused her to have a miscarriage. The physical and emotional intensity of her chosen medium is described in her text for *Video Poem*: 'I travel alone with my Portapak on my back, as Vietnamese women do with their baby. I like Video, because it's heavy ... Portapak tears down my shoulder, backbone and waist. I felt like a Soviet woman, working at a Siberian railway'[15].

'Video is Vacant Apartment'

Although Kubota didn't necessarily identify as a contributor to the feminist movement, there is clear feminist messaging in her work. In the description for one of her installations, she made a radical defence for the value of video art, underpinning its potential to liberate women artists, 'Video is Vengeance of Vagina. Video is Victory of Vagina. Video is Venereal Disease of Intellectuals. Video is Vacant Apartment. Video is Vacation of art. Viva Video ...'[16].

She likened the role of video in our lives to the image of snow on a mountain, 'lightness, speed, the ephemeral quality of the electron set against an unmoving, timeless mass'.

By presenting the video monitor as part of a sculpture, she was able to keep that liquid reality contained inside what she called a 'timeless mass'. It was a technique that led her right back to Duchamp, with her video homage to his painting *Nude Descending a Staircase, No.2*. Kubota created a plywood structure of steps, each containing a monitor showing a nude woman that moved in 'a mass of pulsating foam'[17].

It was a reference to Duchamp as much as the Japanese film *When a Woman Ascends the Stairs* by Mikio Naruse. The profoundly affecting film follows a resourceful Ginza bar hostess who is trying to make ends meet while navigating a workplace filled with leering, whisky-soaked businessmen. Paik warned Kubota not to pursue such an obscure theme, fearing an American audience would never get it, but the piece was purchased by MoMA. 'Nam June was stunned. It was I who had earned cash money'[18], she said.

Even with this success, maintaining an artistic identity independent from Nam June as he became a superstar of video art, became a struggle for Kubota. Though they worked together in the 1970s, even appearing in a group show together, she insisted 'I never collaborated with him'[19], perhaps to keep a distance between their reputations. 'In the very beginning, when they were not married and in the '70s, they were just a couple experimenting in this new medium of video art. I think they really stimulated each other and also her emergence as a video artist coincided with the budding of feminism in America and elsewhere', says Yoshimoto, 'By the early '80s when Nam June became a really big art star, making really huge installations, using hundreds of monitors, he drew the most media attention.'

Kubota maintained a solid artistic reputation within a much smaller circle. Her 1991 retrospective at the American Museum of the Moving Image was described by *The New Yorker* as a 'metaphysical World's fair'[20].

But the vast disparity between her fame and Paik's, despite her enormous contribution to the medium during the same time period, tells us a lot about the visibility given to groundbreaking work made by women. She never received due credit for her innovations in video sculpture during her lifetime.

When Nam June became sick in the late 1990s, she devoted her time to caring for him and supporting him through his shows. 'Because of her love she really focused on Nam June's career', says Yoshimoto, 'After he passed away, she got sick too, so she didn't really have time to give a completely new body of work.' After Nam June Paik died in 2006, Kubota had her first solo show in six years, an homage to him that had echoes of her dialogue with Duchamp more than thirty years before. A metal silhouette decorated with monitors took over the space, each playing a different image of Paik. In the foreword for the show's catalogue, her friend and collaborator Jonas Mekas wrote, 'It's time that we see Shigeko Kubota as an artist, a supreme artist in the art she was so crucial in assisting. Her video/electronic sculptures have been so rarely seen in public. Their modernity, their energy, their impact upon one's entire sensory and mental body is electrifying'[21].

'A video is a ghost of yourself'

Kubota came of age in a time suspended between analogue and digital, but just as video was becoming accessible to the masses through the invention of Portapak recorders, she had all but predicted the digital revolution. All of us are connected through the 'liquid reality' she described. 'Video is a ghost of yourself,' Kubota said, 'It's like your shadow. It reveals your interior. It still exists after you die'[22]. As the Portapak evolved into digital camcorder, and a camcorder shrank into an iPhone camera lens, we began to create video with ease, allowing our 'liquid realities' to become populated by billions of spectres who are left to float online. Every day, we add another step to our digital footprint, and when we die, it is left up to huge, corporate organisations to decide what happens to our posthumous selves.

Memories are no longer static, stored in shoeboxes of photos and shelves of VHS, they exist in a constant stream, and with that, comes a pressure to create them, to preserve at all costs what a hippocampus cannot. This, too, was something Kubota saw coming, even if she made her prediction in wry jest in one of her exhibition catalogues. 'Descartes said "I think therefore I am"', she wrote, 'In the pan-cybernated society, perhaps we will be saying "I video, therefore I am"'[23]. When referencing one of her earliest video sculptures, *Riverrun*, Kubota described it like so, 'Charged electrons flow across our receiver screens like a drop of water ... laden with information carried from some previous time'[24]. Reading these eloquent thoughts on video today, she could just as easily have been talking about a phone screen. She has not been given enough credit for it, but there is still time. Slowly, her name is being heard again. Voices piping up online, sharing her 'ghosts' to thousands of tiny monitors, claiming her as the mother of video art. As I write this, a large-scale retrospective of her work is in motion in Japan. It's like Kubota said, 'A drop of rain becomes a brook, a brook becomes a river'[25].

19
WHERE ARE WE NOW?

I came here to fight art monsters. That's what I expected when I began *More than a Muse*. I'd always known of them, but it was a passage in Jenny Offill's *Dept. of Speculation*, a novel that follows the course of a marriage through an unpredictable mix of memories and facts and literary quotations, where I first saw them take shape. I'll admit, I initially found the passage not in the book itself, but in a *Paris Review* essay by Claire Dederer. Offill's main character, a Brooklyn writer, says, 'My plan was to never get married. I was going to be an art monster instead. Women almost never become art monsters because art monsters only concern themselves with art, never mundane things. Nabokov didn't even fold his own umbrella. Véra licked his stamps for him'[1].

Such monsters do not give in to guilt, or make concessions, or generously make time for others, because they only have an appetite for art. In order to function, the monster needs a manager. Someone to do the lion's share of the childcare. To run errands. To organise the monster's social life. Someone to keep the trivialities of life beyond the door of their art studio, the music room, the writing desk. The art monster, as Offill's character implies, is almost always a man who relies on the support of a partner, at the cost of that person's own time, their own creativity, maybe their own chance for 'greatness'. But the biggest myth of all is the idea that greatness can only come with monstrosity. Never has the banality of domesticity seemed as beautiful and unnerving, as the way Offill writes it in that book.

I wanted to find these 'monsters', and push them out of view, so that I could re-examine the work of the significant others who sacrificed their own art to focus on the 'gifted' one in the family. They live among these pages. Ida

Nettleship gave up painting to acquiesce to every bohemian whim of Augustus John. Dora Maar's mental health and her photography career suffered the fallout of a ten-year relationship with one of history's biggest art monsters. Margaret Keane had her paintings stolen by a man who wanted to occupy the skin of an art monster while doing none of the work.

There is another threat to women's art, one that's even more terrifying than the 'art monster', and that is: the basement.

The archaeologists

When Lee Krasner was in art school, she and a friend disappeared into a basement to paint a still-life of a fish, a subject that was prohibited for women. When Lucia Moholy left her negatives of the architectural photographs she took of the Bauhaus with Walter Gropius, he held on to them tightly, keeping them 'safe' in his Lincoln basement, only to be resurfaced whenever he needed to develop photos for Bauhaus exhibitions, with no credit for Moholy.

When the Whitney Museum was gifted a selection of 3,000 artworks by Josephine and Edward Hopper after their deaths, they siphoned out Edward's works, leaving Jo's to gather dust in its basement. The neglect of art produced by women is a recurring theme. Again and again, it has been pushed underground, banished to the basement. The overshadowing of the women in this book, in the majority of cases, says more about the male-oriented nature of our art institutions than the relationships themselves. Being too closely associated with a prominent male artist could be detrimental for a woman in the same field, but it could have its benefits, too. When Peggy Guggenheim curated the now famous show *Exhibition by 31 Women* in 1943, which exclusively featured female artists, she mainly included women who were married to high-profile men she already knew. Even with such connections, artists like Jacqueline Lamba remained peripheral characters in this landscape built for men. What chance did other women, with zero contacts, have?

While putting together *More than a Muse*, the question I was repeatedly (and understandably) asked was, 'How can you write about these women if they have been overlooked?'.

But this work has all been done before. During the 1970s and 1980s, art historians like Whitney Chadwick, Griselda Pollock, Ann Sutherland Harris and Linda Nochlin had to effectively become art archaeologists, dedicating their energy to unearthing work by women that had been abandoned in gallery storage units. It is through their digging, and their academic writing, that we now have greater awareness of names like Marie Bracquemond and Dora Maar. In the book *Old Mistresses*, Pollock made plain how the erasure of women artists was not just about historical gender imbalance, it was a cognizant choice made by art institutions of the twentieth century. 'There was a tabula rasa with regard to artists who were women ... Women artists only "disappeared" in the twentieth century, in a moment of Modernism, when the first Museum of Modern Art was opened to tell the story of then recent and contemporary art (MoMA, New York, 1929) ... The modern century, politically and socially the "century of women", was, however, to be the first to erase the cultural memory and refuse the current recording of women as creative participants in our culture.'[2]

One of the earliest, and most significant attempts to recover from this erasure was the exhibition *Women Artists: 1550–1950* curated by Ann Sutherland Harris and Linda Nochlin for the Los Angeles County Museum of Art, in 1976. To source the art, they had to hunt for discarded fossils of work by women that had been stashed away, yet again, in gallery basements. 'It was like doing the whole history of art, with a feminist cast,'[3] said Nochlin. Among them was a painting by Dutch Golden Age painter Judith Leyster, which had been so neglected it had, according to Nochlin, a bad case of worms. The exhibition was one of the first to give a large American public platform to the works of Baroque Italian painter Artemisia Gentileschi who, at that point, was not widely known. Now her painting *Self-Portrait as Saint Catherine of Alexandria* sits in the permanent collection of the National Gallery in London. In *The New York Times* review, this exhibition charting 400 years of art by women artists, described Frida Kahlo as overshadowed by her husband Diego Rivera, something that's difficult to fathom considering Kahlo's global cult status today, which has seen her eclipse him.

Despite the hard labour of these archaeologists, only a handful of the artists they recovered were properly canonised.

Breaking the zeitgeist

What a difference three years makes. In 2016, I went to review an art exhibition at The Whitechapel Gallery, a retrospective of the Guerrilla Girls, the gorilla-masked feminist art collective who made a career out of shaming art institutions into change by uncovering stats on the paltry amount of women artists and artists of colour in their collections. The exhibition was constructed from a survey they sent out to 400 art institutions across twenty-nine countries, probing them for answers about their representation of women artists, those who are gender non-conforming and artists of colour. The survey answers were littered with defensive responses from gallery directors that ranged from pained to passive aggressive; they seemed almost hurt to be asked these questions at all. The upshot? The survey concluded that the average representation of women artists across these 400 institutions was 22 per cent. Ironically, that show by the Guerrilla Girls was one of only two major London exhibitions that season dedicated to work by women artists.

Fast forward to 2019, when London's exhibition line-up was telling a very different story. The biggest, most exciting solo shows were mainly by women: Dorothea Tanning at Tate Modern, Faith Ringgold at the Serpentine, Lee Krasner at the Barbican, Dora Maar at Tate Modern, Kara Walker in the Tate Modern's Turbine Hall. It seemed as though these institutions were waking up, at last feeling the embarrassment of the bias they had been carrying for decades. Finally there was something more on offer than just another contrived angle for yet another Picasso show.

Social media has played a significant part in the shift. Instagram accounts, such as *The Great Women Artists*, have offered a new take on the archaeological endeavours of historians like Griselda Pollock and Whitney Chadwick, surfacing images of work by women artists and sharing them with an audience of more than 70,000 on a daily basis, circulating artworks far beyond the academic circles to which they have previously been confined. Katy Hessel founded the account right after she left university in 2015, when she attended an art fair and was shocked by the lack of women artists on display.

While it's a positive that these institutions are rushing to be more inclusive of women, non-binary artists and artists of colour, there is a danger in this sea-change being perceived as part of a zeitgest. *Women Artists 1550–1950* had high-profile press coverage when it opened in 1976, and still the majority of women who appeared in it went straight back into the metaphorical basement when its 'moment' had passed. We need to avoid the trap of 'Google Doodle' feminism, where women are surfaced and celebrated with an illustration that presents a sanitised view of their existence, and disappear after twenty-four hours. Incidentally, Clara Schumann, Varvara Stepanova and Sophie Taeuber-Arp, have all been given the Google Doodle treatment.

The change needs to be permanent, and for that to happen, there needs to be a major overhaul of the permanent art collections at these institutions. 'So often it is like "tick, tick, tick" when actually it is all about museums collecting women artists', says Hessel, 'A gallery does a year of female artists but what do they do next year? You can't just go back to it or revert back to what the world used to be like. It's really important that isn't just a trend, it's important that museums address their collections – I wouldn't be able to remember what happened in 1997 at Tate but I could probably give you loads of names of work in their collection'[4].

Searching for subjects for this book resulted in daily déjà vu. Many of the women mentioned are 'rediscovered' every ten years or so. In 1997, Manchester City Art Gallery held an art show dedicated to the 'forgotten wives, sisters and colleagues of the Pre-Raphaelite movement'[5]. *Pre-Raphaelite Sisters*, an exhibition on the same subject, albeit larger in scope, opened at the National Portrait Gallery in 2019, sold as the untold story of the women of Pre-Raphaelite art. The lack of a solid foundation in art history placed all these artists in a protracted state of recovery. We need to move to the next phase, to stop viewing such artists as 'overlooked' or 'lost' and just accept them as found.

ENDNOTES

Preface

1   S. Preston, 'BY HUSBAND AND WIFE; A Group Show by Teams -- Three Modernists', *The New York Times*, 25 September 1949, available from Proquest Historical Newspapers, (accessed June 4 2019).

2   L. Loofbourow, 'The male glance: how we fail to take women's stories seriously', *The Guardian*. 6 March 2018, https://www.theguardian.com/news/2018/mar/06/the-male-glance-how-we-fail-to-take-womens-stories-seriously, (accessed April 3 2018).

3   Loofbourow, 'The male glance'.

4   Loofbourow.

5   Loofbourow.

6   G. Pollock, *Differencing the Canon: Feminism and the Writing of Art's Histories*, London and New York, Routledge, 1999, p. 24.

7   Legrange, *Gazette des Beaux-Arts*, Paris, 1860, cited in: R. Parker and G. Pollock, *Old Mistresses: Women, Art and Ideology*, London and New York, I.B.Tauris, new edition, 2013, p. 13.

8   L. Nochlin, 'Why Have There Been No Great Women Artists?', in T.B. Hess and E.C. Baker, *Art and Sexual Politics: Women's Liberation, Women Artists, and Art History*, New York, Macmillan, 1973, p. 30.

9   T.T. Latimer, *Acting Out: Claude Cahun and Marcel Moore*, 2006, www.queerculturalcenter.org/Pages/Tirza/TirzaEssay1.html, accessed on 12 June 2019.

10 Jane Alison, interview with the author, 2018.

Pre-Raphaelite women: breaking through the myths

1   R.L. Mégroz, *Dante Gabriel Rosetti: Painter Poet of Heaven in Earth*, New York, Haskell House Publishers, new ed, 1971, p. 50.

2   Mégroz, p. 50.

3   J. Marsh, *Pre-Raphaelite Sisterhood*, London, Quartet, 1985, p. 50.

4   J. Marsh, *Elizabeth Siddal 1829-1862: Pre-Raphaelite Artist*, Sheffield, Ruskin Gallery, Collection of the Guild of St. George/Sheffield Arts Department, 1991, p. 13.

5   Mégroz, p. 89.

6   Dr Serena Trowbridge, interview with the author, 2018.

7   'Fine Arts', *The Spectator*, 26 May 1855, p. 50.

Clara Schumann: the virtuoso

1   B. Litzmann, *Clara Schumann: An Artist's Life, Based on Material Found in Diaries and Letters*, Vol. 2, trans. G.E. Hadow, Cambridge, Cambridge University Press, 2013, p. 312.

2   B. Litzmann, *Clara Schumann: An Artist's Life*, Vol. 1, p. 209.

3   C. Schumann, *Letters of Clara Schumann and Johannes Brahms 1853–1896*, Berthold Litzmann, New York, Vienna House, 1971, p. 169.

4   Schumann, p. 284.

5   Schumann, p. 168.

6   J. Chissell, *Clara Schumann, A Dedicated Spirit: A Study of Her Life and Work*, New York, Taplinger Publishing, 1983, p. xii-xiii.

7   Chissell, p. 1.

8   H.C. Schonberg, *Great Pianists*, New York, Simon and Schuster, 1987, p. 237.

9   N.B. Reich, *Clara Schumann: The Artist and the Woman*, Ithaca, Cornell University Press, 2001, p. 216.

10 Reich, p. 85.

11 Reich, p. 88.

12 Reich, p. 89

13 Reich, p. 91.

14 Reich, p. 91.

15 Reich, p. 119

16 Reich, p. 120

17 J. Duchen, 'Clara Schumann: The Troubled Career of the Pianist', *The Independent*, 7 March 2006, https://www.independent.co.uk/arts-entertainment/music/features/clara-schumann-the-troubled-career-of-the-pianist-468981.html, (accessed 1 December 2018).

18   *The Manchester Guardian*, 'From the classical archive May 1856: Clara Schumann – a musical genius of the highest order', *The Guardian*, 20 September 2016, https://www.theguardian.com/music/2016/sep/20/from-the-classical-archive-1856-clara-schumann-a-musical-genius-of-the-highest-order#img-2, (accessed 1 December 2018).

19   R.P., 'CLARA SCHUMANN; Wife of Robert Was Also a Composer – Opera Excerpts From Singing Stars', *The New York Times*, 13 January 1952, https://www.nytimes.com/1952/01/13/archives/clara-schumann-wife-of-robert-was-also-a-composer-opera-excerpts.html?searchResultPosition=2, (accessed 1 December 2018).

Impressionism: Marie Bracquemond and the feminine influence

1   T. Garb, 'Berthe Morisot and the Feminizing of Impressionism', in T.J. Edelstein (ed.), *Perspectives on Morisot*, New York, Hudson Hills Press, 1990, p. 58.

2   D. Gaze, *Concise Dictionary of Women Artists*, New York, Taylor & Francis, 2001, p. 494.

3   L. Madeline (ed.), *Women Artists in Paris, 1850-1900*, Connecticut, Yale University Press, 2017, p. 56.

4   Madeline, p. 56.

5   Madeline, p. 56.

6   N. Brodskaya and E. Degas, *Edgar Degas*, New York, Parkstone Press International, 2012, p. 68.

7   Becker, J.R., 'Marie Bracquemond, Impressionist Innovator: Escaping the Fury', in L. Madeline (ed.), *Women Artists in Paris, 1850-1900*, Connecticut, Yale University Press, 2017, pp. 55-66.

8   D. Gaze, *Concise Dictionary of Women Artists*, New York, Taylor & Francis, 2013, p. 206.

9   Madeline, p. 58.

10   G. Pollock, 'The National Gallery is erasing women from the history of art', *The Conversation*, 3 June 2015, https://theconversation.com/the-national-gallery-is-erasing-women-from-the-history-of-art-42505, (accessed 23 November 2018).

Camille Claudel: master sculptor

1   O. Ayral-Clause, *Camille Claudel: A Life*, Plunkett Lake Press, 2015, p. 108. Available from: Google Play, (accessed 20 October 2018).

2   Ayral-Clause, p. 108.

3   Ayral-Clause, p. 108.

4   Ayral-Clause, p. 109.

5   Cited in Ayral-Clause, p. 109.

6   Ayral-Clause, p. 61.

7   M. Morhardt, 'Mlle Camille Claudel', *Mercury of France*, Vol XXV, January-March 1898, pp. 709-755. https://www.academia.edu/33400786/Mathias_Morhardt_-_M.lle_Camille_Claudel_1898_, (accessed November 13 2019).

8   L.R. Witherell, 'Camille Claudel Rediscovered', *Woman's Art Journal*, Vol. 6, No. 1, Spring-Summer 1985, p. 6.

9   A. Caranfa, *Camille Claudel: A Sculpture of Interior Solitude*, Lewisburg, Associated University Presses, 1999, p. 46.

10   Ayral-Clause, p. 106.

Bohemian dreams: Ida Nettleship and Hilda Carline

1   M. Holroyd, *Augustus John: The New Biography*, London, Vintage, 1997, p. 67.

2   A. Thomas, *Portraits of Women: Gwen John and Her Forgotten Contemporaries*, Wiley, 1996, p. 68.

3   Thomas, p. 68.

4   A. John, *Chiaroscuro*, Jonathan Cape, 1954, p. 48.

5   Cited in R. John and Michael Holroyd (eds), *The Good Bohemian: The Letters of Ida John*, London, Bloomsbury, 2017, p. 1.

6   John and Holroyd, p. 33.

7   John and Holroyd, p. 35.

8   E. Wilson, *Bohemians: The Glamorous Outcasts*, Tauris Parke, 2003, p. 101.

9   Wilson, p. 101.

10   Holroyd, *Augustus John*, p. 50.

11   John and Holroyd, p. 53.

12   John and Holroyd, p. 50.

13 John and Holroyd, p. 56.

14 John and Holroyd, p. 51.

15 John and Holroyd, p. 69.

16 John and Holroyd, p. 69.

17 I. Chilvers (ed.), The Oxford Dictionary of Art and Artists, Oxford, Oxford University Press, 2009, p. 316.

18 John and Holroyd. p. 93.

19 John and Holroyd, p. 225.

20 John and Holroyd, p. 225.

21 John and Holroyd, p.120.

22 C. Lloyd-Morgan, *Gwen John: Letters and Notebooks*, New York, Harry N. Abrams, 2005, p. 30.

23 John and Holroyd, p. 199.

24 John and Holroyd, p. 210.

25 Holroyd, *Augustus John*, p. 192.

26 S. Spencer and A. Glew, *Stanley Spencer: Letters and Writings*, London, Tate Gallery, 2001, p. 123.

27 Spencer and Glew, p. 209.

28 Spencer and Glew, p. 122.

29 Spencer and Glew, p. 117.

30 Spencer and Glew, p. 121.

31 A. Thomas, *The Art of Hilda Carline: Mrs Stanley Spencer*, Lund Humphries Publishers Ltd., 1999, p. 22.

32 Thomas, p. 28.

33 K. Pople, *Stanley Spencer: A Biography*, Virginia, HarperCollins, 1991, p. 292.

34 Spencer and Glew, p. 125.

35 Thomas, p. 30.

36 M. Thompson, 'Love's deadly cruelty', *The Telegraph*, 22 May 1999, https://www.telegraph.co.uk/culture/4717496/Loves-deadly-cruelty.html, (accessed on 10 February 2019).

37 Thompson, 'Love's deadly cruelty'.

38 U. Spencer, *Lucky To Be An Artist, London*, Unicorn Press, 2015, p. 40.

Gabriele Münter: the blue rider

1   Cited in L. Gossman, 'Gabriele Munter Photographer of America 1898-1900', Department of French and Italian, Princeton University, https://www.princeton.edu/~lgossman/ munter.pdf, (accessed on 5 June 2019).

2   R. Heller, *Gabriele Munter: The Years of Expressionism*, Munich, Prestel, 1997, p. 42.

3   P. Bruno, 'Malweiber', *Simplicissimus*, vol 6, no 15, 1901, pp. 113-122, http://www.simplicissimus.info/index.php?id=5, (accessed 2 November 2019).

4   W. Kandinsky, *Wassily Kandinsky and Gabriele Munter: Letters and Reminiscences 1902-1914*, Munich, Prestel, 1994, p. 31.

5   F.F. Sherman, *Art in America*, vol. 87, Art in America Inc, 1999, p. 90.

6   E. Roditi, *Dialogues on Art*, London, Secker & Warburg, 1960, p. 139.

7   R. Heller, *Gabriele Munter: The Years of Expressionism*, 1903-1920, California, Prestel, 1997, p. 62.

8   G. Munter, *Gabriele Munter: The Search for Expression*, Paul Holberton Publishing, 2005, p. 43.

9   W. Kandinsky, *Wassily Kandinsky and Gabriele Munter: Letters and Reminiscences 1902-1914*, Munich, Prestel, 1994, p. 85.

10 Heller, p. 127.

11 Heller, p. 115.

12 Roditi, *Dialogues on Art*, 120-121.

13 Roditi, *Dialogues on Art*, p. 144.

14 Cited in Gossman, pp. 9-19.

15 Roditi, 1990, p. 15.

16 Heller, p. 58.

Varvara Stepanova: constructing Russian art

1   A.N. Lavrentiev, *Varvara Stepanova: A Constructivist Life*, London, Thames and Hudson, 1988, p. 16.

2   Cited in Lavrentiev, p. 21.

3   Lavrentiev, p. 22.

4   Lavrentiev, p. 18.

5   Professor Alexander Lavrentiev, interview with the author.

6   R. Bolton, *The Contest of Meaning: Critical Histories of Photography*, Massachusetts, MIT Press, 1992, p. 54.

7   Lavrentiev, p. 169.

8   Lavrentiev, p. 169.

9   J.C. Marcadé and E.N. Petrova, *Rodchenko: Constructing the Future*, Ciaxa Catalunya, 2008, p. 104.

10 Lavrentiev, p. 54.

11 Lavrentiev, p. 175.

12 C. Mendes and E.R. Larreta (ed.), *Collective Imagination: Limits and Beyond*, UNESCO, 2001, p. 249.

13 L. Heron and V. Williams (ed.), *Illuminations: Women Writing on Photography from the 1850s to the Present*, I.B. Tauris, 1996, p. 65.

14 Lavrentiev, p. 54.

15 A. Larentiev interview, 2019.

16 Bowlt, J.E. et al., *Amazons of the Avant-Garde*, New York, Guggenheim Museum, 2000, p. 25.

Dada vision: Emmy Hennings and Baroness Elsa von Freytag-Loringhoven

1   H. Ball, *Flight Out of Time: A Dada Diary, London and Los Angeles*, University of California Press, originally published 1927, paperback printing 1996, p. 70.

2   S.G. Blythe, E.D. Powers and Museum of Modern Art, *Looking at Dada*, New York, The Museum of Modern Art, 2006, p. 27.

3   H. Richter, *Dada: Art and Anti-Art*, New York, McGraw-Hill, 1965, p. 132.

4   Richter, p.132.

5   N. Sawelson-Gorse, *Women in Dada: Essays on Sex, Gender and Identity*, Massachusetts, MIT Press, 1998, p. 532.

6   Richter, p. 31.

7   R. Hemus, *Dada's Women*, Connecticut, Yale University Press, 2009, p. 42.

8   Hemus, p. 46.

9   R. Huelsenbeck, *Memoirs of a Dada Drummer*, Berkeley, University of California Press, 1991, p. 24.

10 Huelsenbeck, p. 49.

11 R. Motherwell (ed.), *The Dada Painters and Poets: An Anthology*, Massachusetts, Harvard University Press, 1989, p. 286.

12 Hemus, p. 31

13 S.C. Foster and K. Riha, *Crisis and the Arts: Dada Zurich, A Clown's Game From Nothing*, Michigan, G.K. Hall, 1996, p. 84.

14 Hemus, p. 46.

15 I. Gammel, *Baroness Elsa: Gender, Dada and Everyday Modernity: A Cultural Biography*, Massachusetts, MIT, 2002, p. 184.

16 Sawelson-Gorse, p. 157.

17 E. von Freytag-Loringhoven, *Body Sweats: The Uncensored Writings of Elsa von Freytag-Loringhoven*, Massachusetts, MIT Press, 2011, p. 86.

18 Cited in Gammel, p. 224.

19 B. Wood, 'The Richard Mutt Case', *The Blind Man*, no. 2, 1917, p. 7.

20 Norton, p. 8.

21 Ben Street, interview with the author, 2019.

22 B. Street interview, 2019.

Lucia Moholy: behind the scenes at the Bauhaus

1 N.F. Weber, *Anni Albers*, New York, Guggenheim Museum, 1999, p. 154.

2 'Women and the Bauhaus: Weaving/Anni Albers', MoMA Talks Panels & Symposia, [podcast], MoMA, 2009, https://player.fm/series/moma-talks-panel-discussions-and-symposia/women-and-the-bauhaus-weavinganni-albers, (accessed 10 March 2019).

3 A. Searle, 'Anni Albers review – ravishing textiles that beg to be touched', *The Guardian*, 9 October 2018, https://www.theguardian.com/artanddesign/2018/oct/09/anni-albers-tate-modern-review, (accessed July 15 2019).

4 U. Muller, *Bauhaus Women: Art, Handicraft*, Design, Flammarion, 2009, p. 126.

5 L. Moholy, *Marginalien zu Moholy-Nagy. Moholy-Nagy, Marginal Notes*, Krefeld, Scherpe Verlag, 1972. p. 55.

6 Moholy, p. 55.

7 'Women and the Bauhaus: Public Relations/Ise Gropius, Lucia Moholy', MoMA Talks Panels & Symposia, MoMA, 2010.

8   F. Ambler, *The Story of the Bauhaus*, London, Hachette UK, 2018, pp. 186-188. Available from Google Play, (accessed 2 November 2019).

9   R. Schuldenfrei, 'Images in Exile: Lucia Moholy's Bauhaus Negatives and the Construction of the Bauhaus Legacy', *History of Photography*, vol. 37, issue 2, 2013, pp. 182-203.

10 Schuldenfrei, p. 195.

11 Schuldenfrei, p. 195.

12 Schuldenfrei, p. 195.

13 Moholy, p. 53.

14 Muller, p. 11.

Lil Hardin Armstrong and the Jazz Age: born to swing

1   L. Hardin Armstrong, Hear me Talkin' To Ya, interviewed by Steve Allen, 1967, British Library, London, C1411/104C1411/105; Steve Allen Collection.

2   L. Hardin Armstrong, Hear me Talkin' To Ya, interviewed by Steve Allen, 1967, British Library, London, C1411/104C1411/105; Steve Allen Collection.

3   S. Placksin, *American women in jazz: 1900 to the present: their words, lives, and music*, Seaview Books, 1982, p. 61.

4   J.L. Dickerson, *Just for a Thrill: Lil Hardin Armstrong, First Lady of Jazz*, New York, Cooper Square Publishers Inc, 2002, p. 219.

5   L. Hardin Armstrong, interviewed by Steve Allen, 1967.

6   L. Hardin Armstrong, 1967.

7   L. Hardin Armstrong. 'Satchmo and Me', *American Music*, vol. 25, no. 1, 2007, pp. 109. JSTOR, www.jstor.org/stable/40071645.

8   Placksin, p. 59.

9   L. Hardin Armstrong, 1967.

10 Placksin, p. 59.

11 L. Hardin Armstrong, *'Satchmo and Me'*, p.109.

12 Placksin, p. 59.

13 L. Hardin Armstrong, *'Satchmo and Me'*, p. 110.

14 Dahl, L., *Stormy Weather: The Music and Lives of a Century of Jazzwomen*, New York, Pantheon, 1984, p. 26.

15 L. Armstrong, *Louis Armstrong, in His Own Words*, New York, Oxford University Press, 1999, p. 65.

16 L. Hardin Armstrong, p. 118.

17 L. Hardin Armstrong, 1967.

18 L. Hardin Armstrong, p. 114.

19 Placksin, p. 61.

20 Placksin, p. 61.

21 L. Hardin Armstrong, 1967.

22 L. Hardin Armstrong, 1967.

23 Placksin, p. 62.

24 Placksin, p. 62.

25 L. Hardin Armstrong, 1967.

Alma Reville: the silent partner

1 *Daily Express*, 14 Aug 1974, Available from Proquest Historical Newspapers, (accessed 11 July 2019).

2 J. McBride, 'Mr and Mrs Hitchcock', *Sight & Sound*, Autumn issue, 1976, p. 225.

3 J. McBride, 'Mr and Mrs Hitchcock', p. 225.

4 A. Reville, 'Cutting and Continuity', in E. Allen. and S.Gottlieb, (eds.), *The Hitchcock Annual Anthology: Selected Essays From Volumes 10-15*, London, Wallflower, 2009, p. 66.

5 'Alma in Wonderland' *The Picturegoer*, December 1925. Reprinted in E. Allen. and S.Gottlieb, (eds.), *The Hitchcock Annual Anthology: Selected Essays From Volumes 10-15*, London, Wallflower, 2009, p. 53.

6 'Alma in Wonderland', 1925.

7 McBride, p. 225.

8 R. Grosvenor, "I Don't Scare Easily", Says Mrs Hitchcock', *Sunday Express*, 30 January 1972, Proquest Historical Newspapers, (accessed 15 August 2019).

9 McBride, p. 225.

10 Pamela Hutchinson, interview with the author, 2019.

11 C. Chandler, *It's Only a Movie Alfred Hitchcock: A Personal Biography*, New York and London, Simon & Schuster, 2008, p. 53.

12 A. Guy Blaché and A. Slide, *The memoirs of Alice Guy Blaché*, Scarecrow Press, 1986, p. 73.

13 K. Hepburn, *Me: Stories of My Life*, Knopf, 1991, p. 44.

14 Chandler, p. 54.

15 McBride, p. 225.

16 S. Berg and P. Sierchio. 'Hitched to the Script'. *Written By*, vol. 10, no. 3, 2006, p. 48.

17 S. Berg and P. Sierchio. 'Hitched to the Script', p. 47.

18 McBride, p. 224.

19 R. Grosvenor, "I Don't Scare Easily".

20 C. Champlin, 'Alma Reville Hitchcock – The Unsung Partner', *Los Angeles Times*, July 29 1982, p.7. Available from Proquest Historical Newspapers, (accessed 11 July 2019).

Josephine Nivison Hopper: the recovery

1   G. Souter, *Edward Hopper Light and Dark*, New York, Parkstone Press, 2015, pp. 247-248. Available from Google Play, (accessed 10 November 2019).

2   J.B. Mellow, 'The World Of Edward is Hopper—The drama of light, the artificiality of nature, the remorseless human comedy', *The New York Times*, 5 September, 1971, https://www.nytimes.com/1971/09/05/archives/the-world-of-edward-hopper-the-drama-of-light-the-artificiality-of.html, (accessed 14 May 2019).

3   Mellow, 'The World Of Edward is Hopper'.

4   Mellow, 'The World Of Edward is Hopper'.

5   V. Woolf, *To the Lighthouse*, first published 1927, Oxford and New York, Oxford University Press edition, 2006, p. 132.

6   Woolf, *To the Lighthouse*, p. 132.

7   Woolf, p. 132.

8   G. Levin, *Edward Hopper: An Intimate Biography*, London and Los Angeles, California University Press, 2007 revised edition, p. 171.

9   Levin, p. 171.

10 E. Colleary, 'Josephine Nivison Hopper: Some Newly Discovered Works', *Woman's Art Journal*, vol. 25, no.1, 2004, p. 8.

11 Cited in Levin, p. 354.

12 Levin, p. 173.

13 Levin, p. 179-180.

14 Levin, p. 721.

15 Levin, p. 334.

16 Levin, p. 403.

17 Levin, p. 198.

18 Colleary, *Josephine Nivison Hopper*', p. 10.

19 Levin, p. 335.

20 G. Wood, 'Man and Muse', *The Guardian*, 24 April 2004, https://www.theguardian.com/artanddesign/2004/apr/25/art1, (accessed 3 May 2019).

21 Levin, p. 208.

Shirley Graham Du Bois: renaissance woman

1 S. Schmalenberger, S, 'Debuting Her Political Voice: The Lost Opera of Shirley Graham', *Black Music Research Journal*, vol. 26, no 1, 2006, p.60.

2 Professor Gerald Horne, interview with the author, 2019.

3 G. Horne, *Race Woman: The Lives of Shirley Graham Du Bois*, New York, New York University Press, 2000, p. 17.

4 S. Graham Du Bois, *Paul Robeson: Citizen of the World*, New York, J. Messner, inc, 1946, p. 68.

5 S. Graham Du Bois, p. 95.

6 David DuBois: My Mother, Shirley Graham DuBois, [online video], 2010, oral history archive, Visionary Project, http://www.visionaryproject.org/duboisdavid/, (30 June 2019).

7 W.E.B. Du Bois, *In Battle for Peace: The Story of May 83rd Birthday*, Oxford and New York, Oxford University Press, new ed, 2007, p. 6.

8 Cited in Horne, p. 23.

9 Professor Gerald Horne interview, 2019.

10 W.E.B. Du Bois, *In Battle for Peace: The Story of May 83rd Birthday*, p. 39.

11 Shirley Graham Du Bois speaking at UCLA 11/13/1970, [online video], 2014, https://www.youtube.com/watch?v=u3mhM3bHCZ8, (accessed 2 July 2019).

12 'Shirley Graham DuBois, 69, Writer And Widow of Civil Rights Leader', *The New York Times*, 5 April 1977, https://www.nytimes.com/1977/04/05/archives/shirley-graham-dubois-69-writer-and-widow-of-civil-rights-leader.html, (accessed 2 July 2019).

Surrealist women: Jacqueline Lamba and Suzanne Césaire

1   A. Breton, *Amour Fou*, Lincoln and London, University of Nebraksa Press, 1937, translation by Mary Ann Caws 1987, p. 4.

2   A. Breton, *Nadja*, London, Penguin Modern Classics, p. 160.

3   W. Chadwick, *Women Artists and the Surrealist Movement*, New York, Bulfinch Press, 1985, p. 11.

4   P. Rosemont, *Surrealist Women: An International Anthology*, London, Athlone Press, 1998, p. 77.

5   C. McCormick, 'Dorothea Tanning by Carlo McCormick', *Bomb*, 1990, https://bombmagazine.org/articles/dorothea-tanning/, (accessed July 27 2019).

6   Chadwick, 1985, p. 12.

7   'A Woman's Work: Surrealist Artist Meret Oppenheim', *MoMA*, https://www.moma.org/learn/moma_learning/meret-oppenheim-object-paris-1936/, (Ocotober 10 2018)

8   W. Chadwick, *The Militant Muse*, London, Thames & Hudson, 2017, p. 9.

9   S. Grimberg, 'Jacqueline Lamba: From Darkness, with Light', *Woman's Art Journal*, vol. 22, no. , 5-1, p. 11.

10 Rosemont, p.77.

11 Rosemont, p.77.

12 Eileen Agar, interviewed by Cathy Courtney, 1990, *Artists' Lives*, The British Library, London, C466/01.

13 M.A. Caws, R. Kuenzli, G. Raaberg (eds), *Surrealism and Women*, London, MIT Press, 1991.

14 Grimberg, 2001, p. 10.

15 Grimberg, 2001, p. 10.

16 Grimberg, 2001, p. 5.

17 Grimberg, 2001, p. 12.

18 S. Césaire, *The Great Camouflage: Writings of Dissent (1941-1945)*, Connecticut, Wesleyan University Press, 2012, p. 34.

19 S. Césaire, *The Great Camouflage: Writings of Dissent (1941-1945)*, p. 38.

20 Rosemont, p. 126.

21 Césaire, p. xii.

22 Césaire, p. 27.

23 Césaire, p. 43.

24 Césaire, p. 29-30.

25 Ina Césaire quoted in Césaire, p. 65.

Dora Maar: radical photography

1   J. Lord, *Picasso and Dora: A Memoir*, London, Weidenfield & Nicolson, 1993, p. 102.

2   Lord, *Picasso and Dora: A Memoir*, p. 95.

3   Lord, p. 120.

4   Cited in L. Baring, *Dora Maar: Paris in the Time of Man Ray, Jean Cocteau, and Picasso*, Rizzoli, 2017, p. 33.

5   Cited in L. Baring, 'Dora Maar: Paris in the Time of Man Ray, Jean Cocteau, and Picasso', 21 December 2017, *The Eye of Photography*, https://loeildelaphotographie.com/en/dora-maar-paris-in-the-time-of-man-ray-cocteau-and-picasso/, (accessed 14 July 2019).

6   F. Gilot and C. Lake, *Life With Picasso*, London, Penguin Books Ltd., 1966, p. 341.

7   L. Menand, 'The Norman Invasion', *The New Yorker*, 14 October 2013, https://www.newyorker.com/magazine/2013/10/21/the-norman-invasion, (accessed 14 July 2019).

8   F. Gilot and L. Carlton, *Life With Picasso*, New York, New York Review of Books, new edition, 2019, p. 218.

9   M.A. Caws, 'A tortured goddess', *The Guardian*, 7 October 2000, https://www.theguardian.com/books/2000/oct/07/features.weekend, (accessed 2 July 2019).

10 J.B. Jiminez, *Dictionary of Artists' Models*, New York and London, Routledge, 2013, p. 337.

11 J. L'Enfant, 'Dora Maar and the Art of Mystery', *Woman's Art Journal*, vol. 17, no. 2, 1996, pp. 15–20. JSTOR, www.jstor.org/stable/1358462.

12 I. Chilvers and J. Glaves-Smith, *Oxford Dictionary of Modern and Contemporary Art*, Oxford, Oxford University Press, 2009, p. 420.

13 J. Richardson, 'Trompe l'Oeil', *New York Review of Books*, 3 December, 1964, https://www.nybooks.com/articles/1964/12/03/trompe-loeil-2/, (accessed 2 July 2019).

14 A. Baldassari, *Picasso: Life with Dora Maar: Love and War 1935-1945*, Paris, Flammarion, 2006, p. 12.

15 Cited in J. L'Enfant, 'Dora Maar and the Art of Mystery', pp. 15–20.

Lee Krasner: rip it up, start again

1   T. Jenkins, 'Art show too male? At times, this cry makes no sense', *The Guardian*, 25
    September 2016, https://www.theguardian.com/commentisfree/2016/sep/24/art-show-
    too-male-cry-makes-no-sense (accessed 20 May 2019).

2   F. O'Hara, *Art Chronicles, 1954-1966*, New York, George Braziller, 1975, p. 6.

3   P. Schjeldahl, 'Fragments of An Awesome Whole', *The New York Times*, 19 January 1975,
    https://www.nytimes.com/1975/01/19/archives/fragments-of-an-awesome-whole.html,
    (accessed 20 May 2019).

4   M. Collings, 'Abstract Expressionism, exhibition review: What a load of Pollocks',
    The Guardian, 20 September 2016, https://www.standard.co.uk/go/london/arts/abstract-
    expressionism-exhibition-review-what-a-load-of-pollocks-a3349116.html, (accessed
    20 May 2019).

5   A. E. Gibson, *Abstract Expressionism: Other Politics*, New Haven, Yale University Press, 1997,
    p. 135.

6   N. Gosling, 'A Portent from Brooklyn', *The Observer*, 26 September, 1965. Available from
    Proquest Historical Newspapers, (accessed 20 May 2019).

7   L Krasner, 'Statement' in B. Roberson and B.H. Friedman, *Lee Krasner: Paintings, Drawings and
    Collages*, London, Whitechapel Art Gallery, 1965, p. 13.

8   Gabriel, *Ninth Street Women*, p. 21.

9   D. Holmes, oral history interview with Lee Krasner, 1972, Archives of American Art,
    Smithsonian Institution. https://www.aaa.si.edu/collections/interviews/oral-history-
    interview-lee-krasner-12037#transcript, (accessed 23 May 2019).

10 Cited by J. Marter, 'Negotiating Abstraction: Lee Krasner, Mercedes Carles Matter and the
    Hofmann Years', *Women's Art Journal*, vol. 28, no. 2, 2007, p. 36, JSTOR, www.jstor.org/
    stable/20358129.

11 Gabriel, *Ninth Street Women*, p. 82.

12 D. Seckler, oral history interview with Lee Krasner, 1964 Nov. 2-1968 Apr. 11. Archives of
    American Art, Smithsonian Institution.

13 Inside New York's Art World: Lee Krasner, 1978, [online video], 2008, https://www.
    youtube.com/watch?v=yFdE0bH9FRg (accessed 20 May 2019).

14 Cited in Marter, *'Negotiating Abstraction: Lee Krasner, Mercedes Carles Matter and the Hofmann Years'*,
    p. 38.

15 Marter, p.39.

16 Inside New York's Art World: Lee Krasner, 1978.

17 Gabriel, p. 177.

18 Inside New York's Art World: Lee Krasner, 1978.

19 S. Preston, 'Modern Work in Diverse Shows: Contemporary American and Italian Work in New Displays', *The New York Times*, 2 October 1955, ISSN 03624331. Available from Proquest Historical Newspapers, (accessed 12 May 2019).

20 L. Rago, 'We interview Lee Krasner', School Arts, vol. 60, 1960, p. 32.

21 R. Hobbs, *Lee Krasner*, New York, Independent Curators International in association with Harry N. Abrams, 1999, p. 112.

22 D. Holmes, oral history interview with Lee Krasner, 1972

23 Gosling, 1965.

Margaret Keane: big eyes

1   Big Eyes, Big Lies | The Carpetbagger | *The New York Times*, [online video], 2014, https://www.youtube.com/watch?v=IX7dNpWnf6E, (accessed 25 July 2019).

2   C. Buckley. 'How Amy Adams Overcame Her Resistance to 'Big Eyes''', *The New York Times*, 6 January 2015, (accessed 25 July 2019).

3   Margaret Keane, interview with the author, 2019.

4   Keane interview, 2019.

5   J. Howard. 'The Man Who Paints Those Big Eyes', *Life*, vol. 59, no. 9, 1965, p. 39.

6   A 1964 interview with Walter Stanley Keane, Margaret Keane, Big Eyes Paintings, [online video], 2015, https://www.youtube.com/watch?v=9WgStC6fvtM, (accessed 25 July 2019).

7   Swanson, 'Margaret Keane's Eyes Are Wide Open', Vulture, 18 December 2014, https://www.vulture.com/2014/12/margaret-keanes-eyes-are-wide-open.html, (accessed 25 July 2019).

8   Howard, 'The Man Who Paints Those Big Eyes', p. 40.

9   Howard, p. 42.

10 Howard, p. 42.

11 Howard, p. 42.

12 L. Catterall, 'Walter Keane's tactics make judge see red', *Honolulu Star Bulletin*, 15 May 1986. Available from Proquest Historical Newspapers, (accessed 13 July 2019).

13 Howard, p. 43.

Shigeko Kubota: the mother of video art

1   S. Kubota, *Shigeko Kubota: Video Sculptures*, Essen, Das Museum, 1981, p. 13.

2   Shigeko Kubota, interviewed by Miwako Tezuka, 2009, https://post.at.moma.org/content_items/344-interview-with-shigeko-kubota, (accessed 23 May 2019).

3   P. Bui and S. Kubota, 'Shigeko Kubota with Phong Bui', *The Brooklyn Rail*, 2007, https://brooklynrail.org/2007/09/art/kubota, (accessed 1 August 2019).

4   R. Smith, 'Review/Art; Sleek Video Sculptures By Shigeko Kubota', *The New York Times*, 24 May 1991, https://www.nytimes.com/1991/05/24/arts/review-art-sleek-video-sculptures-by-shigeko-kubota.html, (accessed 1 August 2019).

5   S. Kubota interview, 2009.

6   P. Bui and S. Kubota, Shigeko Kubota with Phong Bui, 2007.

7   P. Bui, *The Brooklyn Rail*.

8   K. Stiles, *Concerning Consequences: Studies in Art, Destruction, and Trauma*, Chicago and London, The University of Chicago Press, p. 147.

9   S. Kubota interview, 2009.

10   Professor Midori Yoshimoto, interview with the author, 2019.

11   S. Kubota interview, 2009.

12   S. Kubota, *Shigeko Kubota: Video Sculptures*, Essen, Das Museum, 1981, p. 13.

13   S. Kubota and M.J. Jacob, *Shigeko Kubota video sculpture*, New York, American Museum of the Moving Image, 1991, p. 35.

14   M. Yoshimoto interview, 2019.

15   Kubota and Jacob, *Shigeko Kubota video sculpture*, p. 74.

16   Kubota and Jacob, p. 74.

17   Yoshimoto, *Into Performance*, p. 191.

18   S. Kubota interview, 2009.

19   S. Kubota interview, 2009.

20   Author uncredited, 'Art', *The New Yorker* archive, 13 May 1991, https://archives.newyorker.com/newyorker/1991-05-13/flipbook/014/, (accessed 1 August 2019).

21   Author uncredited, 'Shigeko Kubota, My Life with Nam June Paik', Stendhal Gallery, http://1995-2015.undo.net/it/mostra/58503, (accessed 2 August 2019).

22   Kubota interview.

23   S. Kubota, *Shigeko Kubota: Video Sculptures*, 1981, p. 34.

24   S. Kubota, *Shigeko Kubota: Video Sculpture*, 1991, p. 41.

25   Kubota, 1991, p. 40.

Where are we now?

1   J. Offill, *Dept. Of Speculation*, London, Granta Books, 2015, p. 15. Available from Apple Books, (accessed 30 September 2019).

2   R. Parker and G. Pollock, *Old Mistresses: Women, Art and Ideology*, new edition, 2013, p. 23-24.

3   G. Glueck. Bredow, 'The woman as artist', *The New York Times*, 25 September 1977, https://www.nytimes.com/1977/09/25/archives/the-woman-as-artist.html, (accessed 29 September 2018).

4   Katy Hessel, interview with the author, August 2019.

5   R. Dorment, 'The Pre-Raphaelite sisterhood', *The Telegraph*, 10 January 1998, https://www.telegraph.co.uk/culture/4711482/The-Pre-Raphaelite-sisterhood.html, (accessed 30 September 2018).

BIBLIOGRAPHY

Preface

Saltz, J., *Seeing Out Louder: Art Criticism 2003-2009*, New York, Woodbridge, 2009.

Gombrich, E.H., *The Story of Art*, 11th edn., London, Phaidon Press, 1966.

Levin, A.K. (ed.), *Gender, Sexuality and Museums*, London, Routledge, 2010.

Frederickson, K. and Webb, S.E. (eds), *Singular Women: Writing the Artist*, Berkeley, University of California Press, 2003.

Chadwick, W. and de Courtivron, I. (eds), *Significant Others*, London, Thames & Hudson, 1993.

Alison, J. and Malissard, C. (eds), *Modern Couples: art, intimacy and the avant-garde*, London, Prestel, 2018.

Chadwick, W., *Women, Art and Society*, 4th edn., London, Thames & Hudson, 2007.

Gaze, D. (ed.), *Concise Dictionary of Women Artists*, London, Fitzroy Dearborn, 2001.

Chadwick, W., *Women, Art and Society*, 5th edition, London, Thames & Hudson, 2012.

Women's Review, vol. 1-12, 1885.

Greer, G., *The Obstacle Race: The Fortunes of Women Painters and Their Work*, London, Secker and Warburg, 1979.

Weidemann, C., Larass, P. and Klier, M., *50 Women Artists You Should Know*, London, Prestel, 2008.

Rosenau, H., *Woman in Art: From Type to Personality*, London, Isomorph, 1944.

Bailey, G.A. et al., *Art in Time: A World History of Styles and Movements*, London, Phaidon Press, 2014.

Chadwick, W. (ed.), *Mirror Images: Women, Surrealism, and Self-Representation*, Cambridge Massachusetts, MIT Press, 1998.

Preston, S., 'BY HUSBAND AND WIFE; A Group Show by Teams -- Three Modernists', *The*

New York Times, 25 September 1949, available from The British Library Newsroom database, (accessed June 4 2019).

Loofbourow, L., 'The male glance: how we fail to take women's stories seriously', *The Guardian*, 6 March 2018, https://www.theguardian.com/news/2018/mar/06/the-male-glance-how-we-fail-to-take-womens-stories-seriously, (accessed April 3 2018).

Pollock, G., *Differencing the Canon: Feminism and the Writing of Art's Histories*, London and New York, Routledge, 1999.

Parker, R. and Pollock ,G., *Old Mistresses: Women, Art and Ideology*, London and New York, I.B.Tauris, new edition, 2013.

Nochlin, L., 'Why Have There Been No Great Women Artists?', in Hess, T.B. and Baker, E.C. *Art and Sexual Politics: Women's Liberation, Women Artists, and Art History*, New York, Macmillan, 1973.

Pollock, G., *Vision and Difference: Feminism, Femininity and Histories of Art*, London and New York, Routledge, 2015.

Latimer, T.T., 'Acting Out: Claude Cahun and Marcel Moore', 2006, www.queerculturalcenter. org/Pages/Tirza/TirzaEssay1.html, (accessed on 12 June 2019).

Nochlin, L., 'Starting from scratch: Linda Nochlin traces the beginnings of feminist art history', *Women's Art Magazine*, Nov/Dec 1994, p. 6+. Gale Academic Onefile, (accessed 16 February 2019).

Tsjeng, Z., *Forgotten Women: The Artists*, London, Cassell, 2018.

Pre-Raphaelite women: breaking through the myths

Mégroz, R.L., *Dante Gabriel Rossetti: Painter Poet of Heaven in Earth*, London, Faber and Gwyer, 1928.

Marsh, J., *Elizabeth Siddal 1829–1862: Pre-Raphaelite Artist*, Sheffield, Ruskin Gallery, Collection of the Guild of St. George/Sheffield Arts Department, 1991.

Tate Gallery, *The Pre-Raphaelites*, London, Tate Gallery, 1984.

Marsh, J., Nunn P.G., MCA Gallery et al. *Pre-Raphaelite Women Artists*, London, Thames & Hudson, 1998.

Mcnay, A., 'Beyond Ophelia: A Celebration of Lizzie Siddal, Artist and Poet', *Studio International*, 28 June 2018, https://www.studiointernational.com/index.php/beyond-ophelia-celebration-of-lizzie-siddal-artist-poet-wightwick-manor-wolverhampton-national-trust, (10

October 2018).

Geffroy, G., *La Vie Artistique*, Paris, 1894.

Marsh, J., *Pre-Raphaelite Sisterhood*, London, Quartet, 1985.

Jiminez, J.B. (ed.), *Dictionary of Artists' Models*, London, Routledge, 2001.

Marsh, J., *The Legend of Elizabeth Siddal*, London, Quartet Books Ltd., 1989.

Hunt, V., *The Wife of Rossetti*, 1932.

'Fine Arts', *The Spectator*, 26 May 1855.

Gerrish Nunn,P., *Victorian Women Artists*, London, The Women's Press Ltd; First Edition,
1987.

Mégroz, R.L., *Dante Gabriel Rosetti: Painter Poet of Heaven in Earth*, New York, Haskell House
Publishers, new ed, 1971.

Barringer, T.J., *Pre-Raphaelites: Victorian Avant Garde*, London, Tate Publishing, 2012.

The Germ, thoughts towards nature in art and literature, 1850.

Siddal, E., *Poems and Drawings of Elizabeth Siddal*, Wolfville N.S., Wombat Pres, 1978.

Clara Schumann: the virtuoso

Reich, N.B., *Clara Schumann: The Artist and the Woman*, Ithaca, Cornell University Press, 2000.

Schumann,C., *Letters of Clara Schumann and Johannes Brahms 1953–1896*, Edward Arnold,
1927.

Schonberg, H.C., *Great Pianists*, New York, Simon and Schuster, 1987.

Chisell, J., *Clara Schumann, A Dedicated Spirit: A Study of Her Life and Work*, New York,Taplinger
Publishing, 1983.

Reich, N.B., *Clara Schumann: The Artist and the Woman*, Ithaca, Cornell University Press, 2001.

No known author, *The Manchester Guardian*, 'From the classical archive May 1856: Clara
Schumann – a musical genius of the highest order', *The Guardian*, 20 September 2016,
https://www.theguardian.com/music/2016/sep/20/from-the-classical-archive-1856-clara-
schumann-a-musical-genius-of-the-highest-order#img-2, (accessed 1 December 2018).

Duchen, J., 'Clara Schumann: The Troubled Career of the Pianist', *The Independent*, 7 March
2006, https://www.independent.co.uk/arts-entertainment/music/features/clara-schumann-
the-troubled-career-of-the-pianist-468981.html, (accessed 1 December 2018).

R.P., 'CLARA SCHUMANN; Wife of Robert Was Also a Composer – Opera Excerpts
From Singing Stars', *The New York Times*, 13 January 1952, https://www.nytimes.

com/1952/01/13/archives/clara-schumann-wife-of-robert-was-also-a-composer-opera-excerpts.html?searchResultPosition=2, (accessed 1 December 2018).

Litzmann, B., *Clara Schumann: An Artist's Life, Based on Material Found in Diaries and Letters*, Vol. 1, trans. G.E. Hadow, Cambridge, Cambridge University Press, 2013.

Reich, N.B., *Clara Schumann: The Artist and the Woman*, 2nd ed., Ithaca, Cornell University Press, 2001.

Beer, A., *Sounds and Sweet Airs: The Forgotten Women of Classical Music*, London, England, Oneworld Publications, 2016.

Hebblethwaite, P., 'Junk Shop Classical On Clara Schumann: Music Stories Told £1 LP By £1 LP', *The Quietus*, 25 June 2018, https://thequietus.com/articles/24841-clara-schumann-junkshop-classical, (30 September 2018).

Kenny, A. and Wollenberg, S. (eds), *Women and the Nineteenth Century Lied*, Surrey, Ashgate, 2015.

Chissell, J., *Clara Schumann: A Dedicated Spirit*, London, Hamilton, 1983.

Thiel, L. et al., *A Victorian Quartet: Four Forgotten Women Writers*, Pied Piper, 2008.

Impressionism: Marie Bracquemond and the feminine influence

Mauclair, C., *The French Impressionists:(1860–1900)*, trans. P.G. Konody, London, Duckworth & Co., 1903.

Lucie-Smith, E., *Impressionist Women*, London, Weidenfeld and Nicolson, 1989.

Meyers, J., 'Women Impressionists: Berthe Morisot, Mary Cassat, Eva Gonzales, Marie Bracquemond', *Apollo: The International Magazine of Art and Antiques*, 2008, pp. 127-129.

Garb, T., Women Impressionists, New York, Rizzoli, 1986.

Pfeiffer, I. and Hollein, M., *Women Impressionists*, Ostfildern, Hatje Cantz, 2008.

Pollock, G., 'The National Gallery is erasing women from the history of art', *The Conversation*, 3 June 2015, https://theconversation.com/the-national-gallery-is-erasing-women-from-the-history-of-art-42505, (accessed 23 November 2018).

Brodskaya, N. and Degas, E. *Edgar, Degas*, New York, Parkstone Press International, 2012.

Lipton, E., *Alias Olympia: A Woman's Search for Manet's Notorious Model & Her Own Desire*, London, Thames and Hudson, 1993.

Valadon, S., *Suzanne Valadon*, Flammarion, 1981.

Main, V.R., *A Woman With No Clothes On: A Novel*, London, Delancey, 2008.

Madeline, L., *Women Artists in Paris, 1850–1900*, Connecticut, Yale University Press, 2017.

Ash, R. and Higton, B. (eds), *Renoir's Women*, London, Pavilion, 1994.

Pollock, G., *Mary Cassatt: Painter of Modern Women*, London, Thames & Hudson, 1998.

Higonnet, A., *Berthe Morisot*, Berkeley, University of California Press, 1995.

Edelstein, T.J. (ed.), *Perspectives on Morisot*, New York, Hudson Hills Press, 1990.

Vigué, J., *Great Women Masters of Art*, New York, Watson-Guptill, 2002.

Gaze, D. (ed.), *Concise Dictionary of Women Artists*, London, Fitzroy Dearborn, 2001.

Gaze, D., *Concise Dictionary of Women Artists*, New York, Taylor & Francis, 2013.

Vigué, J., *Great Women Masters of Art*, New York, Watson-Guptill, 2002.

Myers, N., 'Women Artists in Nineteenth-Century France', in *Heilbrunn Timeline of Art History*, New York: The Metropolitan Museum of Art, 2000, published September 2008, http://www.metmuseum.org/toah/hd/19wa/hd_19wa.htm, (accessed 19 December 2018).

Camille Claudel: master sculptor

Le Normand-Romain, A., *Camille Claudel & Rodin: Time Will Heal Everything*, Editions Du Musée Rodin, 2003.

Paris, R.M., *Camille: The Life of Camille Claudel*, Rodin's Muse and Mistress, trans. L.E. Tuck, London, Aurum, 1988.

Lampert, C., 'The Genius of Camille Claudel', *Apollo* Magazine, 13 May 2017, https://www.apollo-magazine.com/the-genius-of-camille-claudel/, (accessed 10 September 2018).

Akbar, Arifa., 'How Rodin's tragic lover shaped the history of sculpture', *The Independent*, 11 August 2012, https://www.independent.co.uk/arts-entertainment/art/features/how-rodins-tragic-lover-shaped-the-history-of-sculpture-8026836.html, (accessed 13 September 2018).

Chadwick, W. and de Courtivron, I. (eds), *Significant Others*, London, Thames & Hudson, 1993.

O. Ayral-Clause, *Camille Claudel: A Life*, Plunkett Lake Press, 2015.

M. Morhardt, 'Mlle Camille Claudel', *Mercury of France*, Volume XXV, January-March 1898, pp. 709-755, https://www.academia.edu/33400786/Mathias_Morhardt_-_M.lle_Camille_Claudel_1898_, (accessed November 13 2018).

Witherell, L.R., 'Camille Claudel Rediscovered', *Woman's Art Journal*, Vol. 6, No. 1, Spring-Summer 1985.

Rodin, A. 'Letter from Auguste Rodin to Camille Claudel', date unknown, http://www.musee-rodin.fr/en/collections/archives/letter-auguste-rodin-camille-claudel, (accessed August 13 2019).

Author unknown, *Camille Claudel and Nogent-sur-Seine*, Musée Camille Claudel, http://www.museecamilleclaudel.fr/en/collections/visitors-trails/camille-claudel-and-nogent-sur-seine, (accessed 13 September 2018).

Charles, V., *Camille Claudel*, New York, Parkstone Press International, 2018.

Caranfa, A., *Camille Claudel: A Sculpture of Interior Solitude*, Lewisburg, Associated University Presses, 1999.

Bohemian dreams: Ida Nettleship and Hilda Carline

Clarke Hall, E., *Edna Clarke Hall: Drawings and Watercolours 1895–1947*, London, d'Offay Couper Gallery, 1971.

Spencer, U., *Lucky To Be An Artist*, London, Unicorn Press, 2015.

Holroyd, M. and John, R. (eds), *The Good Bohemian: The Letters of Ida John*, London, Bloomsbury, 2017.

John, A., *Chiaroscuro*, Jonathan Cape, 1954.

Thomas, A., *Portraits of Women Gwen John and her Forgotten Contemporaries*, Cambridge, 1994.

C. Lloyd-Morgan, *Gwen John: Letters and Notebooks*, New York, Harry N. Abrams, 2005.

Wilson, E., *Bohemians: The Glamorous Outcasts*, Tauris Parke, 2003.

I. Chilvers (ed.), *The Oxford Dictionary of Art and Artists*, Oxford, Oxford University Press, 2009.

Holroyd, M., *Augustus John: The New Biography*, London, Vintage, 1997.

McLaughlin, R., 'What Happened to the Women Artists who Won Prizes in 1918?', *Frieze*, 14 May 2018, https://frieze.com/article/what-happened-women-artists-who-won-prizes-1918, (accessed 4 April 2019).

Nochlin, L., 'Starting from scratch: Linda Nochlin traces the beginnings of feminist art history', *Women's Art Magazine*, Nov-Dec. 1994, p. 6. Gale Academic Onefile, (accessed 20 April 2019).

MacDonald, M., 'Arts: The secret kept by artist's wife and her lover', *The Independent*, 29 May 1996, https://www.independent.co.uk/arts-entertainment/arts-the-secret-kept-by-artists-wife-and-her-lover-1349650.html, (accessed 4 April 2019).

Hughes, J., 'Spencer: portraits of a failed marriage', *The Independent*, 10 January 1999, https://www.independent.co.uk/news/spencer-portraits-of-a-failed-marriage-1046116.html, (accessed 4 April 2019).

Jenkins, D.F. and Stephens, C. (eds), *Gwen John and Augustus John*, London, Tate Publishing, 2004.

Thomas, A., *The Art of Hilda Carline: Mrs Stanley Spencer*, Lund Humphries Publishers Ltd., 1999.

Hill, R., 'One's self-washed drawers', *London Review of Books*, May 2017, https://www.lrb.co.uk/v39/n13/rosemary-hill/ones-self-washed-drawers, (accessed 15 April 2019).

Schama, S., 'The Church of Me', *The New Yorker*, 9 February 1997, https://www.newyorker.com/magazine/1997/02/17/the-church-of-me, (accessed 15 April 2019).

Spencer, S., *Images of Hilda Spencer: Summer Exhibition 1985*, Berkshire, Stanley Spencer Gallery, 1985.

Pople, K., *Stanley Spencer: A Biography*, Virginia, HarperCollins, 1991, p. 292.

Rothenstein, J., *Stanley Spencer: The Man: Correspondence and Reminiscences*, London, Elek, 1979.

Thompson, M., 'Love's deadly cruelty', *The Daily Telegraph*, 22 May 1999, https://www.telegraph.co.uk/culture/4717496/Loves-deadly-cruelty.html, (accessed on 10 February 2019).

Sickert, W., *Walter Sickert: The Complete Writings on Art*, Oxford, Oxford University Press, 2002.

Islington, Libraries, *The Sickerts in Islington: Catalogues of the Works of Walter Sickert*, Thérèse Lessore and Their Families in Islington Libraries Local History Collection, London, Islington Libraries, 1987.

Hughes, J., 'Spencer: portraits of a failed marriage', *The Independent*, 10 January 1999, https://www.independent.co.uk/news/spencer-portraits-of-a-failed-marriage-1046116.html, (accessed 18 March 2019).

Gabriele Münter: the blue rider

Meskimmon, M., *We Weren't Modern Enough: Women Artists and the Limits of German Modernism*, London, I.B. Tauris, 1999.

Tanner, E., 'Between life crisis and world war', *Schirn Mag*, February 2016, https://www.schirn.de/en/magazine/context/between_life_crisis_and_world_war/, (accessed 10 May 2019).

Lankheit, K. (ed.), *The Blaue Reiter Almanac*, London, Thames & Hudson, 1974.

Roditi, E., *Dialogues: Conversations With European Artists at Mid-Century*, 3rd edn., London, Lund Humphries, 1990.

Behr, S., *Women Expressionists*, London, Phaidon Press Ltd, 1988.

Wistuba, S., 'Gabriele Münter and the Modern World', *School of Communication and Creative Industries*, Charles Sturt University, 2018, p. 1. Available from Academia.edu, (accessed on 14 June 2019).

Sherman, F.F., *Art in America*, vol. 87, Art in America Inc, 1999.

Lanfermann, P., 'Marianne Werefkin – From the Blue Rider to the Great Bear: An Exhibition in Retrospect', *Avant Garde Critical Studies*, vol. 33, 2017, pp. 20-34.

Gossman, L., 'Gabriele Münter Photographer of America 1898-1900', Department of French and Italian, Princeton University, https://www.princeton.edu/~lgossman/munter.pdf, (accessed on 5 June 2019).

Elger, D., *Expressionism: A Revolution in German Art*, Koln, Benedikt Taschen, 1994.

Hoberg, A., *Wassily Kadinsky and Gabriele Münter: Letters and Reminiscences 1902–1914*, Munich/ London, Prestel, 2001.

Münter, G., *Gabriele Münter: The Search for Expression*, Paul Holberton Publishing, 2005.

Jansen, I. and Muhling, M. (eds), *Gabriele Münter 1877–1962: Painting to the Point*, Munich, Prestel Verlag, 2017.

Roditi, E., *Dialogues on Art*, London, Secker & Warburg, 1960.

Heller, R., *Gabriele Münter: The Years of Expressionism*, Munich, Prestel, 1997.

Smith, R., 'Art; Lost in the Glow Of the Man at Her Side', *The New York Times*, 16 August 1998, https://www.nytimes.com/1998/08/16/arts/art-lost-in-the-glow-of-the-man-at-her-side.html, (accessed 3 May 2019).

Delistraty, C., 'When Female Artists Stop Being Seen as Muses', *The Paris Review*, 6 July 2018, https://www.theparisreview.org/blog/2018/07/06/when-female-artists-stop-being-seen-as-muses/, (accessed 3 May 2019).

McNay, A., 'Gabriele Münter: Painting to the Point', *Studio International*, 26 December 2018, https://www.studiointernational.com/index.php/gabriele-munter-painting-to-the-point-review-museum-ludwig-cologne, (accessed 10 May 2019).

'Storm Women', *Schirn*, http://schirn.de/sturmfrauen/digitorial/en/, (accessed 10 May 2019).

Bruno, P., 'Malweiber', *Simplicissimus*, vol. 6, no. 15, 1901, pp. 113–122.

Varvara Stepanova: constructing Russian art

Antifashistskii Komitet Sovietskikh Zhenshchin (RUSSIA), 'Soviet Woman', Soviet Fascist
Committee and the Central Council of Trade Unions of the U.S.S.R., Moscow. 1946.

Lavrentiev, A.N., *Varvara Stepanova: A Constructivist Life*, London, Thames and Hudson, 1988.

Bolton, R., *The Contest of Meaning: Critical Histories of Photography*, Massachusetts, MIT Press,
1992.

Marcadé, J.C. and Petrova, E.N., *Rodchenko: Constructing the Future*, Ciaxa Catalunya, 2008.

Mendes. C. and Larreta, E.R. (eds), *Collective Imagination: Limits and Beyond*, UNESCO, 2001.

Heron, L. and Williams, V. (ed.), I*lluminations: Women Writing on Photography from the 1850s to the
Present*, I.B. Tauris, 1996.

Lodder, C., *Russian Constructivism*, New Haven, Yale University Press, 1983.

Armstrong, H. (ed.), *Graphic Design Theory: Readings from the Field*, New York, Princeton
Architectural 2009.

Rickey, G., *Constructivism: Origins and Evolution*, New York, George Braziller, 1969.

Rodchenko, A.M., *Alexander Rodchenko*, Oxford, Museum of Modern Art, 1979.

Gray, C., *The Russian Experiment in Art 1863–1922*, London, Thames and Hudson, 1986.

Gayford, M., 'Exhibitions Revolution: Russian Art 1917–1932', *The Spectator*, 18 February 2017,
p. 46.

Kiaer, C., *Imagine No Possessions: The Socialist Objects of Russian Constructivism*, Massachusetts, MIT
Press, 2005.

Wilson, J.C., 'Varvara Stepanova, the pioneer who brought constructivist design to proletarian
life', *It's Nice That*, 26 October 2017, https://www.itsnicethat.com/articles/varvara-
stepanova-contructivist-design-port-magazine-fashion-261017, (accessed 10 June 2019).

Bowlt, J.E. et al., *Amazons of the Avant-Garde*, New York, Guggenheim Museum, 2000.

Rodchenko, A.M., *The Future is Our Only Goal*, Prestel, 1991.

Ash, J., 'A Catalogue of Russian Avant-Garde Books, 1912–1934 and 1969–2003', *Solanus*, vol.
20, 2006, pp. 86–88.

Dangerous Art: From Varvara Stepanova to Pussy Riot, [online video], 2013, https://www.
youtube.com/watch?v=mAlQxDzL46E, (accessed 14 April 2019).

Dada Vision: Emmy Hennings and Baroness Elsa von Freytag-Loringhoven

Gammel, I., *Baroness Elsa: Gender, Dada and Everyday Modernity: A Cultural Biography*, Massachusetts, MIT, 2002.

Huelsenbeck, R., *Dada Manifesto 1949*, Wittenborn, Schultz, 1951.

Burmeister, R. et al, *Dada Africa: Dialogue with the other*, Scheidegger and Spiess, 2016.

Huelsenbeck, R., *Memoirs of a Dada Drummer*, Berkeley, University of California Press, 1991.

Bailey, B., 'Duchamp's Fountain: The Baroness theory debunked', *The Burlington magazine*, vol. 161, no. 1399, pp. 804–810.

Norton, L., 'The Richard Mutt Case', *The Blind Man*, no. 2, 1917.

von Freytag-Loringhoven, E., *Body Sweats: The Uncensored Writings of Elsa von Freytag-Loringhoven*, Massachusetts, MIT Press, 2011.

Blythe, S.G. and Powers, E.D., and Museum of Modern Art, *Looking at Dada*, New York, The Museum of Modern Art, 2006.

Ball, H., *Flight Out of Time: A Dada Diary, London and Los Angeles*, University of California Press, originally published 1927, paperback printing 1996.

Karpel, B., *The Dada Painters and Poets: An Anthology*, Massachusetts, Harvard University Press, 1989.

Tomkins, C., *Duchamp*, New York, H. Holt, 1996.

Foster, S.C. and Riha, K., *Crisis and the Arts: Dada Zurich, A Clown's Game From Nothing*, Michigan, G.K. Hall, 1996.

Sawelson-Gorse, N., *Women in Dada: Essays on Sex, Gender and Identity*, Massachusetts, MIT Press, 1998.

Hemus, R., *Dada's Women*, Connecticut, Yale University Press, 2009.

Richter, H., *Dada: Art and Anti-Art (World of Art)*, London, Thames & Hudson, 1997.

Dada and Surrealism: Europe After the Rain documentary (1978), [online video], 2018, https://www.youtube.com/watch?v=sdBaS8fgwNs, (accessed 27 April 2019).

Hustvedt, S., 'A woman in the men's room: when will the art world recognise the real artist behind Duchamp's Fountain?', *The Guardian*, 29 March 2019, https://www.theguardian.com/books/2019/mar/29/marcel-duchamp-fountain-women-art-history, (accessed 27 April 2019).

Ades, D., 'Duchamp's Fountain and the feminist avant garde in New York', *The Guardian*, 3 April

2019, https://www.theguardian.com/artanddesign/2019/apr/03/duchamps-fountain-and-the-feminist-avant-garde-in-new-york, (accessed 27 April 2019).

Rugh, T.F., 'Emmy Hennings and the Emergence of Zurich Dada', *Woman's Art Journal*, vol. 2, no. 1, 1981, pp. 1-6. Available from JSTOR, www.jstor.org/stable/1357892, (accessed 27 April 2019).

Lucia Moholy: behind the scenes at the Bauhaus

Moholy-Nagy, L., [Malerei, Fotografie, Film.] *Painting, Photography, Film*, trans. J. Seligman, Massachusetts, MIT Press, 1969.

History of Photography, vol, 2, Taylor and Francis, 2013.

Moholy, L., *Marginalien zu Moholy-Nagy*, (Moholy-Nagy, Marginal Notes), Krefeld, Scherpe Verlag, 1972.

Muller, U., *Bauhaus Women: Art, Handcraft, Design*, Paris Flammarion, 2009.

Weltge, S.W., *Bauhaus Textiles: Women Artists and the Weaving Workshop*, London, Thames and Hudson, 1993.

'Women and the Bauhaus: Public Relations/Ise Gropius, Lucia Moholy', MoMA Talks Panels & Symposia, MoMA, 2010, https://player.fm/series/moma-talks-panel-discussions-and-symposia/women-and-the-bauhaus-public-relationsise-gropius-lucia-moholy, (accessed 10 March 2019).

Weber, N.F., *Anni Albers*, New York, Guggenheim Museum, 1999.

Searle, A., 'Anni Albers review – ravishing textiles that beg to be touched', *The Guardian*, 9 October 2018, https://www.theguardian.com/artanddesign/2018/oct/09/anni-albers-tate-modern-review, (accessed July 15 2019).

Saletnik, J. and R. Schuldenfrei, *Bauhaus Construct: Fashioning Identity, Discourse and Modernism*, Routledge, 2013.

Ambler, F., *The Story of Bauhaus*, London, Hachette UK, 2018.

'Women and the Bauhaus: Weaving/Anni Albers', MoMA Talks Panels & Symposia, [podcast], MoMA, 2009, https://player.fm/series/moma-talks-panel-discussions-and-symposia/women-and-the-bauhaus-weavinganni-albers, (accessed 10 March 2019).

Schuldenfrei, R., 'Images in Exile: Lucia Moholy's Bauhaus Negatives and the Construction of the Bauhaus Legacy', *History of Photography*, vol. 37, issue 2, 2013, pp. 182–203.

Oelze, S., 'Forgotten and unrecognized: Female artists at the Bauhaus', *DW*, 12 April 2019,

https://www.dw.com/en/forgotten-and-unrecognized-female-artists-at-the-
bauhaus/a-48306352, (accessed 24 April 2019).

Greenspan, S., Photo Credit: Negatives of the Bauhaus, [podcast], 16 August 2018,
https://99percentinvisible.org/episode/photo-credit-negatives-bauhaus/, (accessed 24 April
2019).

Lil Hardin Armstrong and the Jazz Age: born to swing

Dahl, L., *Stormy Weather: The Music and Lives of a Century of Jazzwomen*, New York, Pantheon,
1984.

Gioia, T., *The Jazz Standards: A Guide to the Repertoire*, Oxford, Oxford University Press, 2012.

Armstrong, L., 'Jazz Lips: Louis Armstrong, in His Own Words', *The New Republic*, vol. 4427,
1999, pp. 29–35.

Placksin, S., *American Women in Jazz: 1900 to the Present; Their Words, Lives and Music*, Wideview,
1982.

Shaw, A., *The Jazz Age: Popular Music in the 1920s*, Oxford, Oxford University Press, 1987.

'Hear me Talkin' To Ya'/Lil Hardin Armstrong, interviewed by Steve Allen, 1967, British
Library, London, C1411/104C1411/105; Steve Allen Collection.

Armstrong, L.H., 'Satchmo and Me', *American Music*, vol. 25, no. 1, 2007, pp. 109. JSTOR, www.
jstor.org/stable/40071645. (accessed July 21 2019).

Dickerson, J.L., *Just for a Thrill: Lil Hardin Armstrong, First Lady of Jazz*, New York, Cooper Square
Publishers Inc, 2002.

Provost, S.C., 'Bringing Something New: Female Jazz Instrumentalists' Use of Imitation and
Masculinity', *Jazz Perspectives*, 2017, vol. 10, pp. 141–57. Available from Taylor & Francis
Online, (accessed 24 April 2019).

Alma Reville: the silent partner

Bridges, M. and Robson, C. (eds), *Silent Women*, Supernova Books, 2016.

Gaines, J., *Pink-Slipped: What Happened to Women in the Silent Film Industries?*, Urbana, University of
Illinois Press, 2018.

Allen, R. and Gottlieb, S. (eds), *The Hitchcock Annual Anthology: Selected Essays From Volumes 10–15*,
London, Wallflower, 2009.

Simon, J. (ed.), *Alice Guy Blaché: Cinema Pioneer*, New Haven, Yale University Press, 2009.

Blaché, A.G. and Slide, A., *The Memoirs of Alice Guy Blaché*, Scarecrow Press, 1986.

Meuel, D., *Women Film Editors: Unseen Artists of American Cinema*, North Carolina, McFarland & Company Inc, 2016.

Slide, A., *The Silent Feminists: America's First Women Directors*, London, Scarecrow Press, 1996.

Hepburn, K., *Me: Stories of My Life*, Knopf, 1991.

Grosvenor, R., '"I Don't Scare Easily", Says Mrs Hitchcock', *Sunday Express*, 30 January 1972, Proquest Historical Newspapers, (accessed 15 August 2019).

Morris, N. 'Alma Reville.' In Gaines, J., Vatsal, R. and Dall'Asta, M., eds. Women Film Pioneers Project, New York, NY: Columbia University Libraries, 2016. <https://doi.org/10.7916/d8-rkt5-8s39>.

Chandler, C., *It's Only a Movie Alfred Hitchcock: A Personal Biography*, New York and London, Simon & Schuster, 2008.

'Alma in Wonderland' *The Picturegoer*, December 1925. Reprinted in Allen, E., and Gottlieb, S. (eds.), *The Hitchcock Annual Anthology: Selected Essays From Volumes 10–15*, London, Wallflower, 2009.

Davis, I., 'One woman who has never been frightened by Alfred Hitchcock...' *Daily Express*, 14 Aug 1974, Available from Proquest Historical Newspapers, (accessed 11 July 2019).

Reville, A., 'Cutting and Continuity', in Allen, E., and Gottlieb, S. (eds.), T*he Hitchcock Annual Anthology: Selected Essays From Volumes 10–15*, London, Wallflower, 2009.

No known author, 'Obituary, Alma Reville', *Screen International*, no. 353, 1982.

Champlin, C., 'Alma Reville Hitchcock – The Unsung Partner', *Los Angeles Times*, July 29 1982, p.7. Available from Proquest Historical Newspapers, (accessed 11 July 2019).

Berg, S. and Sierchio, P., 'Hitched to the Script'. *Written By*, vol 10, no. 3, 2006, pp. 45-55.

McBride, J., 'Mr and Mrs Hitchcock', *Sight & Sound*, vol. 45, no. 4, 2010, p. 224-225.

Stamp, S., *Lois Weber in Early Hollywood*, California, University of California Press, 2015.

Diu, N.L., 'Mrs Alfred Hitchcock: "The Unsung Partner"', *The Telegraph*, 8 February 2013, https://www.telegraph.co.uk/culture/film/film-news/9832084/Mrs-Alfred-Hitchcock-The-Unsung-Partner.html, (accessed 7 June 2019).

Bridges, M. and C. Robson (eds.), *Silent Women: Pioneers of Cinema*, London, Supernova Books, 2016.

Josephine Nivison Hopper: the recovery

Mepham, J., *To the Lighthouse by Virginia Woolf*, Basingstoke, Macmillan Education, 1987.

Hopper, E. and Goodrich, L., *Edward Hopper*, New York, H.N. Abrams, 1971.

Colleary, E.T., 'Josephine Nivison Hopper: Some Newly Discovered Works', *Woman's Art Journal*, vol. 25, no. 1, 2004, pp. 3-11.

Mellow, J.B., 'The World Of Edward is Hopper – The drama of light, the artificiality of nature, the remorseless human comedy', *The New York Times*, 5 September, 1971, https://www.nytimes.com/1971/09/05/archives/the-world-of-edward-hopper-the-drama-of-light-the-artificiality-of.html, (accessed 14 May 2019).

Souter, G., *Edward Hopper Light and Dark*, New York, Parkstone Press, 2015.

Stone, C.B., Hurt, *The Shadow: The Josephine Hopper Poems*, Dos Madres Press, 2013.

Woolf, V., *To the Lighthouse*, first published 1927, Oxford and New York, Oxford University Press edition, 2006.

Wood, G., 'Man and Muse', *The Observer*, 24 April 2004, https://www.theguardian.com/artanddesign/2004/apr/25/art1, (accessed 3 May 2019).

Levin, A.K. (ed.), *Gender, Sexuality and Museums*, London, Routledge, 2010.

Mecklenburg, V.M., *Edward Hopper: The Watercolors*, London, W.W. Norton, 1999.

Levin, G., *Edward Hopper: An Intimate Biography*, New York, Rizzoli, 2007.

Frederickson, K. and Webb, S.E. (eds), *Singular Women: Writing the Artist*, Berkeley, University of California Press, 2003.

Laing, O., *The Lonely City: Adventures in the Art of Being Alone*, Edinburgh, Canongate, 2017.

Hilsdale, A., *My Dear Mr Hopper*, New Haven, Yale University Press, 2013.

Shirley Graham Du Bois: renaissance woman

Du Bois, W.E.B., *In Battle for Peace: The Story of My 83rd Birthday*, Masses & Mainstream Inc., 1952.

Freedomways, vol. 10, 1970.

Sherrard-Johnson, C., *Portraits of the New Negro Woman: Visual and Literary Culture in the Harlem Renaissance*, New Brunswick/London, Rutgers University Press, 2007.

Bracks, L.L. and Smith, J.C. (eds), *Black Women of the Harlem Renaissance Era*, Maryland, Rowman & Littlefield, 2014.

Graham, S., *Paul Robeson, Citizen of the World*, Connecticut, Negro Universities Press, 1971.

Kaiser, E. (ed.), *A Freedomways Reader: Afro-America in the Seventies*, New York, International Publishers, 1977.

Du Bois, S.G., *His Day is Marching On: A Memoir of W.E.B Du Bois*, New York, J.B. Lippincott Co., 1971.

Graham, S., *The Story of Phillis Wheatley*, New York, J. Messner, 1949.

Horne, G., *Race Woman: The Lives of Shirley Graham Du Bois*, New York, New York University Press, 2000.

Schmalenberger, S., 'Debuting Her Political Voice: The Lost Opera of Shirley Graham', *Black Music Research Journal*, vol. 26, no 1, 2006.

David DuBois: My Mother, Shirley Graham DuBois, [online video], 2010, oral history archive, Visionary Project, http://www.visionaryproject.org/duboisdavid/, (30 June 2019).

Shirley Graham DuBois, 69, Writer And Widow of Civil Rights Leader, *The New York Times*, 5 April 1977, https://www.nytimes.com/1977/04/05/archives/shirley-graham-dubois-69-writer-and-widow-of-civil-rights-leader.html, (accessed 2 July 2019).

Shirley Graham Du Bois speaking at UCLA 11/13/1970, [online video], https://www.youtube.com/watch?v=u3mhM3bHCZ8, 2014, (accessed 30 April 2019).

Joseph-Gabriel, A., 'Shirley Graham Du Bois and Black Liberation', *Black Perspectives*, 13 March 2019, https://www.aaihs.org/shirley-graham-du-bois-and-black-liberation/, (accessed 12 May 2019).

The Crisis, vol. 42, no. 4, 1935, pp. 1-28.

Surrealist women: Jacqueline Lamba and Suzanne Césaire

Rosemont, P. (ed.), *Surrealist Women: An International Anthology*, London, Athlone Press, 1998.

Breton, A., *Arcanum 17*, trans. Z. Rogow, Toronto, Coach House Press, 1994.

Cottenet-Hage, M., 'Surrealist Women: An International Anthology', *Journal of Gender Studies*, vol. 8, no. 3, 1999, pp. 363-364.

Chadwick, W., *Women Artists and the Surrealist Movement*, New York, Bulfinch Press, 1985.

Grimberg, S., 'Jacqueline Lamba: From Darkness, with Light', *Woman's Art Journal*, vol. 22, no. 1, 5-1. doi:10.2307/1358725. (accessed 5 March 2019).

Kuenzli, R., Caws, M.A. and Raaberg, G., *Surrealism and Women*, London, The MIT Press, 1990.

Breton, A., *Mad Love*, Lincoln and London, University of Nebraska Press, translated by Mary

Ann Caws,1987.

Agar, E., interviewed by Cathy Courtney, 1990, *Artists' Lives* interview, The British Library, London, C466/01.

Césaire, S., *The Great Camouflage: Writings of Dissent (1941–1945)*, Connecticut, Wesleyan University Press, 2012.

Ithaca, Kay Sage 1898–1963, New York, Ithaca, 1977.

Carrington, L., Down Below, New York, *New York Review of Books*, 2017.

Pace, A.R., *Jacqueline Lamba: Peintre Rebelle, Muse de l'Amour Fou*, Paris, Gallimard, 2010.

McCormick, C., 'Dorothea Tanning by Carlo McCormick', *Bomb*, 1 October 1990. https://bombmagazine.org/articles/dorothea-tanning/. (accessed March 27 2019).

Miller, L.E., *Lou Harrison: Composing a World*, Oxford, Oxford University Press, 1998.

Lichtenstein, T., *Twilight Visions: Surrealism and Paris*, Berkeley, University of California Press, 2009.

Breton, A., *Nadja*, trans. R. Howard, London, Penguin, 1999.

Breton, A., *Selections*, University of California Press, 2003.

Chadwick, W., *Women Artists and the Surrealist Movement*, New York, Bulfinch Press, 1985.

Chadwick, W., *The Militant Muse*, London, Thames & Hudson, 2017.

Hubert, R.R., *Magnifying Mirrors: Women, Surrealism, and Partnership*, Nebraska, University of Nebraska Press, 1994.

Chadwick, W. (ed.), *Mirror Images: Women, Surrealism, and Self-Representation*, Cambridge Massachusetts, MIT Press, 1998.

Sharpley-Whiting, T.D., *Negritude Women*, Minneapolis, University of Minnesota Press, 2002.

Rabaka, R., *The Negritude Movement: W.E.B. Du Bois, Leon Damas, Aime Césaire, Leopold Senghor, Frantz Fanon, and the Evolution of an Insurgent Idea*, Maryland, Lexington Books, 2015.

Rabbitt, K., 'In Search of the Missing Mother: Suzanne Césaire, Martiniquaise', *Research in African Literatures*, vol. 44, no. 1, 2013, pp. 36-54.

Dora Maar: radical photography

Lord, J., *Picasso and Dora: A Memoir*, London, Weidenfield & Nicolson, 1993.

Baring, L., *Dora Maar: Paris in the Time of Man Ray, Jean Cocteau, and Picasso*, Rizzoli, 2017.

Caws, M.A., *Dora Maar – With and Without Picasso: A Biography*, London, Thames & Hudson, 2000.

Mailer, M., *Portrait of Picasso as a Young Man: An Interpretive Biography*, New York, Atlantic Monthly Press, 1995.

Mailer, A., *The Last Party: Scenes From My Life With Norman Mailer*, New York, Barricade Books, 1997.

Baldassari, A., *Picasso: Life with Dora Maar: Love and War 1935–1945*, Paris, Flammarion, 2006.

Gilot, F., *Life With Picasso*, London, Penguin Books Ltd., 1966.

Freeman, J., *Picasso and the Weeping Women: The Years of Marie-Thérèse Walter & Dora Maar*, New York, Rizzoli, 1994.

Jiminez, J.B., *Dictionary of Artists' Models*, New York and London, Routledge, 2013, p. 337.

Menand, L., 'The Norman Invasion', *The New Yorker*, 14 October 2013, https://www.newyorker.com/magazine/2013/10/21/the-norman-invasion, (accessed 14 July 2019)

Caws, M.A., 'A tortured goddess', *The Guardian*, 7 October 2000, https://www.theguardian.com/books/2000/oct/07/features.weekend, (accessed 2 July 2019).

Valdes, Z., *The Weeping Woman*, New York, Arcade Publishing, 2016.

L'Enfant, J., 'Dora Maar and the Art of Mystery', *Woman's Art Journal*, vol. 17, no. 2, 1996, pp. 15–20. JSTOR, www.jstor.org/stable/1358462, (accessed 14 July 2019).

Richardson, J., 'Trompe l'Oeil', *New York Review of Books*, 3 December, 1964, https://www.nybooks.com/articles/1964/12/03/trompe-loeil-2/, (accessed 2 July 2019).

Baring, L., 'Dora Maar: Paris in the Time of Man Ray, Jean Cocteau, and Picasso', 21 December 2017, *The Eye of Photography*, https://loeildelaphotographie.com/en/dora-maar-paris-in-the-time-of-man-ray-cocteau-and-picasso/, (accessed 14 July 2019).

Gopnik, A., 'Escaping Picasso', *The New Yorker*, 8 December 1996, https://www.newyorker.com/magazine/1996/12/16/escaping-picasso, (accessed 6 July 2019).

Dillon, B., 'The Voraciousness and Oddity of Dora Maar's Pictures', *The New Yorker*, 21 May 2019, https://www.newyorker.com/culture/photo-booth/the-voraciousness-and-oddity-of-dora-maars-pictures, (accessed 6 July 2019).

Lee Krasner: rip it up, start again

Landau, E., *Lee Krasner: A Catalogue Raisonné*, New York, Abrams, 1995.

O'Hara, F., *Art Chronicles, 1954–1966*, New York, George Braziller, 1975.

Rose, B. (ed.), *Lee Krasner: A Retrospective*, Houston, Museum of Fine Arts, 1983.

Brach, P. 'Lee Krasner: Front and Center', *Art in America*, vol. 89, no. 2, 2001, pp. 90-99.

Anfam, D. (ed.), *Abstract Expressionism*, London, Royal Academy of Arts, 2016.

Fortune, B.B., *Elaine de Kooning: Portraits*, Washington D.C., Prestel, 2015.

Engelmann, I.J., *Jason Pollock and Lee Krasner*, London, Prestel, 2007.

Jenkins, T., 'Art show too male? At times, this cry makes no sense', *The Observer*, 25 September 2016, https://www.theguardian.com/commentisfree/2016/sep/24/art-show-too-male-cry-makes-no-sense (accessed 20 May 2019).

Schjeldahl, P., 'Fragments of An Awesome Whole', *The New York Times*, 19 January 1975, https://www.nytimes.com/1975/01/19/archives/fragments-of-an-awesome-whole.html, (accessed 20 May 2019).

Collings, M., 'Abstract Expressionism, exhibition review: What a load of Pollocks', *Evening Standard*, 20 September 2016, https://www.standard.co.uk/go/london/arts/abstract-expressionism-exhibition-review-what-a-load-of-pollocks-a3349116.html, (accessed 20 May 2019).

Gabriel. M., *Ninth Street Women*, New York, Little, Brown and Company, 2019.

Holmes, D., oral history interview with Lee Krasner, 1972. Archives of American Art, Smithsonian Institution.https://www.aaa.si.edu/collections/interviews/oral-history-interview-lee-krasner-12037#transcript, (accessed 23 May 2019).

Krasner, L., 'Statement' in Roberson, B. and Friedman, B.H., *Lee Krasner: Paintings, Drawings and Collages*, London, Whitechapel Art Gallery, 1965.

Gosling, N., 'A Portent from Brooklyn', *The Observer*, 26 September, 1965. Available from Proquest Historical Newspapers, (accessed 20 May 2019).

Marter, J., 'Negotiating Abstraction: Lee Krasner, Mercedes Carles Matter and the Hofmann Years', *Women's Art Journal*, vol. 28, no. 2, 2007, p. 36, JSTOR, www.jstor.org/stable/20358129. (accessed 25 June 2019).

C. Nemser, *Art Talk: conversations with 15 women artists*, New York, Scribner, 1975.

Inside New York's Art World: Lee Krasner, 1978, [online video], 2008, https://www.youtube.com/watch?v=yFdE0bH9FRg (accessed 20 May 2019).

Pearson. S, *The New York Times*, 1955.

Rago, L., 'We interview Lee Krasner', *School Arts*, vol. 60, 1960.

Janis, S., *Abstract & Surrealist Art in America*, New York, Reynal & Hitchcock, 1944.

Hobbs, R., *Lee Krasner*, New York, Abrams, 1999.

Marter, J.M. (ed.), *Women of Abstract Expressionism*, Colorado, Denver Art Museum in association with Yale University Press, 2016.

Puniello, F.S., *Abstract Expressionist Women Painters: An Annotated Bibliography*, London, Scarecrow Press, 1996.

Gibson, A., 'Lee Krasner and Women's Innovations in American Abstract Painting', *Woman's Art Journal*, vol. 28, no. 2, 2007, pp.11-19. http://www.jstor.org/stable/20358126, (accessed 6 May 2019).

Pierpont, C.R., 'How New York's Postwar Female Painters Battled for Recognition', *The New Yorker*, 8 October 2018, https://www.newyorker.com/magazine/2018/10/08/how-new-yorks-postwar-female-painters-battled-for-recognition, (accessed 6 May 2019).

Roueché, B., 'Unframed Space', *The New Yorker*, 5 August 1950, https://www.newyorker.com/magazine/1950/08/05/unframed-space, (accessed 6 May 2019).

Preston, S., 'Modern Work in Diverse Shows: Contemporary American and Italian Work in New Displays', *The New York Times*, 2 October 1955, ISSN 03624331. Available from Proquest Historical Newspapers, (accessed 12 May 2019).

Seckler, D., Oral history interview with Lee Krasner, 1964 Nov. 2-1968 Apr. 11. Archives of American Art, Smithsonian Institution.

Margaret Keane: big eyes

Gallo, L., *Big Eyes: The Flim, The Art*, London, Titan Books, 2014.

Blythe, B., *Big Eye Art: Resurrected & Transformed*, London, Merrell, 2008.

Big Eyes, Big Lies | The Carpetbagger | *The New York Times*, [online video], 2014, https://www.youtube.com/watch?v=IX7dNpWnf6E, (accessed 25 July 2019).

Buckley, C., 'How Amy Adams Overcame Her Resistance to "Big Eyes"', *The New York Times*, 6 January 2015, https://carpetbagger.blogs.nytimes.com/2015/01/06/how-amy-adams-overcame-her-resistance-to-big-eyes/, (accessed 25 July 2019).

Howard. J., 'The Man Who Paints Those Big Eyes', *Life*, vol. 59, no. 9, 1965.

A 1964 interview with Walter Stanley Keane, Margaret Keane, Big Eyes Paintings, [online video], 2015, https://www.youtube.com/watch?v=9WgStC6fvtM, (accessed 25 July 2019).

Swanson, C., 'Margaret Keane's Eyes Are Wide Open', *Vulture*, 18 December 2014, https://

www.vulture.com/2014/12/margaret-keanes-eyes-are-wide-open.html, (accessed 25 July 2019).

Catterall, L., 'Walter Keane's tactics make judge see red', *Honolulu Star Bulletin*, 15 May 1986. Available from Proquest Historical Newspapers, (accessed 13 July 2019).

Ronson, J., 'The big-eyed children: the extraordinary story of an epic art fraud', *The Guardian*, 26 October 2014, https://www.theguardian.com/artanddesign/2014/oct/26/art-fraud-margaret-walter-keane-tim-burton-biopic, (accessed 10 May 2019).

Shigeko Kubota: the mother of video art

Schimmel, P. et al., *Out of Actions: Between Performance and the Object, 1949–1979*, London, Thames & Hudson Ltd. 1998.

Rush, M., *New Media in Art (World of Art)*, 2nd edn., London, Thames & Hudson Ltd., 2005.

Higgins, H., *Fluxus Experience*, Berkeley, University of California Press, 2002.

Kellein, T., *Fluxus*, London, Thames and Hudson, 1995.

Kubota. S., *Shigeko Kubota: Video Sculptures*, Essen, Das Museum, 1981.

Kubota, S., interviewed by Miwako Tezuka, 2009, https://post.at.moma.org/content_items/344-interview-with-shigeko-kubota, (accessed 23 May 2019).

Bui, P. and Kubota, S., 'Shigeko Kubota with Phong Bui', *The Brooklyn Rail*, 2007, https://brooklynrail.org/2007/09/art/kubota, (accessed 1 August 2019).

Smith, R., 'Review/Art; Sleek Video Sculptures By Shigeko Kubota', *The New York Times*, 24 May 1991, https://www.nytimes.com/1991/05/24/arts/review-art-sleek-video-sculptures-by-shigeko-kubota.html, (accessed 1 August 2019).

Stiles, K., *Concerning Consequences: Studies in Art, Destruction, and Trauma*, Chicago and London, The University of Chicago Press, 2016.

Kubota, S. and Jacob, M.J., *Shigeko Kubota Video Sculpture*, New York, American Museum of the Moving Image, 1991.

Author uncredited, 'Art', *The New Yorker* archive, 13 May 1991, https://archives.newyorker.com/newyorker/1991-05-13/flipbook/014/, (accessed 1 August 2019).

Author uncredited, 'Shigeko Kubota, My Life with Nam June Paik', Stendhal Gallery, http://1995-2015.undo.net/it/mostra/58503, (accessed 2 August 2019).

Yoshimoto, M., *Into Performance: Japanese Women Artists in New York*, London, Rutgers University Press, 2005.

Kubota, S., *Shigeko Kubota: Video Sculptures*, Essen, Das Museum, 1981.

Brill, D., *Shock and the Senseless in Dada and Fluxus (Interfaces: Studies in Visual Culture)*, Hanover, Dartmouth College Press: University Press of New England, 2010.

Jones, C.A., 'Shigeko Kubota 1937-2015', *Artforum*, 15 October 2015, https://www.artforum. com/passages/caroline-a-jones-on-shigeko-kubota-1937-2015-55566, (accessed 10 June 2019).

Where are we now?

Offill, J., *Dept. Of Speculation*, London, Granta Books, 2015. Available from Apple Books, (accessed 30 September 2019).

Chadwick, W., *Women, Art and Society*, 5th edition, London, Thames & Hudson, 2012.

Parker, R. and Pollock, G., *Old Mistresses: Women, Art and Ideology*, new edition, 2013.

Glueck. G., 'The woman as artist', *The New York Times*, 25 September 1977, https://www. nytimes. com/1977/09/25/archives/the-woman-as-artist.html, (accessed 29 September 2018).

Dorment, R., 'The Pre-Raphaelite sisterhood', *The Daily Telegraph*, 10 January 1998, https:// www.telegraph.co.uk/culture/4711482/The-Pre-Raphaelite-sisterhood.html, (accessed 30 September 2018).

Dederer, C. 'What Do We Do with the Art of Monstrous Men?', *The Paris Review*, 20 November 2017, https://www.theparisreview.org/blog/2017/11/20/art-monstrous-men/, (accessed 1 September 2018).

Hess T.B. and Baker, E.C., *Art and Sexual Politics: Women's Liberation, Women Artists, and Art History*, London and New York, Collier Macmillan, 1973.

Butler, C. and Mark, L.G. (eds), *WACK!: Art and the Feminist Revolution*, Los Angeles and London, MoCa and MIT Press, 2007.

Pollock, G. and Sauron, V.T., (eds), *The Sacred and the Feminine: Imagination and Sexual Difference*, London and New York, I.B. Tauris, 2007.

G. Pollock, *Differencing the Canon: Feminism and the Writing of Art's Histories*, London and New York, Routledge, 1999.

Harris, A.S., *Women Artists 1550-1950*, Los Angeles, Los Angeles County Museum of Art, 1976.

PICTURE CREDITS

Jazz pianist and composer Lil Hardin at the centre of King Oliver's Creole Jazz Band, c. 1922.
Pictorial Press Ltd / Alamy Stock Photo

Film editor and assistant director Alma Reville at work on the set of *The Mountain Eagle* with actor Bernhard Goetzke, c. 1926.
Everett Collection Inc / Alamy Stock Photo

Shirley Graham Du Bois, playwright, biographer and activist, c. 1946.
Granger Historical Picture Archive / Alamy Stock Photo

Lee Krasner, abstract expressionist painter at work in her studio, c. 1981.
Ernst Haas / Getty Images

Margaret Keane in her studio, with Walter Keane in the shadows, c. 1965.
Bill Ray / The LIFE Picture Collection via Getty Images

Pioneering video artist Shigeko Kubota with her Portapak camera, c. 1972.
© Tom Haar

ACKNOWLEDGEMENTS

More than once in this book, I have discussed how important it is to recognise the value of collaboration, and I can't stress enough how much of a collective effort this has been. It started with my commissioning editor Zena Alkayat, who came up with the concept for the book, pushed to get it made, and took a big chance by signing me up to write it. And without the hard work of my intelligent, patient and ever-understanding editor Susannah Otter, copy editor Tamsin English, and fact-checker Nick Funnell, it would not exist. Thank you to Kathleen McNamee, Grace Goslin and Nisha Woolford, who helped with transcribing and referencing. And to everyone who read pages and offered edits: Steve Pill, Jan Page, Alice Saville, Kate Lloyd and so many others, I am so grateful.

I also owe a huge debt to the interviewees quoted in the book, who offered not just their time but their expertise and experience: Jane Alison, Dr. Serena Trowbridge, Professor Gerald Horne, Professor Alexander Lavrentiev, Ben Street, Pamela Hutchinson, Professor Midori Yoshimoto, Professor Ann Sutherland Harris, Katy Hessel and artist Margaret Keane.

Thanks to my colleagues at *Time Out* London, who let me disappear on a sabbatical to put the necessary time in, especially Alexandra Sims, who looked after everything while I was gone. Special thanks to my supportive friend Eddy Frankel, who commissioned me for my first *Time Out* art review. Thanks to the women of 'the corridor', and to the extremely sound security staff at the British Library, who were often the only people I'd speak to for the entire day.

Thanks to my parents, Pat and Margot, for reading every word of every chapter long before the book was published, and for raising me in a house filled with dusty art books and copies of *Films and Filming* magazine that I would constantly steal. To my sister Ellen, and my niece and nephew Leah and Chris, two electric, smiley sources of joy who charged me with enough energy to make it through some very late nights.

And to Adam Jackson-Nocher, who is the only person I really believe when he says 'it's going to be ok'.

Thanks to the following libraries and archives:

The British Library reading rooms, London. 96 Euston Rd, London NW1 2DB.

The Women's Art Library, Goldsmiths, University of London, New Cross SE14 6NW.

The Slade Collections, UCL Art Museum, University College London, Gower Street, London WC1E 6BT.

ABOUT THE AUTHOR

Katie McCabe is an Irish writer and editor based in London who previously practised as an Occupational Therapist before switching careers and moving into media. She is the former editor of *Artists & Illustrators* magazine and has written for *Vice*, *Little White Lies* and the *Time Out* art and features sections as a freelance contributor. She is currently the Events Editor at *Time Out London*.